AL LEONARD

HARMONY

MW00580685

PART 1 • DIATONIC

HAL LEONARD

HARMONY & THEORY

PART 1 • DIATONIC

GEORGE HEUSSENSTAMM

HAL•LEONARD®

ISBN 978-1-4234-9887-2

Published by:
Hal Leonard Corporation
7777 W. Bluemound Road
P.O. Box 13819
Milwaukee, WI 53213

In Australia Contact:
Hal Leonard Australia Pty. Ltd.
4 Lentara Court
Cheltenham, Victoria, 3192 Australia
Email: ausadmin@halleonard.com.au

Printed in the U.S.A.

First Edition

Visit Hal Leonard Online at
www.halleonard.com

CONTENTS

CHAPTER 1 FUNDAMENTALS

For many readers, Chapter One will act as a review of basic materials learned from previous musical experience: major scales, minor scales (natural, harmonic, melodic), all keys and key signatures, recognition and spelling of intervals, three-note chords (triads), fundamentals of meter and rhythm, and at least a rudimentary grasp of proper musical notation. For those requiring additional study, gaps in these areas may be filled by any of the many excellent texts on music fundamentals.

PITCH AND NOTE

Pitch refers to the highness or lowness of a musical tone. It is the frequency at which sound vibrates. On a particular instrument or voice, a single pitch may be sounded in a variety of ways, including variations in volume and duration. A pitch, along with how that pitch is sounded, is called a **note**. A written note consists of a notehead, and, unless it is a whole note, a stem.

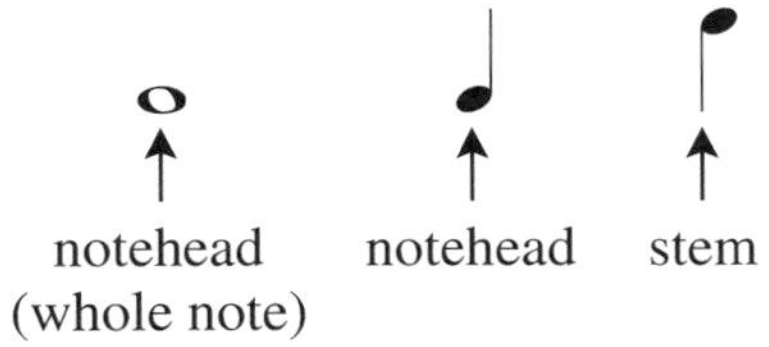

The first seven letters of the alphabet (A, B, C, D, E, F, G) are employed to name pitches. These letters are played on the piano keyboard by the white keys.

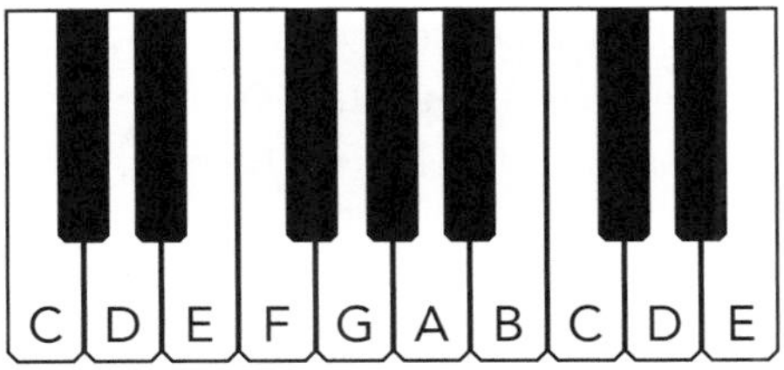

STAFF

In musical notation, pitch is indicated by notes written on a **staff**. The staff has five lines and four spaces.

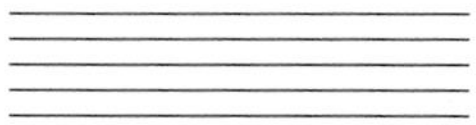

Notes may be written on the lines or in the spaces.

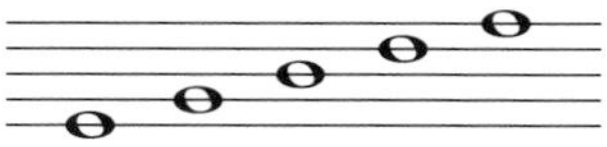

CLEFS

A **clef** sign is used to show which range of pitches are to be encompassed on a staff. This is necessary because there are only seven letters, and many more than seven different pitches. The **treble clef** (G clef) identifies the second line from the bottom of the staff as G.

With this clef added, the entire staff is now referred to as the **treble staff**, with notes on this staff belonging to pitches of medium to high frequency.

Medium to low frequency notes are indicated by placing the **bass clef** on the staff, resulting in the **bass staff**. This clef is attached to the second line from the top indicating the letter F and is therefore also referred to as the **F clef**.

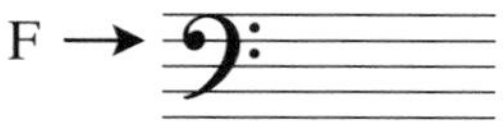

Since it encompasses a very wide range of pitches, the piano needs two clefs and thus two staves. The treble staff above the bass staff is referred to as the **grand staff**. On the piano, the right hand usually plays the notes on the treble staff and the left hand usually plays the bass staff notes.

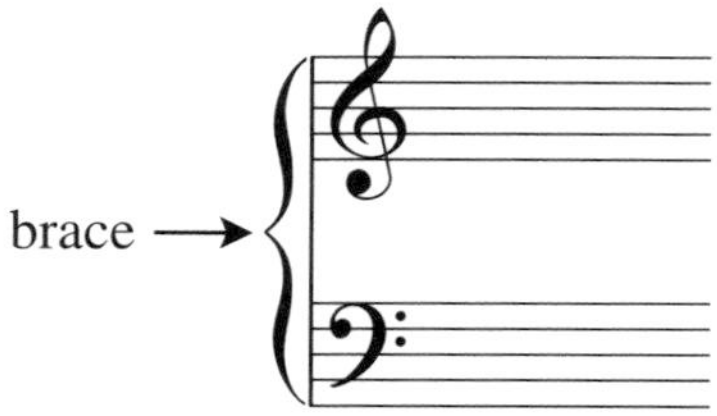

LEDGER LINES

Ledger lines, above and below both staves, are often used to indicate the pitches that lie outside the staff.

ACCIDENTALS

As shown earlier, the white piano keys play the notes represented by the seven letter names. The black keys, which sound pitches in between the letter names, are represented by **accidentals**. On the piano, from one key to the next, whether black or white, is called a **half step**. A **sharp** (♯) sign raises a letter name by half step, while a **flat** (♭) lowers it by a half-step. A natural sign restores a note to its original white key.

Any black key may be identified as a sharp note or a flat note. For example, a D raised a half-step by a sharp sign is called D♯, while an E lowered a half-step by a flat sign is called an E♭. E♭ and D♯ are two different names for the same pitch, the same black key on the piano. These two pitches are said to be **enharmonic** of each other.

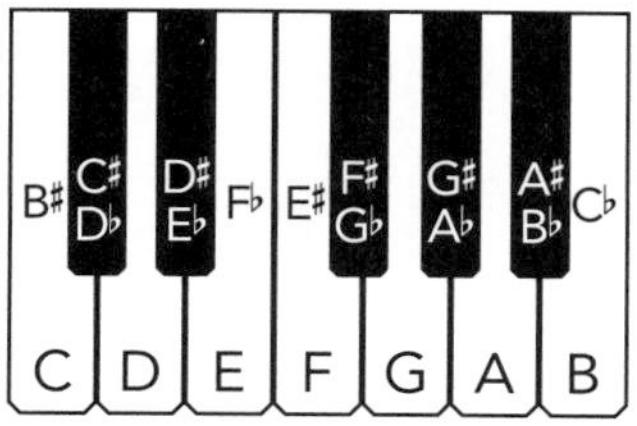

INTERVALS

An **interval** is the distance between two pitches. A half step is just one kind of interval. The interval from one key, skipping just one key (black or white, whichever is closest), to the next key is called a **whole step**.

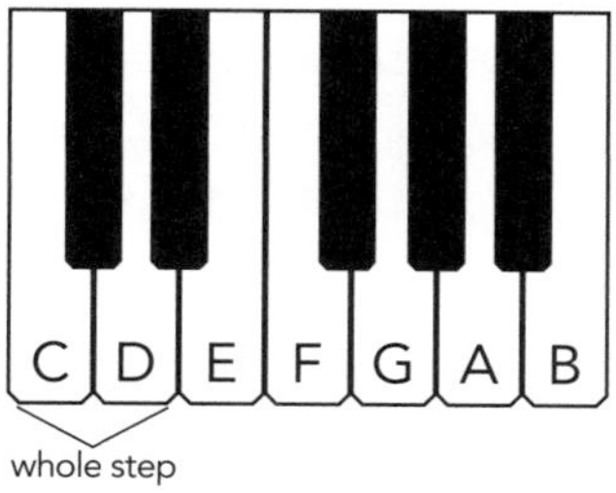

Intervals can also be labeled by their arithmetic name. The **arithmetic interval** from one letter name to the next letter of the alphabet is called a **second**. Both the half step and the whole step may be referred to as seconds if they are named by adjacent letter names. These two kinds of seconds are differentiated by descriptions of **quality** (or color). Two basic types of quality are the **major** and **minor**. The half step from C to D♭ is a **minor** second. The whole step from C to D is a **major** second. (Further discussion of "quality" will follow later.)

The distance from one letter name to another letter name, skipping a letter in between, is referred to as a **third**. Skipping two letter names is a fourth, three a fifth, and so on.

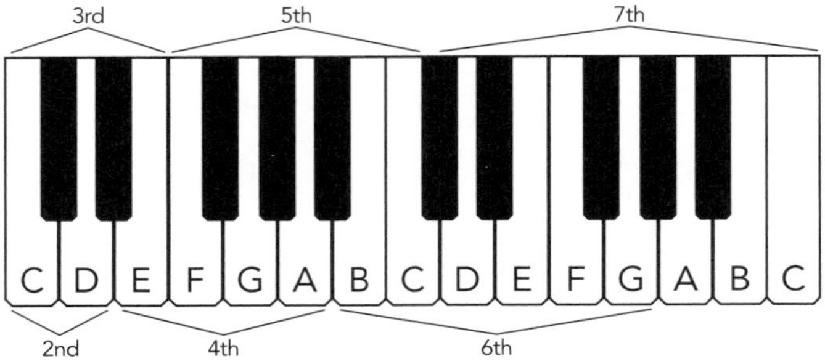

An octave is the distance from one letter name to the next instance of that same letter name, up or down.

The following example shows major intervals within an octave, on just the white keys, beginning on C. The unison, octave, fifth, and fourth cannot be major or minor, rather they exist as **perfect**, **augmented**, or **diminished**.

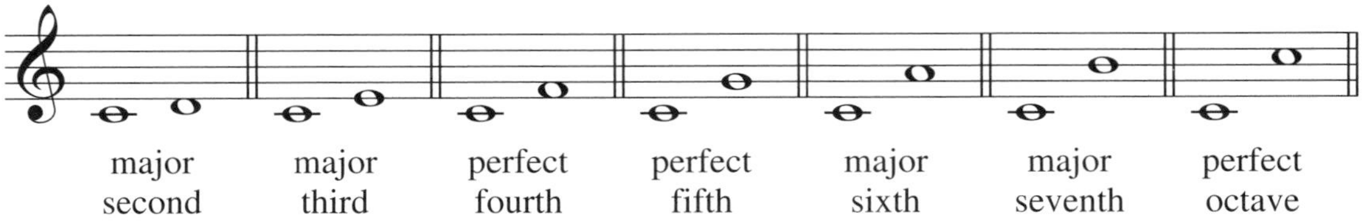

When identifying and writing intervals, find the arithmetic distance first. Two adjacent letter names will always be a second of some kind. Skipping one letter name will always be a third, etc. In determining quality, one method consists of memorizing the number of half steps from one pitch to the next. For example, a C up to an E is a third of some kind. Then, knowing that the distance from C up to E is four half steps, the next step is using the knowledge that a third consisting of four half steps is a major third. Minor intervals are one half step smaller than major intervals; e.g., C up to E♭ is a minor third.

The following example takes the major intervals from the previous example and lowers them by a half step to form minor intervals.

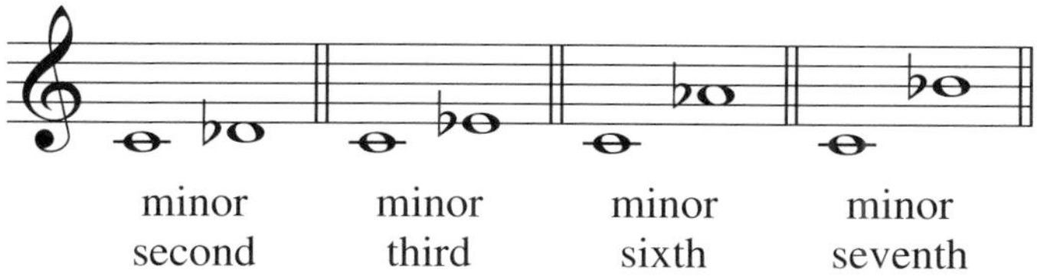

Now back to the perfect intervals. The perfect fourth is five half steps and the perfect fifth seven half steps, while the octave is 12 half steps. Remember that perfect intervals may also be augmented or diminished. Raising a perfect interval by a half step results in an augmented interval. Lowering a perfect interval by half step results in a diminished interval.

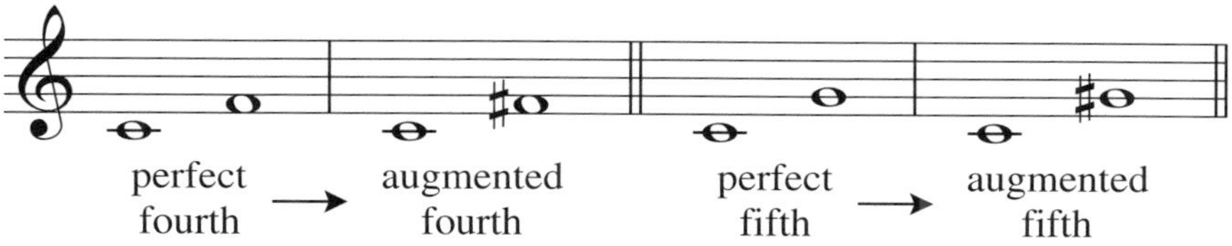

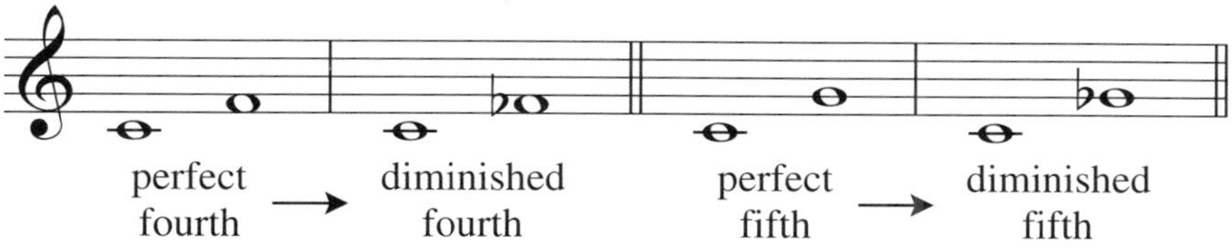

Both the augmented fourth and the diminished fifth are comprised of six half steps.

Counting half steps can be a foolproof yet tedious method to figure out an interval's quality. This method also does not put an interval's quality within the context or function of a specific key. (See the section on scales and keys that follows.) For now, begin by memorizing and counting half steps. Eventually, when scales and key signatures are understood, you can use that knowledge to better identify and spell intervals as well as understand how they work within real music.

Melodic and Harmonic Intervals

On instruments such as the piano, organ, guitar, and harp, among others, more than one pitch may be sounded at the same time. This results in a **harmonic** interval. Sounding two pitches consecutively is called a **melodic** interval. Harmonic intervals are notated vertically.

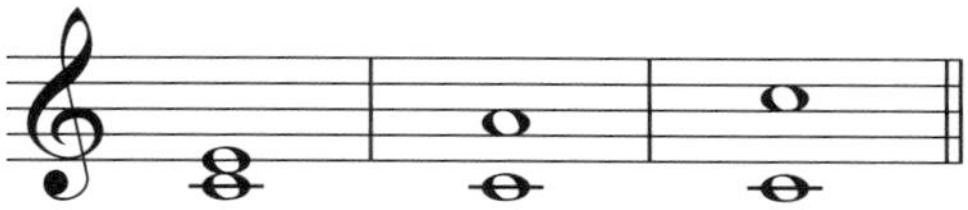

Melodic intervals are notated consecutively, from left to right.

SCALES

A scale is a series of pitches in a pattern of steps (whole and/or half); it is played melodically. The pitches of a scale may form the basic pitch material for a composition. The two most basic scales that govern much of Western art music from before the 20th century are the **major scales** and the **minor scales**.

Major Scale

The pattern of steps for the **major scale** is as follows: whole, whole, half, whole, whole, whole, half. When beginning on C, the major scale consists of all "natural" pitches (only white keys).

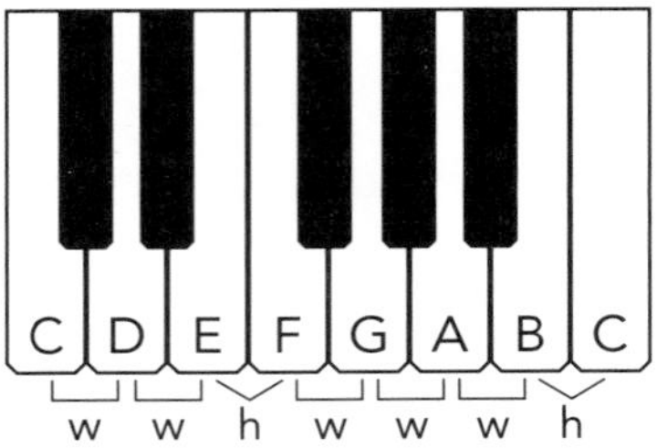

Note that the natural half steps occur between E-F and B-C. This knowledge is essential when spelling **any** scale. See the Exercises at the end of the chapter to spell all the major scales..

When beginning on any pitch other than C, the major scale will consist of at least one "black key" note. Beginning on G, F♯ is included and not F♮. (Note: when referring to pitches, always include its accidental, especially when it is a sharp or flat pitch. F and F♯ are two different pitches as much as F and A are two different pitches.) Beginning on F, the major scale includes B♭.

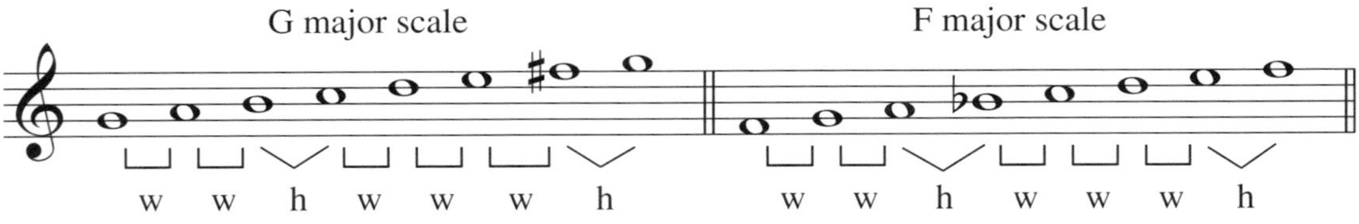

Minor Scale

The **minor scale** consists of pitches following the pattern whole, half, whole, whole, half, whole, whole. When beginning on A, the minor scale consists of all natural pitches.

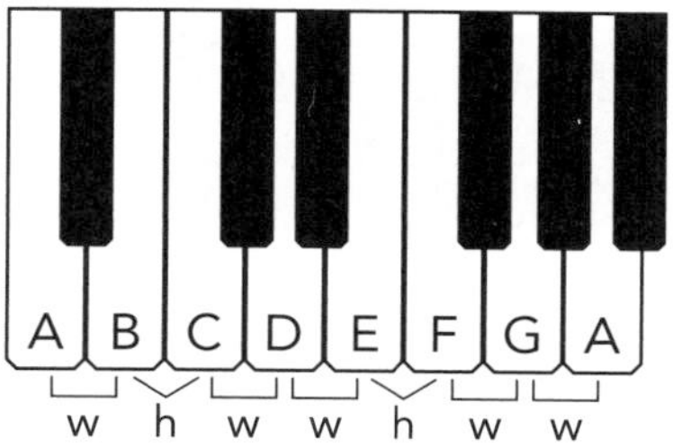

Just like the major scale, only one minor scale will consist of only the white keys (A minor). Here are minor scales built on E and G.

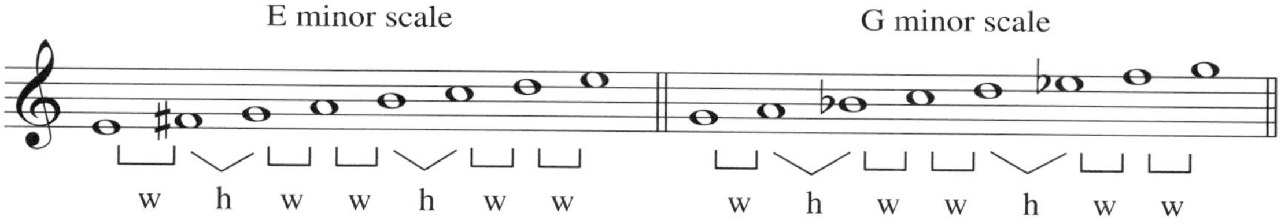

There are three different kinds of minor scales. Referred to in the previous examples is the **natural minor scale**. The two other forms of the minor scale are the **harmonic minor** and **melodic minor**. To form the harmonic minor, take the natural minor and raise the seventh degree (tone) a half step, but remember to retain its letter name!

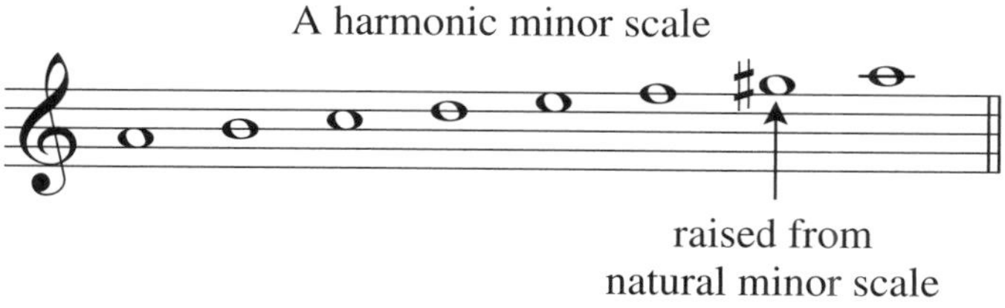

The melodic minor takes the natural minor and raises both the sixth and seventh degrees a half step. In addition, when the melodic minor scale descends, it is restored to its natural minor form.

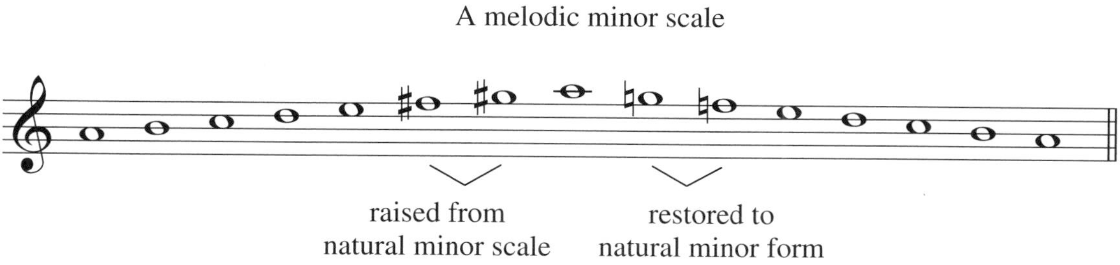

KEY SIGNATURES AND CIRCLE OF FIFTHS

A scale often constitutes the basic pitch material for a composition. A musical work using the pitches of the G major scale may be said to be "in the key of G major." Since all major scales follow the same pattern, a system has been developed to indicate more succinctly which pitches are to be sharped or flatted throughout a composition. A **key signature** is placed to the right of the clef. This consists of flat or sharp signs showing which pitches are affected by these accidentals throughout the work. For example, we learned that the G major scale contains an F♯. Instead of notating a sharp sign before every F in the piece, just one sharp sign (on just one F) at the beginning indicates that *all* Fs (in all octaves) are to be played as F♯.

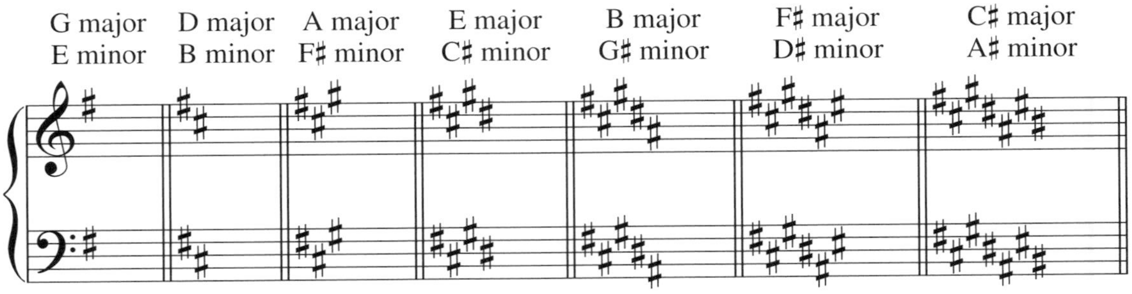

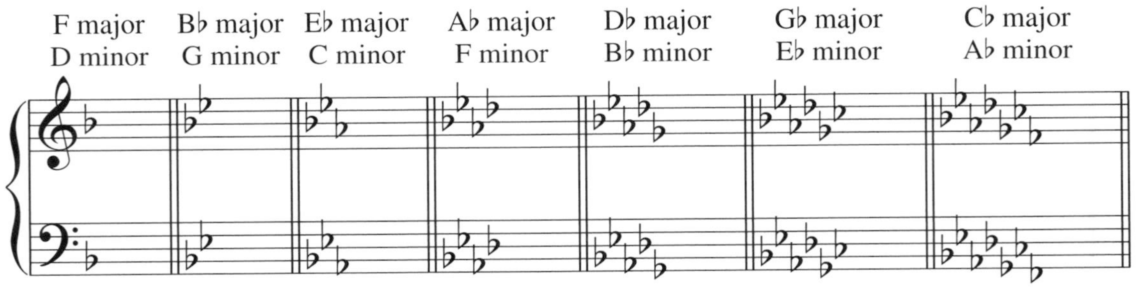

As they practice their instruments, musicians should begin to memorize the look, sound, and feel of the different keys. As this process unfolds, they will discover that they do not need to focus their attention on remembering exactly what pitches are to be played sharp or flat every time they occur—this becomes automatic.

Patterns emerge when viewing all the key signatures in the previous example. First, there is only one key signature with one sharp, only one key signature with two sharps, and the same with flats, etc. Second, the interval between the pitches that name the different keys is always the same. For example, D major, which has two sharps, is a fifth above G major, which has one sharp. In the flat keys, this interval pattern is reversed: F major, which has one flat, is a fifth above B♭, which has two flats. This pattern is known as the **Circle of Fifths** (or Cycle of Fifths).

The order in which the accidentals themselves appear on the staff follows the circle of fifths. Sharp signs follow the order F♯, up a fifth to C♯, up a fifth to G♯, etc. For flats, the order is B♭, down a fifth to E♭, down a fifth to A♭, etc.

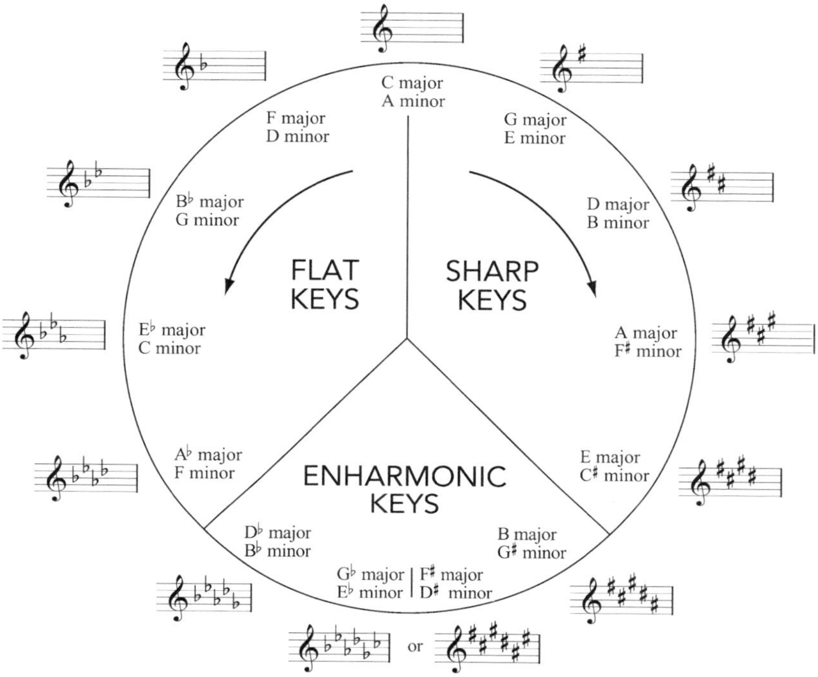

Note above that the minor keys are also listed. Each minor scale/key shares a key signature with a major scale. C major and A minor both include no sharps or flats. The key of A minor is considered to be the **relative minor** of C major, and vice-versa.

CHORDS

While two pitches sounded at the same time form a harmonic interval, three or more pitches played at the same time are called a **chord**.

Triads

A **triad** consists of three pitches, stacked in thirds. A triad built from the starting pitch (tonic) of a major scale is a **major chord** (or **major triad**). This one is built on C.

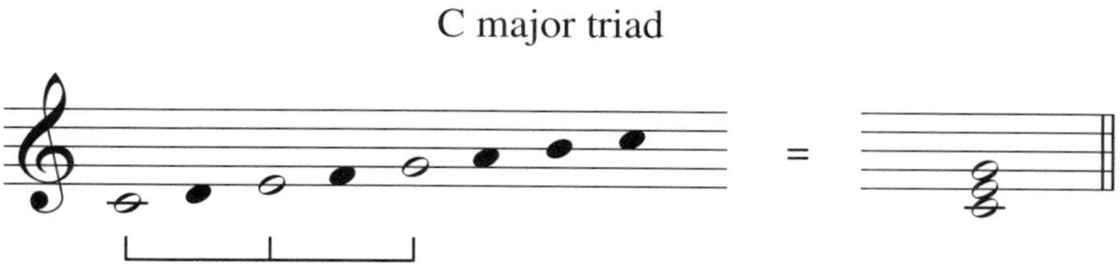

The **minor triad** is built from the first, third, and fifth pitches of the natural minor scale. This one is built on A.

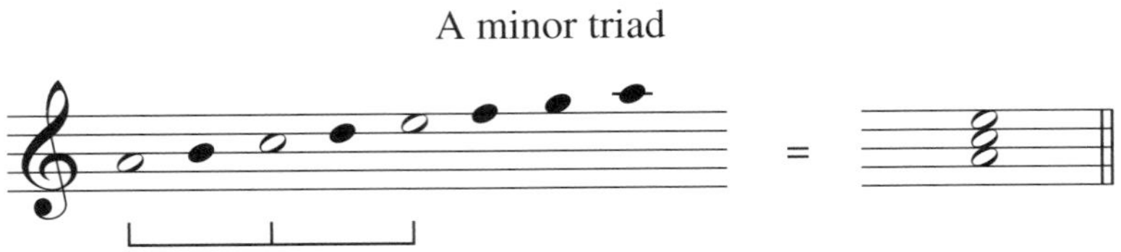

The **root** of a triad is the note upon which it is built. The next pitch up is the **third**, while the top pitch is called the **fifth**. These names or parts of a triad are referred to as **chord tones**.

Triads are identified by the qualities of the stacked thirds. In a major triad, from root up to third is a major third. From third up to fifth is a minor third. In minor triads, the distance from root up to third is a minor third, and from third up to fifth is a major third. In both triads, the interval from root up to fifth is a perfect fifth.

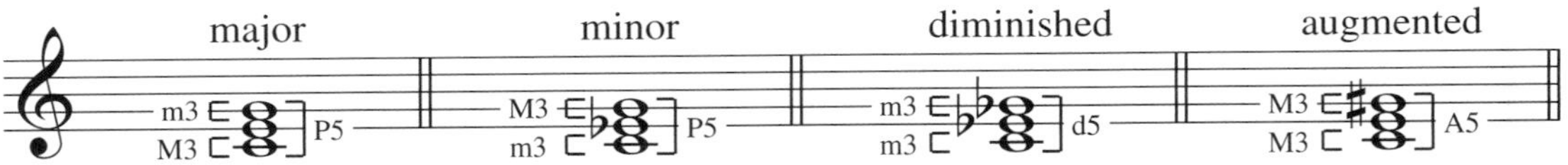

There are two more types of triads shown above, the **diminished** and **augmented**. One method of identifying and writing these triads is to start from a major and/or minor triad and work from there. A diminished triad is like a minor triad with the fifth lowered one half step, retaining the same letter name. For example, to spell a C diminished triad, first determine the spelling of the C minor triad (C-E♭-G), then lower the fifth a half step, keeping the same letter name. The result is C-E♭-G♭.

An augmented triad may be constructed beginning with a major triad. The augmented triad sees the fifth raised a half step. So, a C augmented triad is spelled C-E-G♯.

Major and minor triads form the basis of most of the chords used in tonal music. The diminished triad is not often found in **root position**, that is, with the root of the chord is in the lowest voice. The augmented triad is very rarely used and will be considered in *Hal Leonard Harmony & Theory, Part 2*. For the time being we will deal only with chords in root position, which means that only major and minor triads will be chosen.

Seventh Chords

Larger chords may result from stacking more thirds from the bottom note up. A **seventh chord** consists of four pitches built in thirds. Just like a triad, a seventh chord also has a root, third, and fifth, with the addition of the top chord tone, the **seventh**. There are five types of seventh chords.

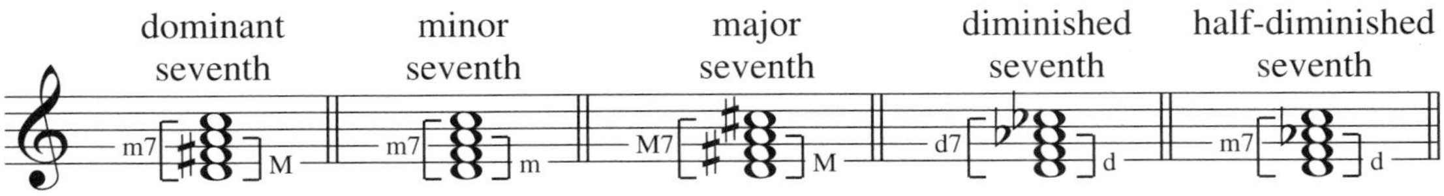

The dominant seventh chord is by far the most common seventh chord in tonal music, followed by the minor seventh. The three remaining chords are used less often, though all are essential.

The Structure of Seventh Chords

type of seventh chord	triad basis	interval of seventh above the root	abbreviation
dominant seventh	major	minor seventh	Mm
minor seventh	minor	minor seventh	mm
major seventh	major	major seventh	MM
diminished seventh	diminished	diminished seventh	dd
half-diminished seventh	diminished	minor seventh	dm

Type of triad
Interval of seventh above root

In due time we will examine the seventh chords in all their various usages, but our full attention will first be given to triads as they are employed in diatonic harmony, beginning in Chapter Two.

RHYTHM AND NOTE VALUES

So far, we've dealt with matters of pitch, which help define a note and the music that makes use of these notes. **Duration**, the length of time a note is held, is also an important facet in defining it. In music, there are also spaces of silence called **rests**. The combination of notes and rests, along with the **tempo** (speed) of a piece of music make up the concept of **rhythm**.

To show duration, different types of notes are used, indicated by their notehead, their stem (except the whole note, which has no stem), and their **flag(s)**. The following example shows several basic types of notes, in order from shortest duration to longest.

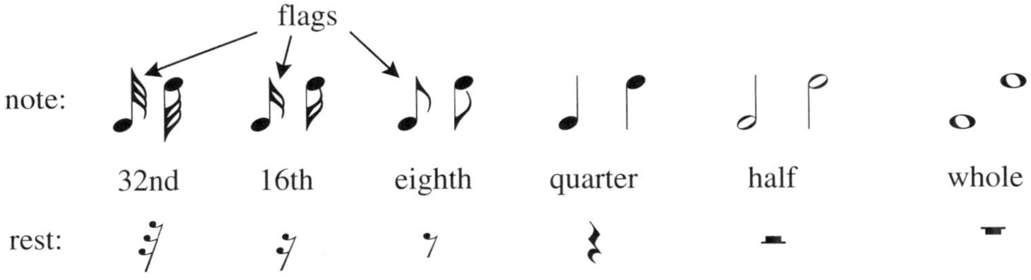

Note that the 32nd note has three flags, the 16th note has two flags, the eighth note has one flag, etc. As we progress from the 32nd note to the 16th note, the value doubles. Therefore, the 16th may be viewed as twice as long as the 32nd. The eighth is twice as long as the 16th, etc.

Multiple notes smaller than the quarter, when following each other consecutively, get beamed together. The number of horizontal **beams** is the same as the number of flags that note receives.

Different combinations of note values may be notated with various arrays of beams. Beams are often used to indicate combination of notes that equal either one or two quarter notes. For example, because four 16ths equal one quarter, they are usually beamed into groups of four.

Placing a dot after a note increases its duration by one half. For example:

(The curved line connecting the notes is a **tie**; the two are performed as a single note value.)

METER

Music can be organized into small metrical units consisting of the same length of time within each. These units are called **measures** and are marked off by **bar lines**.

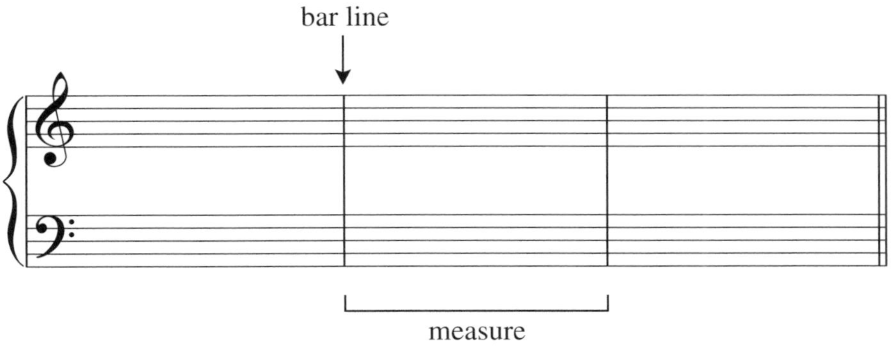

Meter is determined by the amount of time in each measure. Time is generally measured by the pulse or **beat** of the music, so different types of notes may be defined by how many beats they receive in a given meter. A **time signature** is placed immediately to the right of the key signature, and indicates how many beats each measure receives in a composition (or until a different meter is indicated by a new time signature). One of the most frequently used meters is $\frac{4}{4}$ or **C**, also known as "common time."

Here is an array of regularly used time signatures:

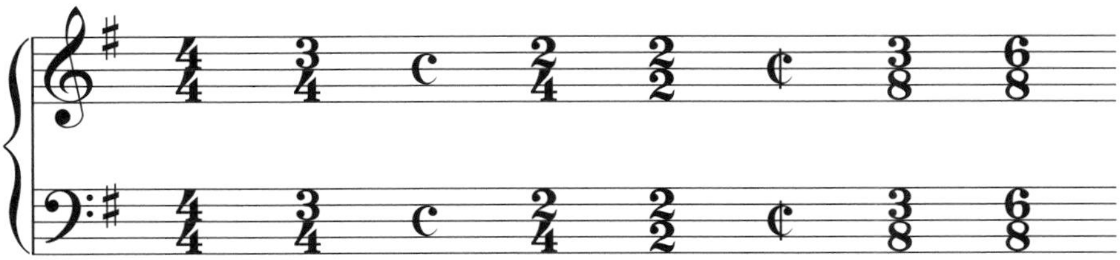

The top number indicates the number of beats per measure, while the bottom number indicates which type of note receives the beat. A measure may have any number of beats, from one (rare) to four (most common) to a maximum of 12. Other common time signatures include $\frac{2}{4}$, $\frac{3}{4}$, and $\frac{6}{8}$. The bottom number is more restricted, with "4" indicating the quarter note and "2" the half. Time signatures may also include an eighth-note pulse ("8" on the bottom) or even "16."

You can count the number of beats at a steady tempo to feel and more accurately perform any given meter. In 4/4, counting to four each measure indicates the quarter-note pulse. Because notes smaller than the quarter may occur between beats, other counting methods must be employed. Exactly halfway between each beat may be counted with the word "and."

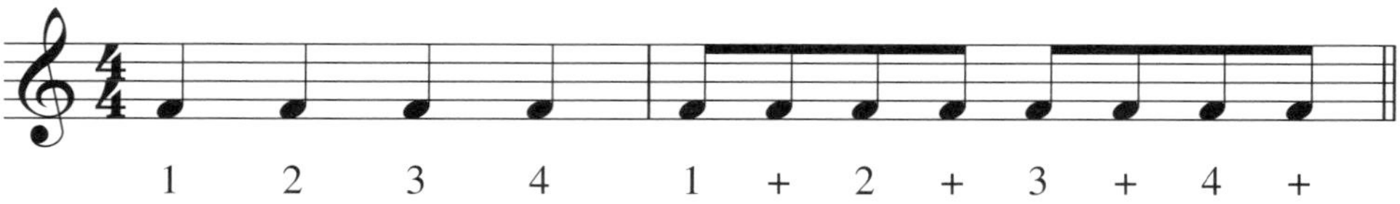

The quarter-note beat may be further divided into four, eight, 16, or (very rarely) 32 equal parts. For now, though, we'll limit ourselves to dividing the beat into four parts. The following example indicates a counting system for all these **subdivisions** of the beat.

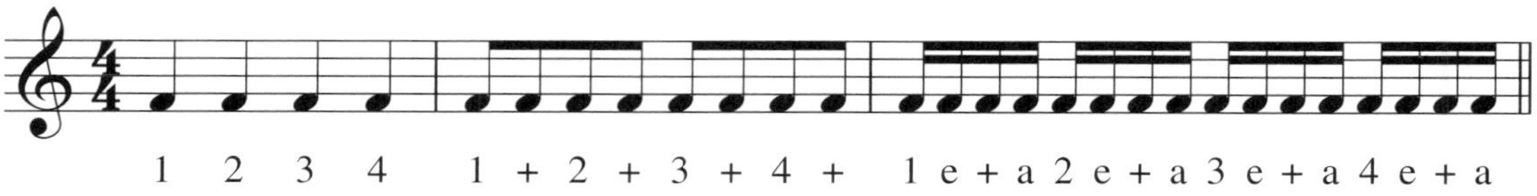

Simple and Compound Meter

Simple meters are those that divide the pulse into multiples of two (two, four, eight, etc.). Such meters include 4/4, 2/4, and 3/4. There are additional time signatures that indicate simple meters and include a "2" on the bottom. The most common is 2/2 (two half-note beats per measure). It is usually referred to as "cut-time," and can be notated as ₵.

Compound meters divide the beat into multiples of three. The most common is 6/8. While one may count up to six in each measure (for the six eighth notes per measure), the pulse is actually felt as two larger beats per measure, with each beat consisting of three eighth notes. Referring back to the section on rhythm and note values, you'll notice that one of the notes included a small dot to the right of the notehead. A dot on any note adds half of the original note value (without the dot). Since a half note (in a meter with a "4" on the bottom) receives two beats, a dot on a half note gives it another beat, indicating that the dotted-half note receives three beats. Similarly, a dotted quarter note receives one and a half beats (three eighth notes, total). So, the pulse in 6/8 meter, which is divided into three eighth notes, would be the dotted-quarter note. Very often, when practicing a composition in the early stages, a musician might count each of the six eighth-note beats. Then, as the work becomes more comfortable and can be played faster, the player may count just the two beats per measure.

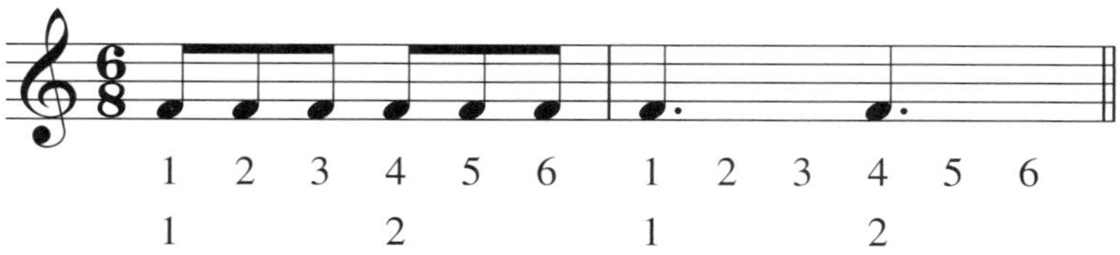

EXERCISES

1. Label the following pitches by letter name and, where applicable, accidental.

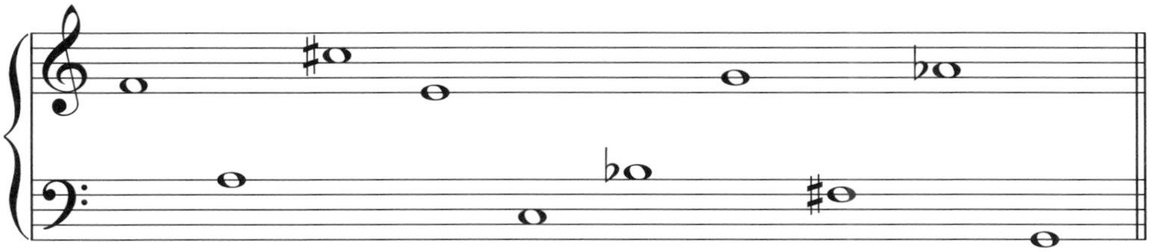

____ ____ ____ ____ ____ ____ ____ ____ ____ ____

2. Practice drawing the treble and bass clef below. Turn the two staves into a grand staff. Finally, on the grand staff write at least one instance of the given letter name using whole notes.

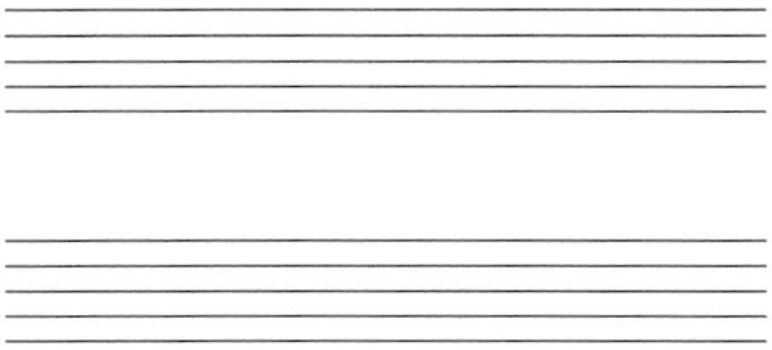

3. The key signature for C♯ major is shown below. Use this key signature as a guide and write the key signature for each of the indicated keys on the grand staff.

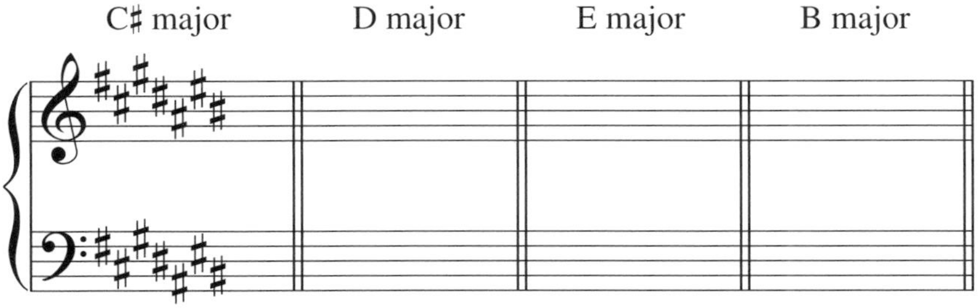

4. The key signature for C♭ major is shown below. Use this key signature as a guide and write the key signature for each of the indicated keys on the grand staff.

C♭ major   E♭ major   F major   D♭ major

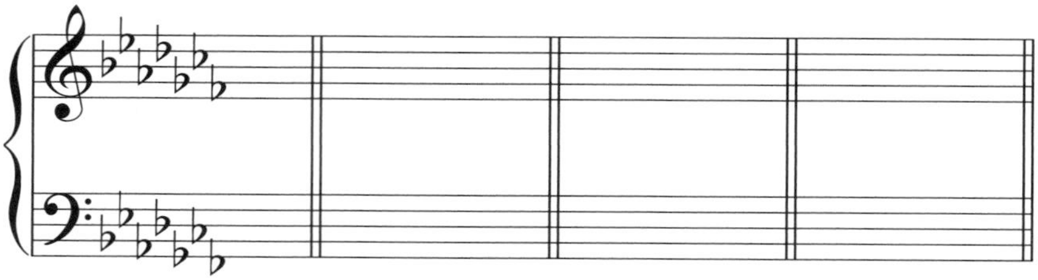

5. Using accidentals (not key signatures), write the following major scales on the grand staff. The first one has been done for you.

D major

E♭ major

A major

A♭ major

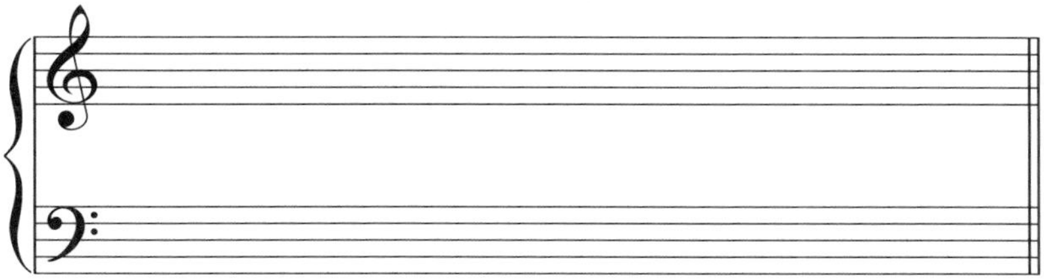

6. Write the following harmonic and melodic minor scales on the grand staff. The natural minor is given.

G natural minor

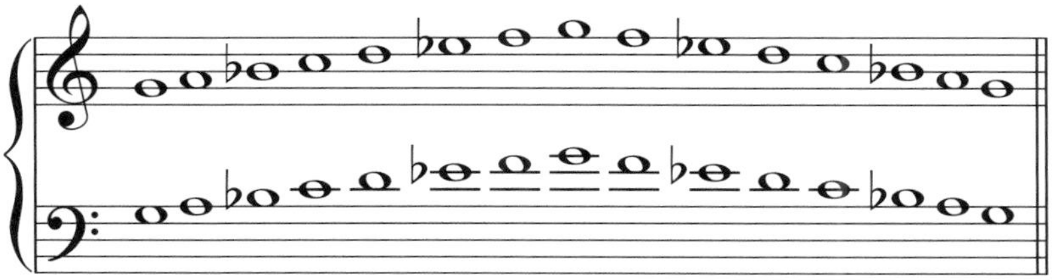

G harmonic minor

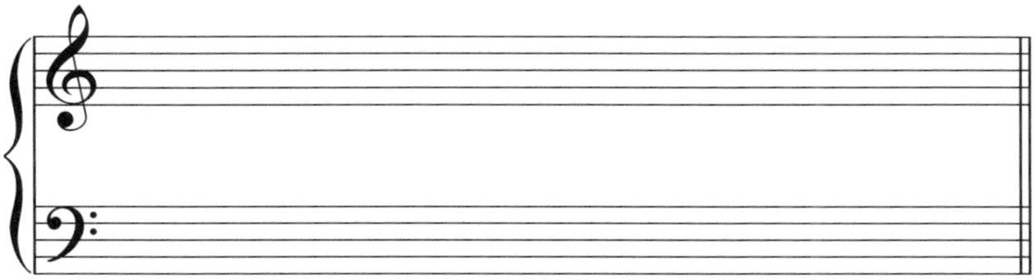

G melodic minor

B natural minor

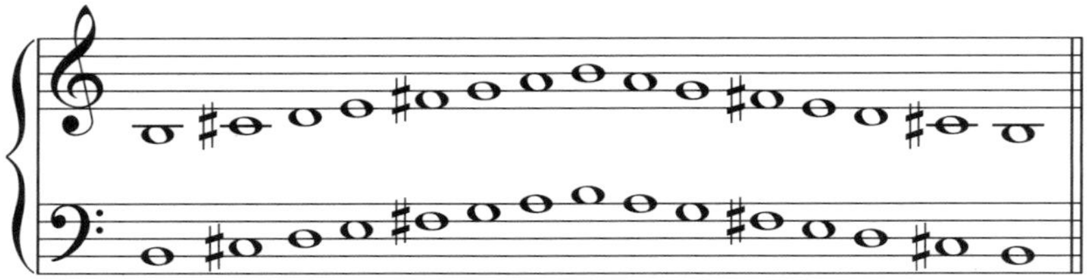

B harmonic minor

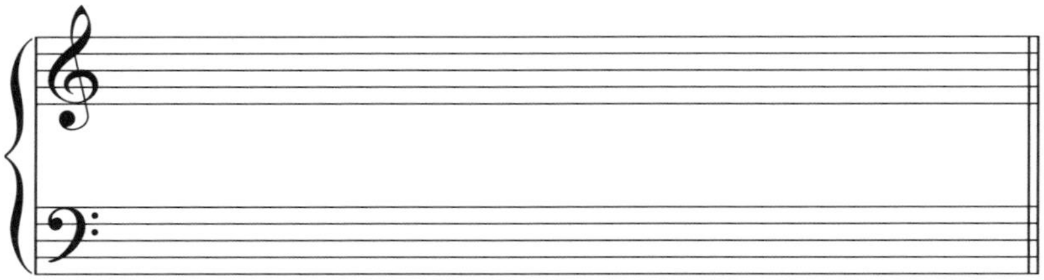

B melodic minor

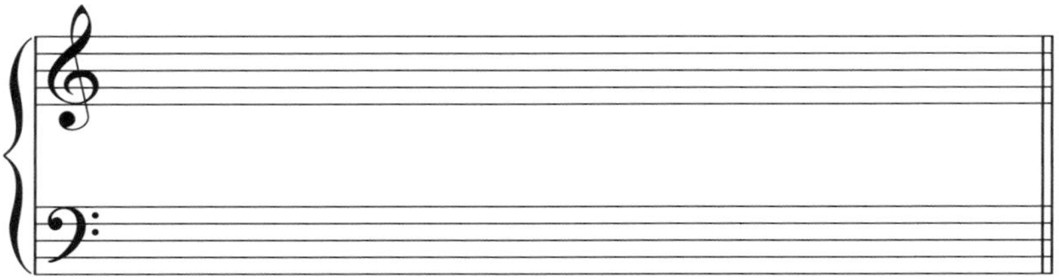

7. Identify the following intervals by arithmetic distance and quality.

8. Identify the following triads by letter name and quality (major or minor).

9. Provide proper bar lines for the time signatures shown below.

CHAPTER 2 FURTHER PRELIMINARIES

Tonal harmony is divided into two main classifications, **diatonic** and **chromatic**.

Diatonic harmony confines itself to chords that do not use any accidentals outside the key. Only the seven unaltered tones of a given diatonic scale are used to form chords. (Note: The raised seventh degree of the minor scale and the occasionally raised sixth degree of the minor scale are exceptions. The chords formed by these accidentals are considered an integral part of diatonic harmony.) Diatonic harmony is the subject of this book.

Chromatic harmony uses accidentals outside the key signature to form chords. Tonal music is rich in such chords. They are the subject of *Hal Leonard Harmony & Theory, Part 2*.

VOCAL RANGES

The study of harmony is approached from the perspective of vocal music. **Four-part harmony** is the norm: soprano, alto, tenor, and bass. For convenience, these vocal parts are written on two staves, using treble and bass clefs:

Soprano and alto share a staff in treble clef, while tenor and bass share a staff in bass clef. Notice the direction of the stems for each part. This so-called "divided stemming" is used consistently. Stem length is approximately the span of the interval of a fifth or sixth. The ranges of the four voices are shown below:

CHORD LAYOUT

Since triads contain three pitches, one of these must be doubled when writing in four-part harmony. In root position, the usual procedure is to double the root. We will call this "normal" doubling. Other doublings in root position will be considered later. In each of the chords shown below, the root has been doubled, and the third and fifth are present. Arrows indicate the doubled roots:

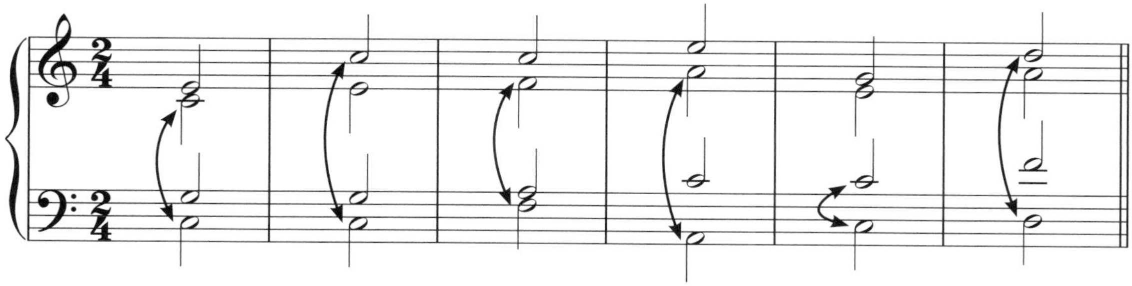

Doubling at the unison is perfectly good as long as the note doubled is within the range of both voices:

For now, only the tenor and bass may be doubled at the unison, since we are doubling only the root, which is confined to the bass in root position. Unison doublings among the upper voices will be encountered later.

CLOSE STRUCTURE AND OPEN STRUCTURE

When the tones of the soprano, alto, and tenor are as close together as possible, you have **close structure**. If a chord tone can be inserted between S and A, or A and T, you have **open structure**. Both are equally good.

close

no room for chord tones
between upper voices

open

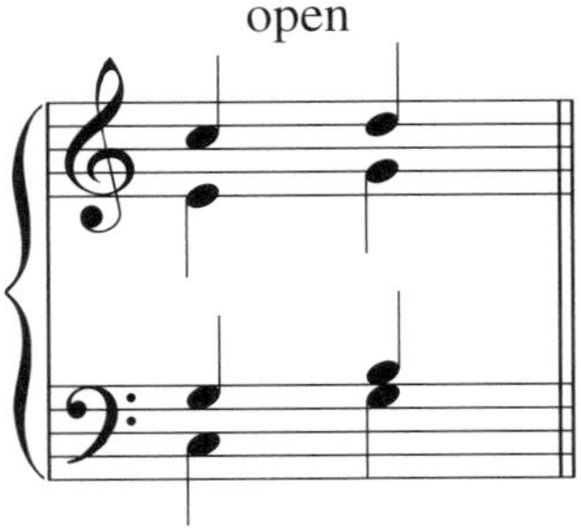

room for chord tones
between upper voices

SPACING

Do not exceed an octave between soprano and alto or between alto and tenor. The following are to be avoided:

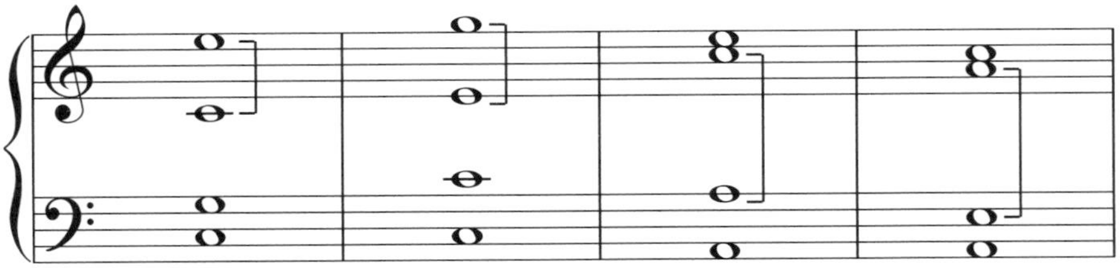

This principle does not apply to the space between tenor and bass. All of the following are good:

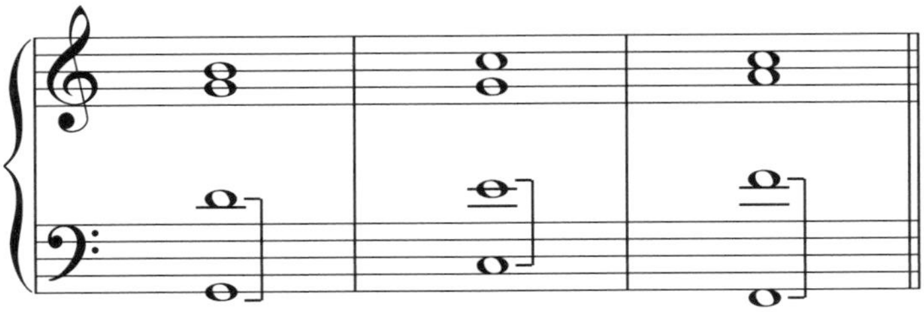

CHORD REPETITION

A chord in root position, when repeated, offers the possibility of rearranging the chord tones among the upper parts. Also, the bass line might skip an octave if its range permits. The most important line is the melody, the soprano part. Chord repetition can be made more interesting by a change in the soprano part.

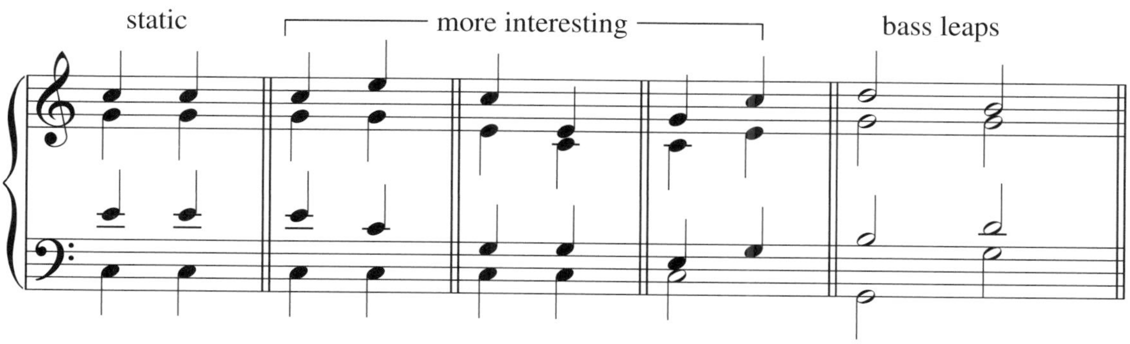

Notice that the doubled root is maintained in each chord, and that the third and fifth are always present.

NAMES OF THE SCALE DEGREES

Each scale degree has a name in both major and minor. In major:

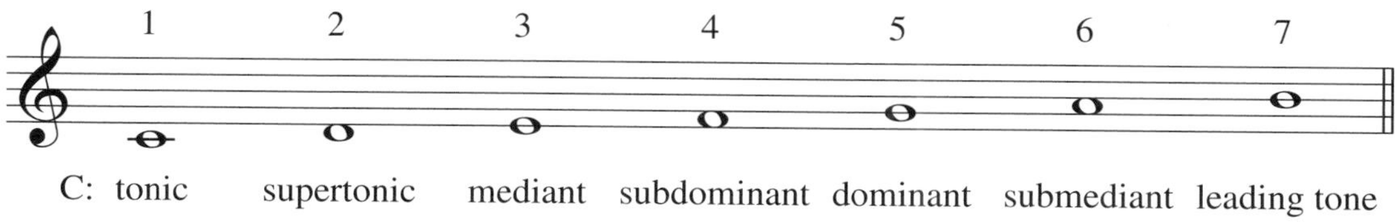

In minor keys, the natural seventh degree is called the **subtonic**, while the raised seventh degree, found in harmonic and melodic ascending minor scales, is called the **leading tone**:

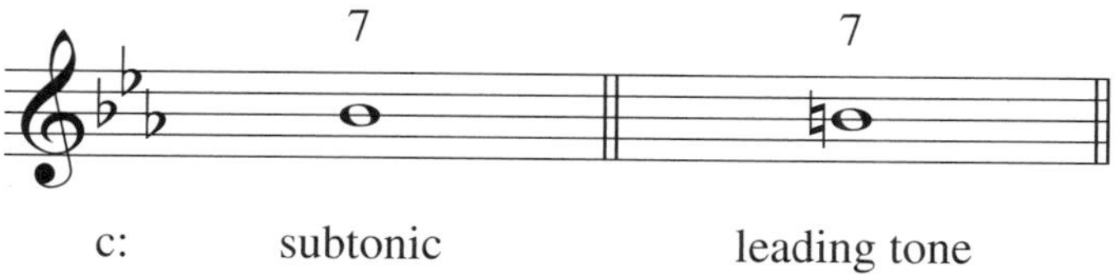

LABELING TRIADS

It is customary to use Roman numerals to designate triads. Upper case is used for major triads, lower case for minor triads. Augmented triads use upper case with a + sign after, and diminished triads use lower case with a small circle to the upper right.

Triads in Major

Note that I, IV, and V are major, ii, iii, and vi are minor, while vii° is a diminished triad.

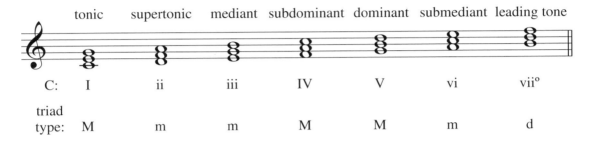

	tonic	supertonic	mediant	subdominant	dominant	submediant	leading tone

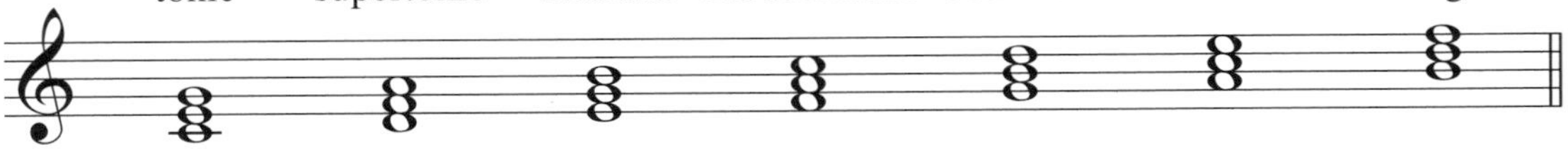

C:	I	ii	iii	IV	V	vi	vii°
triad type:	M	m	m	M	M	m	d

Triads in Minor

Because it is possible to have the raised seventh degree (leading tone) and the raised sixth degree, many more chords are possible in minor keys than in major keys. There are 13 possible chords. Those chords that are most commonly found in diatonic harmony are marked with an asterisk. These will form the basis of our study, although the remaining six chords have their place in music.

	*	*		*		*			*	*			*

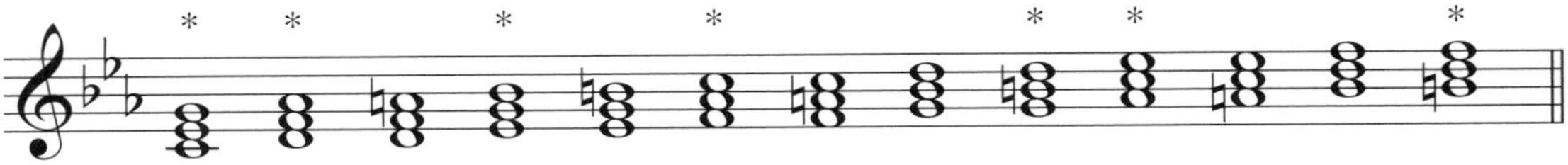

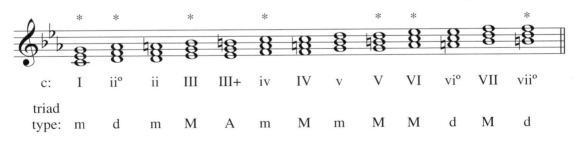

c:	I	ii°	ii	III	III+	iv	IV	v	V	VI	vi°	VII	vii°
triad type:	m	d	m	M	A	m	M	m	M	M	d	M	d

Eliminating the more rarely used chords, we have the following:

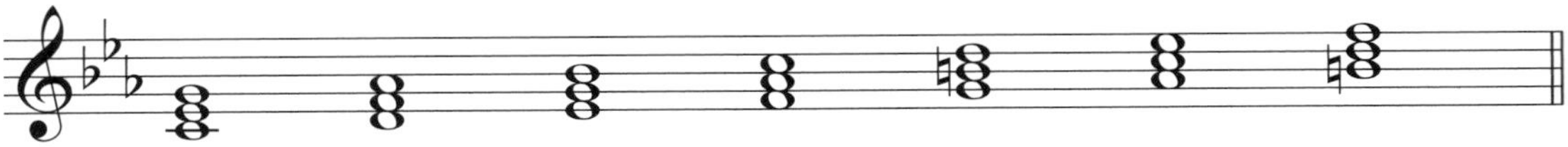

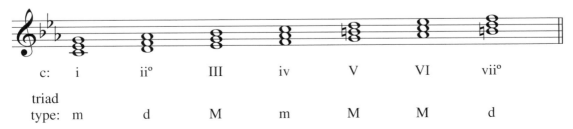

c:	i	ii°	III	iv	V	VI	vii°
triad type:	m	d	M	m	M	M	d

Notice that ii° and vii° are diminished triads. Notice also how the succession of roots forms the harmonic minor scale. With the exception of III, all of the chords are derived from the tones of the harmonic minor scale.

Before moving on to the next chapter, complete the following exercises.

EXERCISES

1. Find errors in terms of doubling, spacing, and ranges. Some examples are without error.

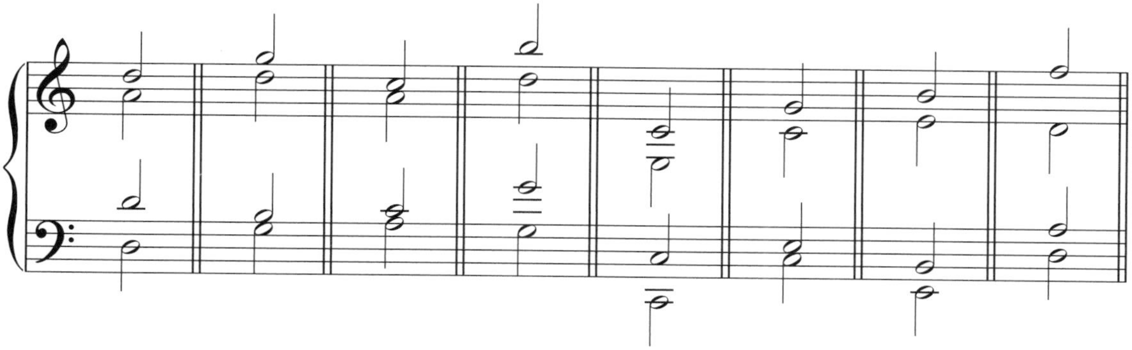

2. Using Roman numerals, identify these chords:

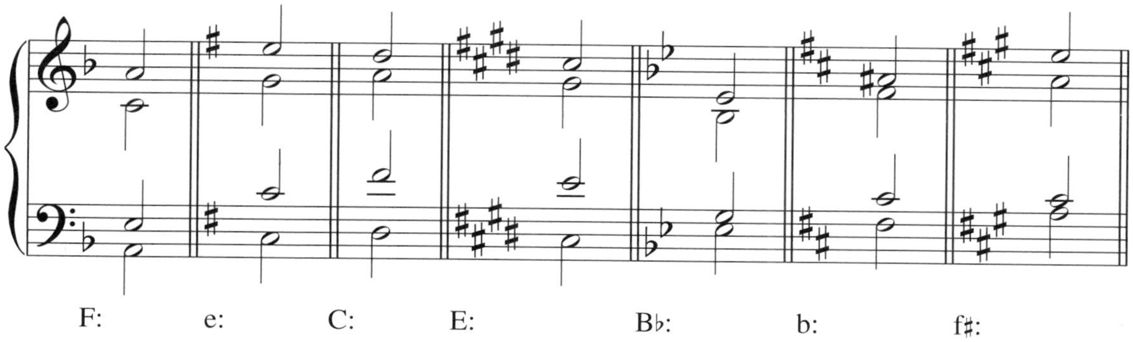

3. Using proper doubling and spacing, fill out these chords:

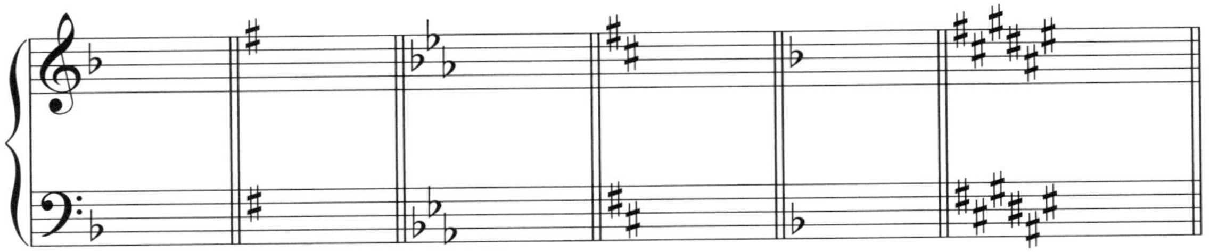

d: iv G: V c: VI D: iii F: ii d♯: V

4. Fill in the chords as specified:

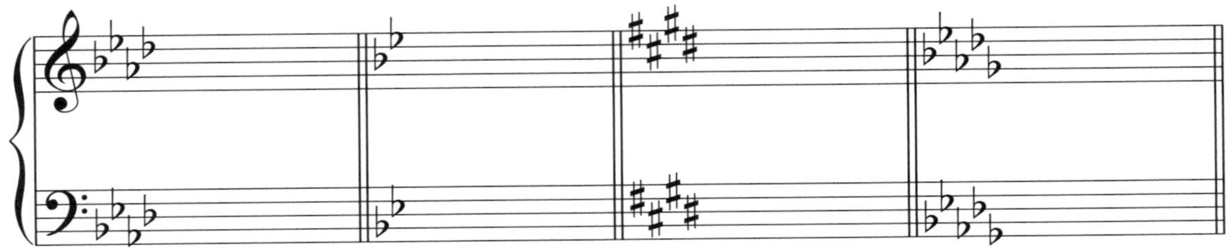

f: dominant B♭: submediant E: mediant D♭: dominant

CHAPTER 3

TRIADS IN ROOT POSITION

The most important chord is the **tonic chord** (I, i). The tonic chord may move to any other chord. The next most important chord is the **dominant chord** (V). It has a very strong tendency to move to the tonic chord. In the progression V–I, the root of V moves down a fifth (or up a fourth) to the root of the I chord. This form of root movement represents the most common type of chord progression in tonal music. This pattern of root movement (down a fifth or up a fourth) is true for other degrees of the scale and the chords built upon them: ii–V, I–IV, vi–ii, iii–vi, for example. (IV–vii° and vii°–iii are less common.)

The reverse progression (up a fifth or down a fourth) is also used, especially I–V and IV–I. ii–vi and vi–iii are less common, and V–ii, vii°–IV, and iii–vii° are very rare. As mentioned earlier, the triad on the seventh degree (vii°) is rarely used in root position and will not be included in instructions that follow. The leading tone triad becomes very important, however, when we examine first inversion (Chapter Four). For now, let us confine ourselves to chord connection in root position.

CONNECTING CHORDS WITH ROOTS A P5 (OR P4) APART

There are three basic methods:

Method #1

1. Write in the bass note of both chords.
2. Write the remaining tones (S, A, T) of the first chord in any of the many ways possible.
3. Hold over the tone that is common to both chords.
4. The remaining two voices move by step to the nearest chord tones. This movement may be upward or downward.

I-IV in D major

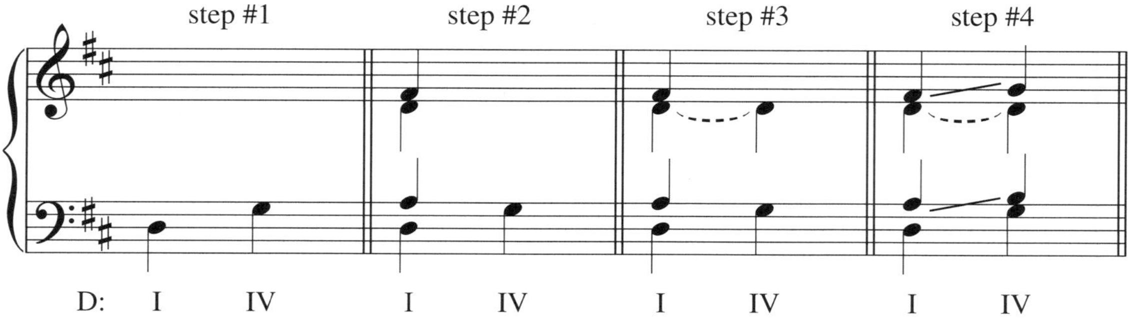

Exactly the same procedure was used in all of the following:

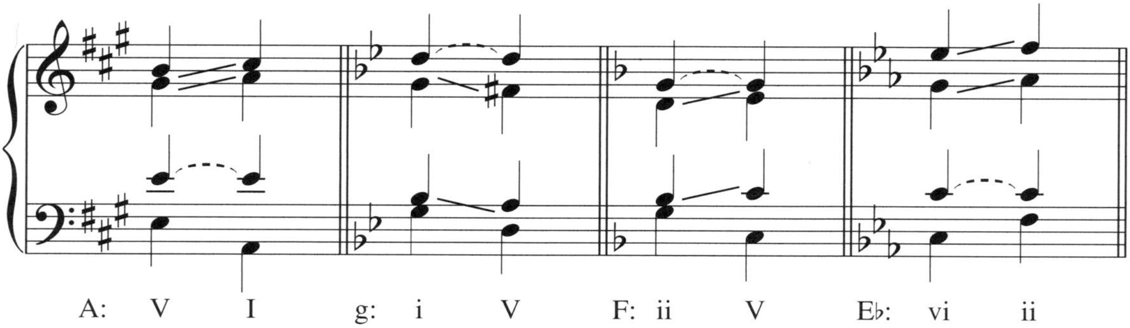

Method #2

1. Write the bass notes of both chords.
2. Write in the remaining chord tones of the first chord in any acceptable way.
3. The upper three voices all move in the same direction to the nearest chord tones. This movement may be upward or downward. In either case, no part moves by more than the interval of a third. One part will move by step, and the others will skip a third.

i-iv in B minor

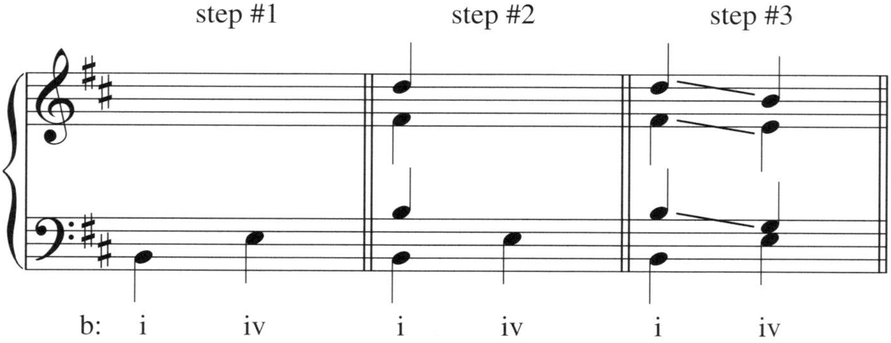

All of the following utilize exactly the same procedure:

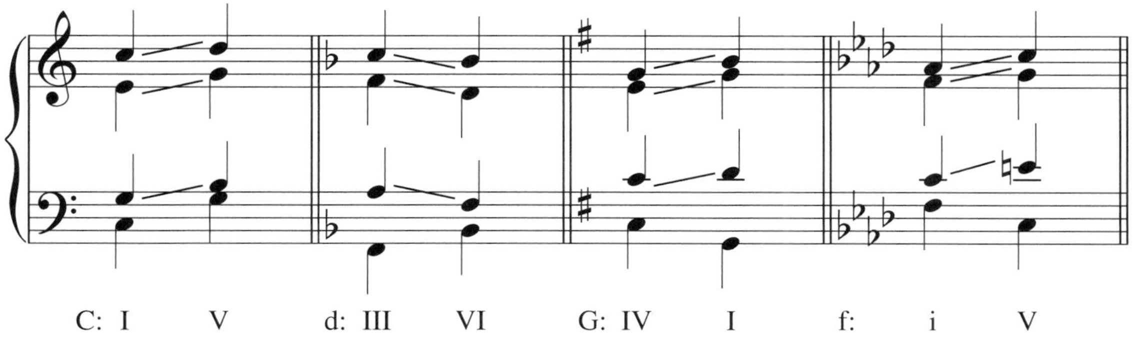

Method #3

This method is not always available because it can present problems in spacing and/or voice leading in certain chord layouts. In this method, the chord third remains in the same part in both chords. And, as in Method #1, the common tone is held over. All this is illustrated in the stepwise procedure shown below and in the examples that follow:

1. Write in the bass notes of both chords.
2. Fill in S, A, and T of the first chord.
3. Hold over the common tone of both chords.
4. Whatever part contains the third of the first chord moves to the third of the second chord.
5. The remaining part moves by step to the root or fifth of the second chord.

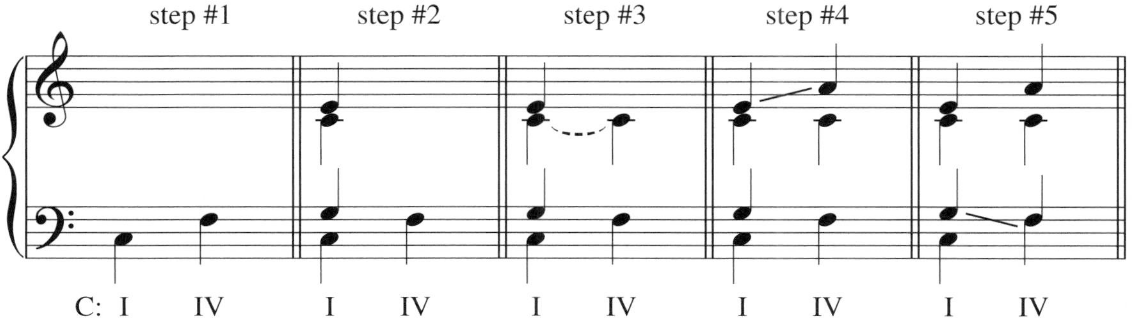

The same procedure was used in these progressions:

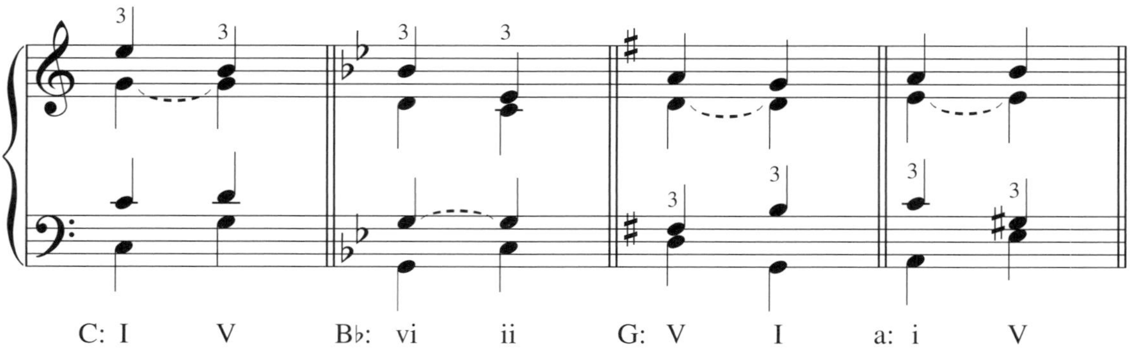

When the third of the triad is in the alto part, problems in spacing and/or voice leading arise. In the first example, the second chord is incorrect, since there is more than an octave between soprano and alto. In the second example, the alto and tenor have crossed parts. Crossed parts are possible between these two voices, but they should revert to their normal positions as soon as possible. Crossed parts should not take place between soprano and alto, or between tenor and bass.

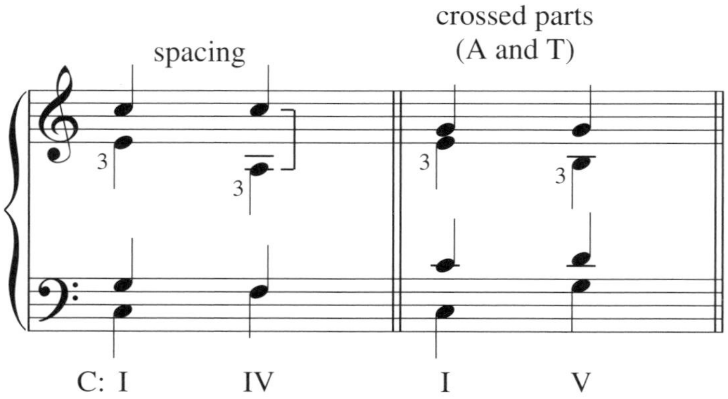

VOICE LEADING

When connecting chords with one another, careful attention must be given to the melodic motion of each of the parts in order to avoid awkward melodic intervals. Also, certain harmonic intervals are problematic and must be avoided. These very important considerations represent some of the most difficult aspects of harmony, and they are all too often overlooked by the student.

The Leading Tone

In the progression V–I, care must be given to the movement of the **leading tone** as the chord moves to I. The leading tone (LT) has a very strong pull to the tonic note. When the LT is in the soprano, it must resolve up by step to the tonic note (as happens in Method #1 only). Method #2 is not usable in this instance. Method #3 is also not acceptable.

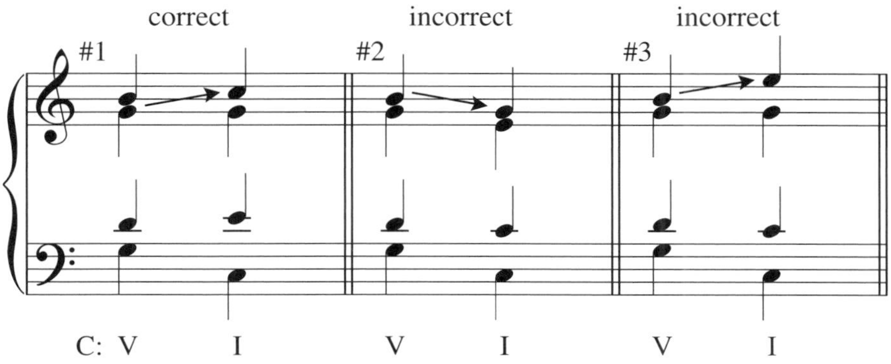

However, if the LT is in an inner voice (alto or tenor), it has the option of either resolving to the tonic note or to move as in Methods #2 or #3:

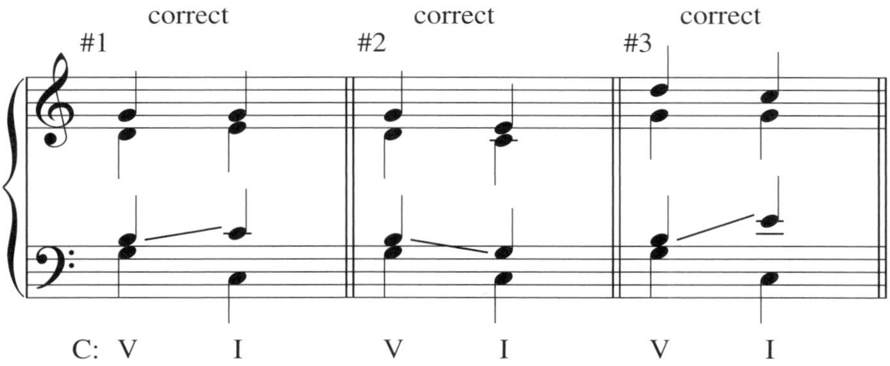

Furthermore, it is possible to resolve the LT in such a way as to produce a tonic chord with three roots and a third (no fifth). This departure from normal doubling is perfectly acceptable:

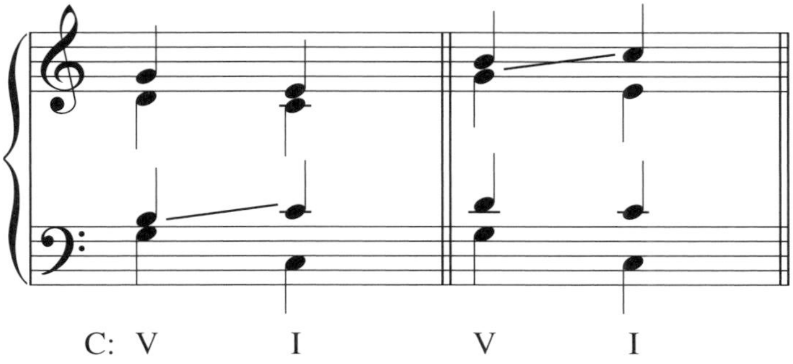

In chord repetition, the LT may be freely transferred from one voice to the next. Only upon resolution must the LT be attended to:

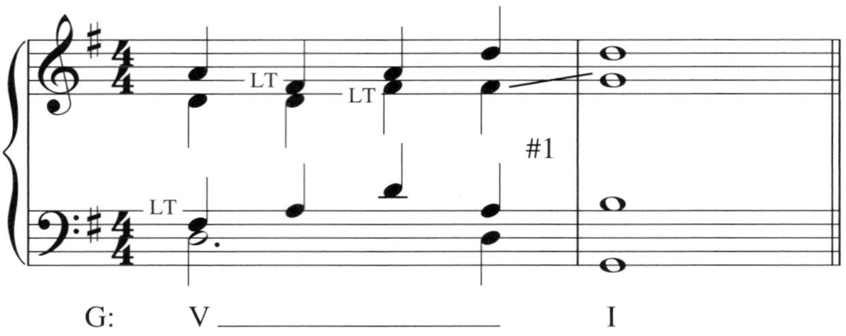

Melodic Intervals

In any voice, there are certain **melodic intervals** that should be avoided. These are the augmented intervals, such as seconds, fourths, and fifths:

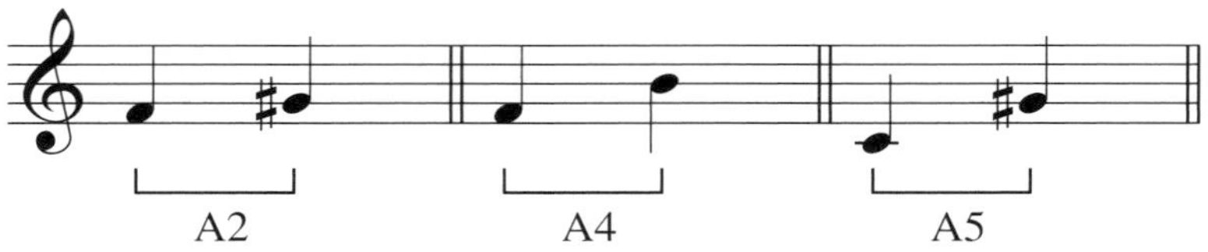

All sevenths and ninths:

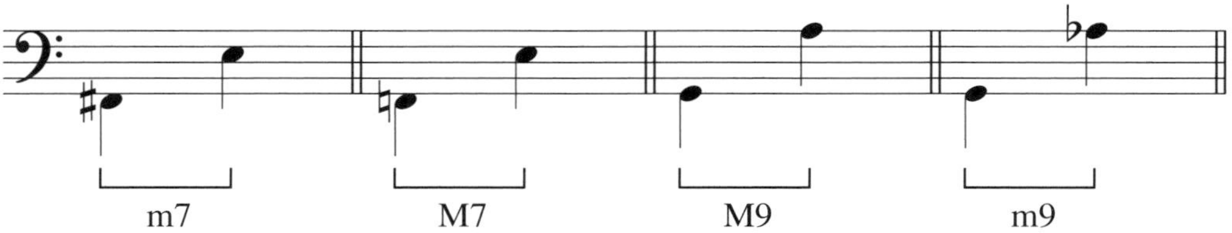

Melodic intervals that may be used freely are: m2, M2, m3, M3, d4 (see exception below), P4, d5, P5, m6, M6, d7 (later), and P8. The diminished fourth occurs between the third degree of the scale and the LT in minor keys. The first example that follows is good, but the second is unacceptable, since the LT is not properly resolved.

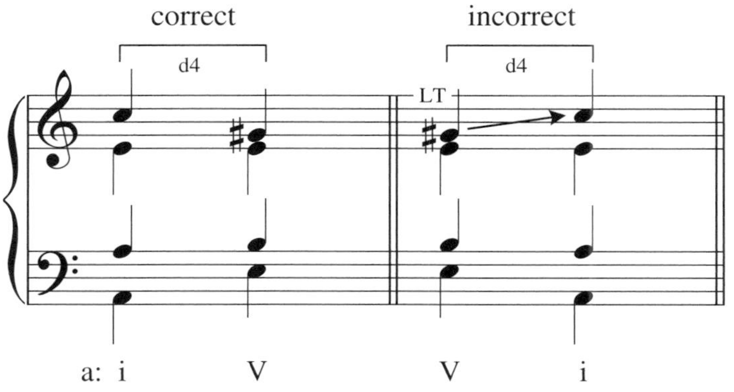

Two skips in the same direction should outline all or part of a triad, or dominant seventh chord (V7), or a supertonic seventh chord (ii7):

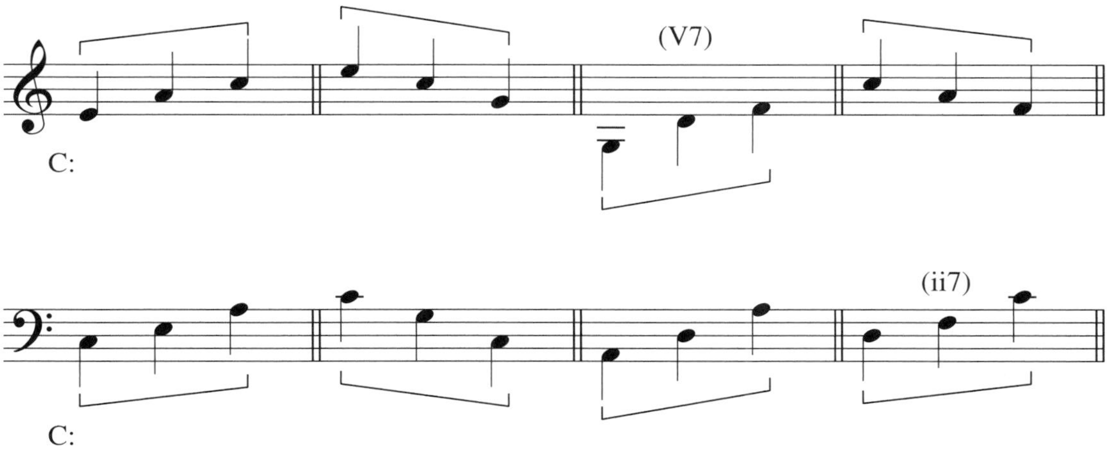

The following examples do not fulfill the above conditions and should be avoided. The last example (#8) does outline a triad, but the span of two sixths in succession is too wide and should not be used:

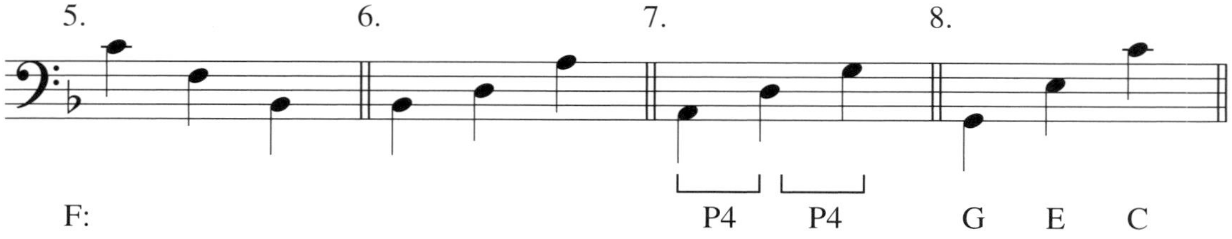

The ascending perfect fourths in #7 above are seen occasionally in the bass line in slow passages. In general, however, avoid this pattern of movement in either direction.

It is important to pay attention to the soprano line's overall shape. Somewhere along the line look for a single high point. Although this isn't always necessary, it is a good principle to follow. The high point in each of the following melodies is indicated with an arrow:

Avoid monotony; don't hover around a particular pitch (or pitches) too much:

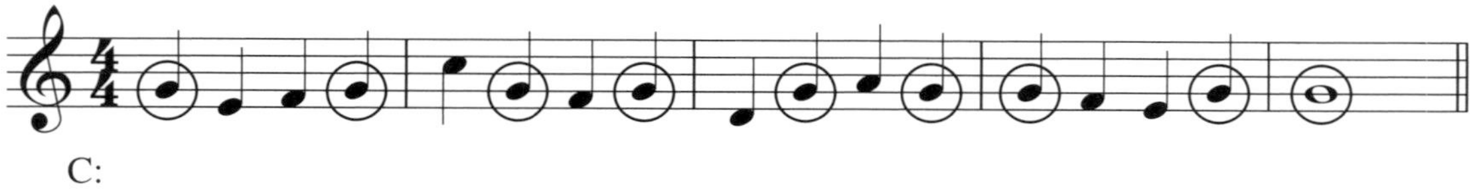

Don't confine the range of the melody within too narrow a limit. The following melody covers a span of only a P4:

Next in importance to the soprano line is the bass line. The same principles apply here. Alto and tenor parts are less crucial. In the hands of a master composer such as J.S. Bach, the inner voices can be melodically very interesting; nevertheless, they are often somewhat static, their primary function being to provide substance to the harmony and solid support for the outer voices.

Parallel Perfect Fifths

Avoid parallel (or contrary motion) perfect fifths between any two parts:

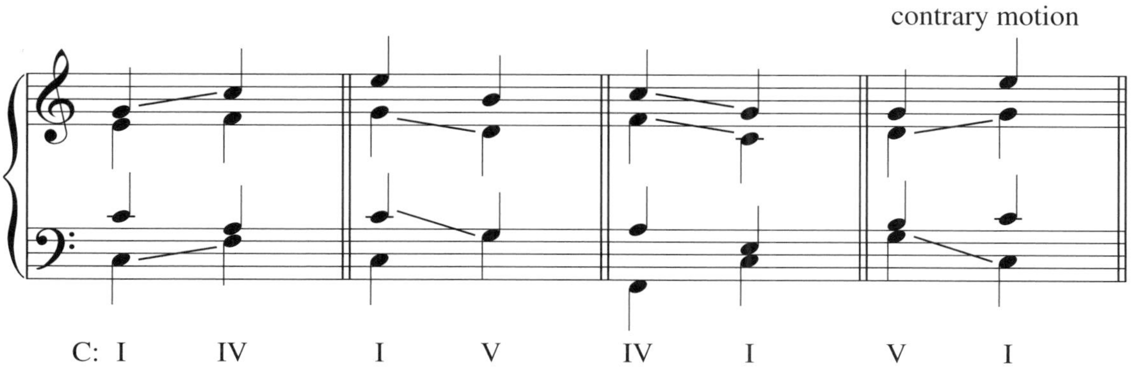

Parallel Perfect Octaves

Avoid parallel (or contrary motion) octaves between any two parts:

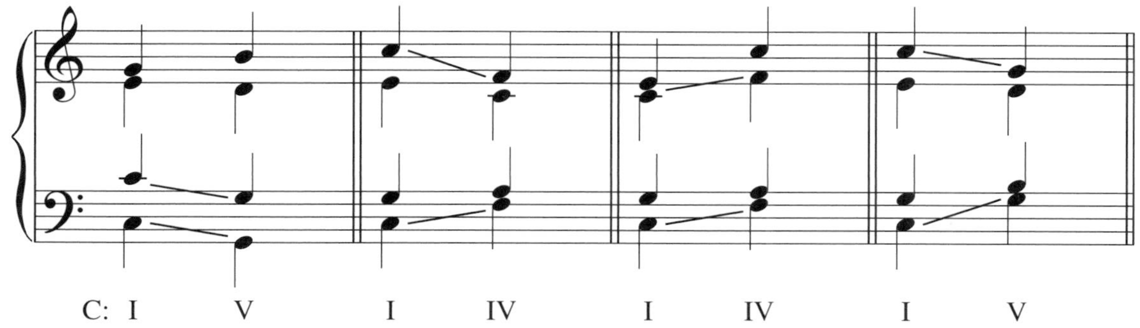

Note: Parallel unisons are equivalent to parallel octaves, as are combinations of unisons and octaves (see page 44, #5 as an example).

Repeated fifths and octaves are not a problem. Parallel fifths and octaves require movement in both parts to different pitches.

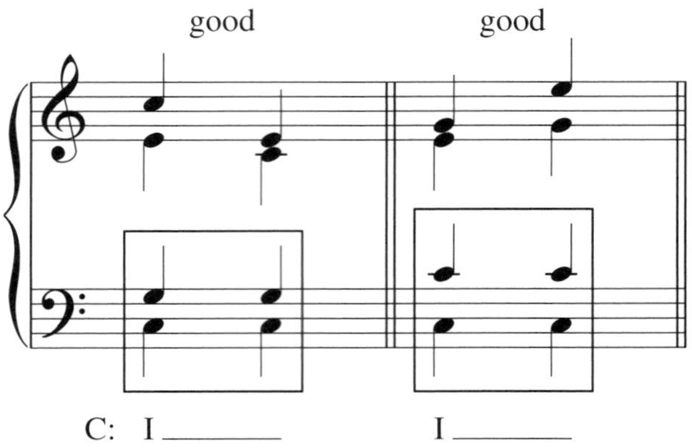

Proper use of Methods #1, #2, or #3 will automatically eliminate any parallel fifths or octaves, but these methods are applicable only to root position movement and movement of the roots up or down a fifth or fourth. As we incorporate movement by different intervals, and as we move into using inversions of triads, extra caution must be brought to bear on avoidance of parallels. One of the great pitfalls in student work is failure to eliminate parallels from their work.

Overlap

Overlap can result from the melodic motion of any two adjacent voices (S and A, A and T, T and B). If, for example, the alto moves to a note higher than the soprano's previous note, overlap occurs. Overlap becomes a problem only when the interval of the overlap is larger than a second, as in #1 and #2 below. Number 3 and #4 are acceptable.

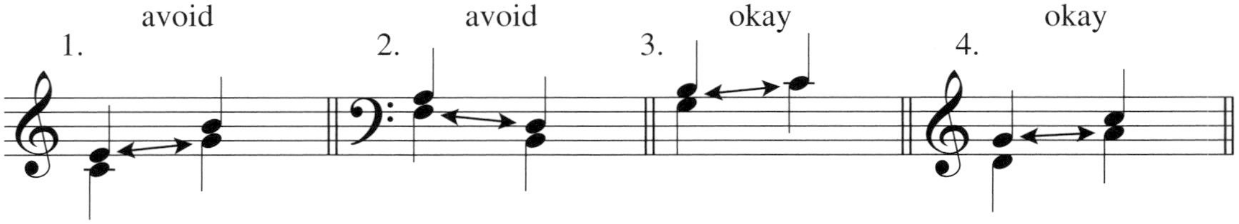

Overlap does not become a problem in chord repetition. In the following example of chord repetition, overlap occurs between soprano and alto and between alto and tenor, but since there is no change of chord, the effect is acceptable:

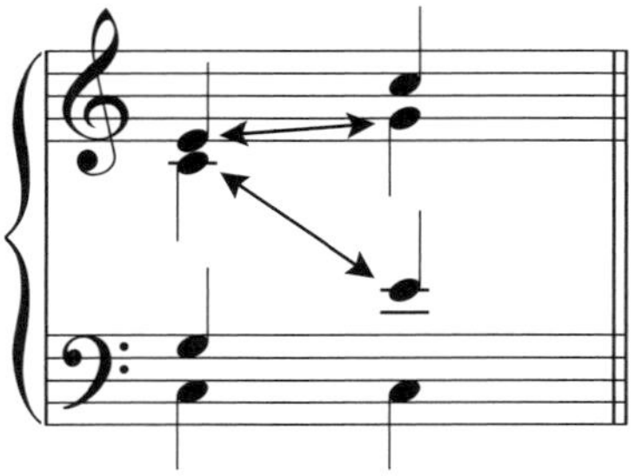

Before examining chord connection in which the roots move in intervals other than fourths or fifths, here are some examples for study. Only tonic, dominant, and subdominant chords are used:

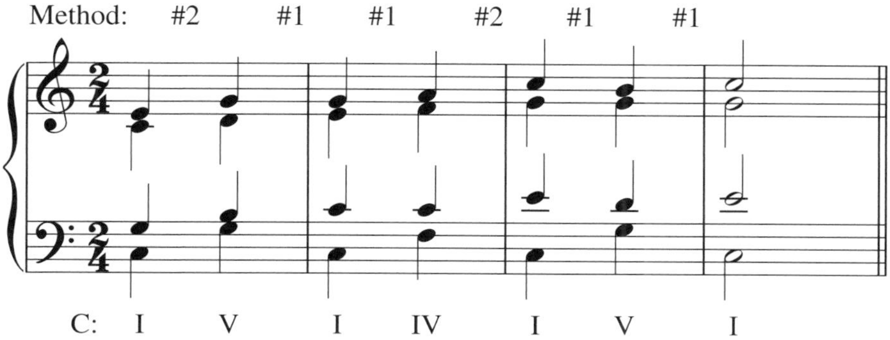

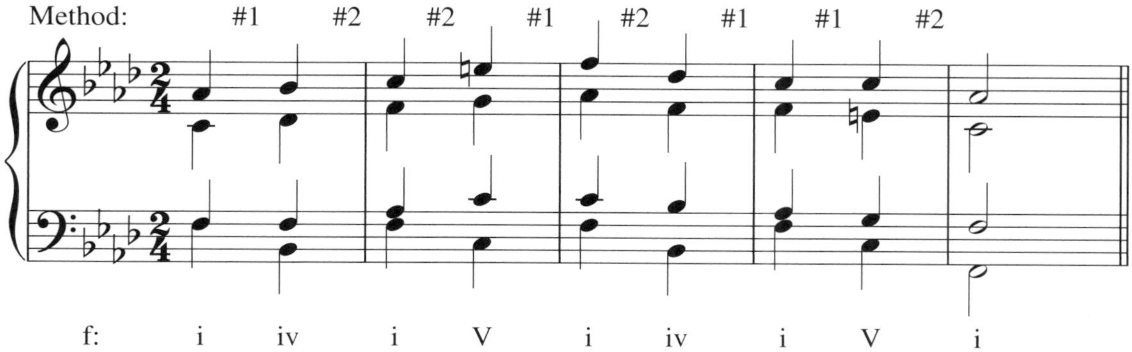

The following examples employ chord repetition liberally. Notice how chord repetition slows down the rate of change of harmony, resulting in a slower **harmonic rhythm**.

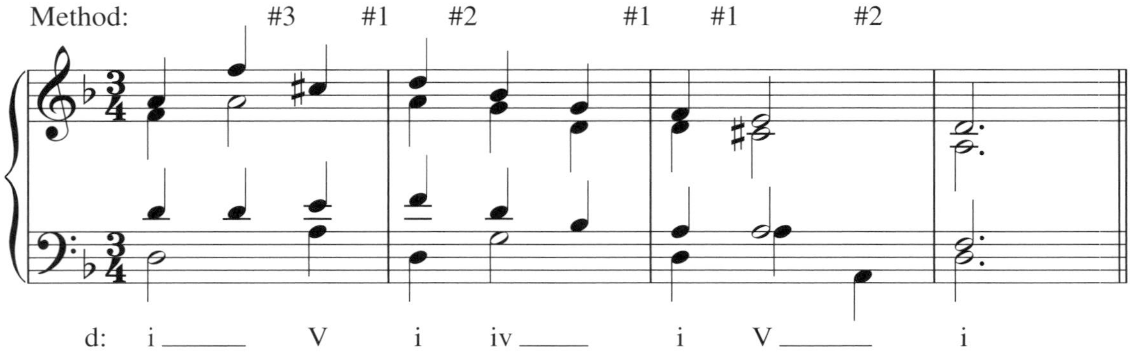

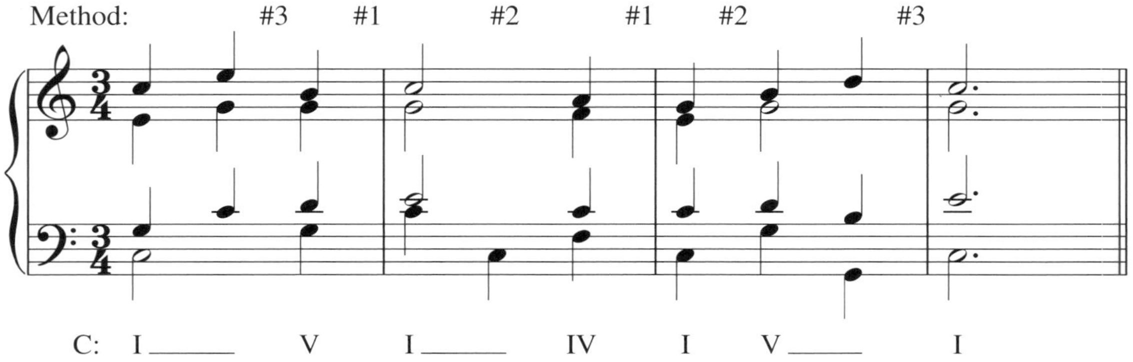

CONNECTING CHORDS WHOSE ROOTS ARE A SECOND APART

Root movement up a second is much more common than root movement down a second. Both are considered strong progressions, however. Examples: IV–V, V–vi. These are the most common by far. Others: iii–IV, I–ii, ii–iii. For downward movement, vi–V is most often used. Others: ii–I, IV–iii, iii–ii, V–IV.

There is a very simple procedure that avoids serious problems in voice leading. Let us demonstrate by using the most common up-a-step root progression, IV–V:

1. Write in the root (bass note) of both chords.
2. Fill out the tones of the first chord.
3. Move all three upper voices down to the nearest chord tones of the second chord.

IV-V in F major

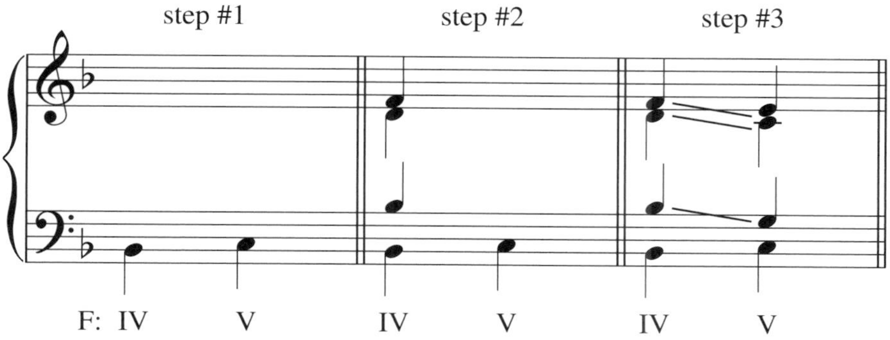

Other examples using this procedure:

In the progression V–vi (V–VI in minor), there is an important difference: resolve the LT up a step to the tonic note. The two remaining voices move down to the nearest chord tones of the second chord. This will result in a double third of the vi chord. This is the desired doubling. Let us take V–VI in A minor as an example:

1. Write the bass note of both chords.
2. Fill out the tones of the first chord.
3. Resolve the LT up a step to the tonic note.
4. Move the two remaining voices down to the nearest chord tones of VI.

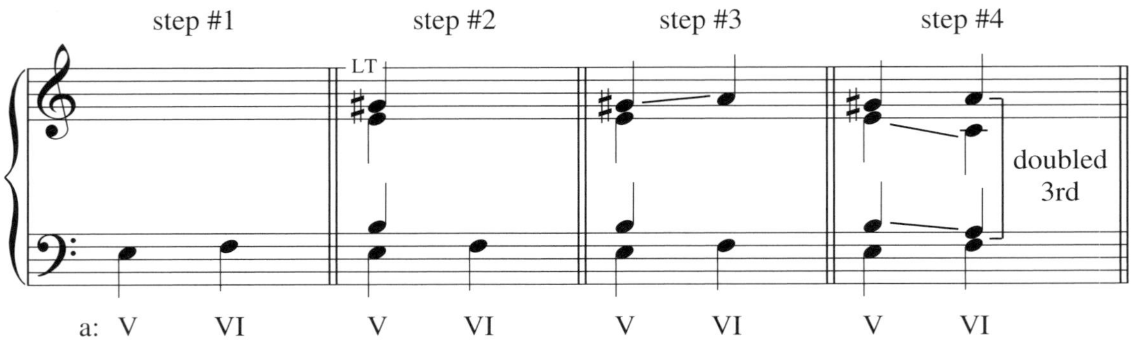

This voice leading is absolutely mandatory in minor keys. In major keys it is possible for the LT to move down a step, especially if the LT is in an inner voice. Even if the LT is in the soprano, this voice leading is possible if the soprano melody is moving in a downward direction:

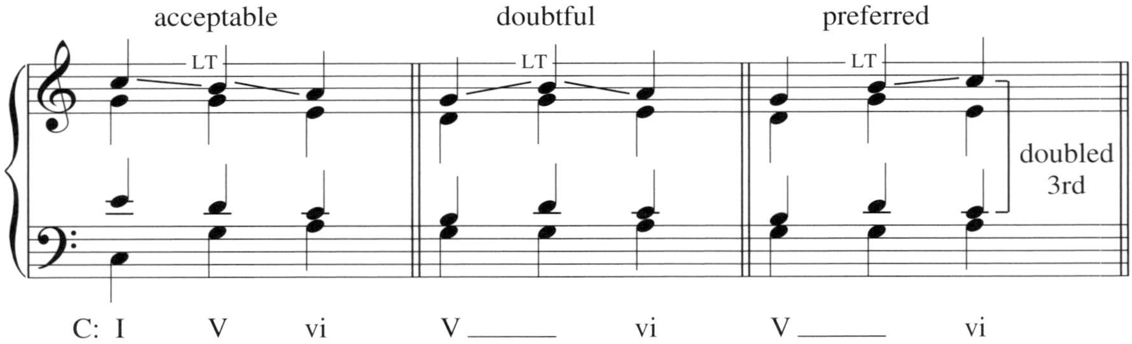

The LT may not move down in the progression V–VI in minor, because of the very awkward augmented second that would result:

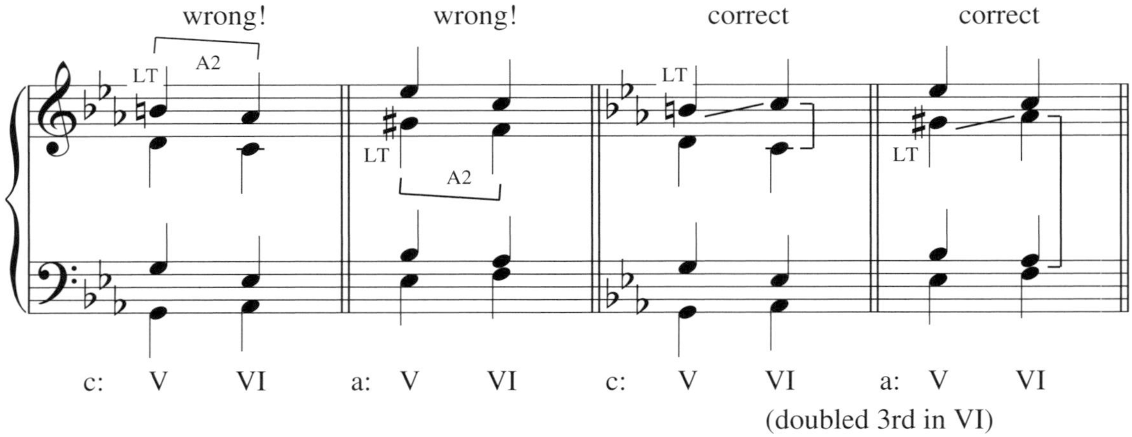

In major keys (not minor!) it may be possible to write the progression IV–V using voice leading different from the usual (upper voices moving down), but great caution must be taken to avoid parallel fifths and octaves, doubling and spacing must be proper, and there must be no awkward melodic intervals. Both of the following are possible, for example:

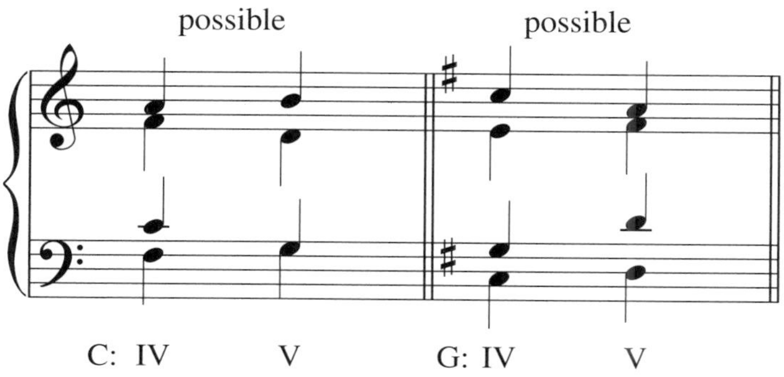

The voice leading in progressions that move down a step is just the reverse of the foregoing procedures: the upper voices move up to the nearest chord tones. The examples that follow illustrate. In VI–V (minor key), it is best to double the third of VI.

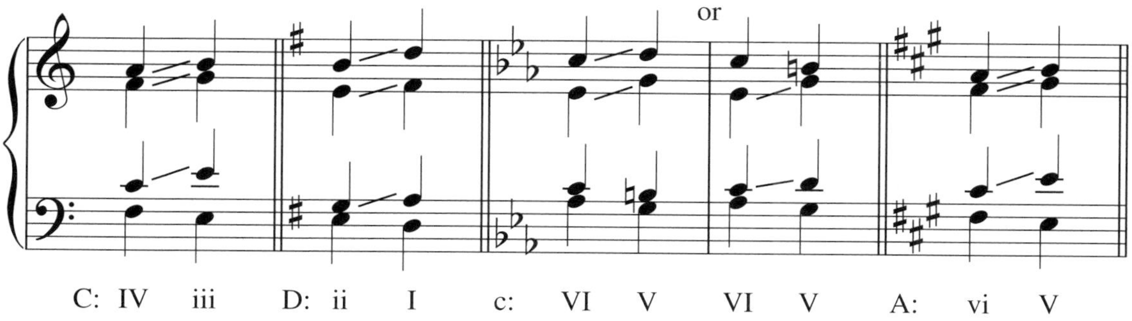

Often a passage will contain several up-a-step root progressions in succession, such as iii–IV–V–vi. If the student is asked to harmonize such a passage, he must keep in mind the spacing between tenor and bass in the first chord in this succession. The spacing must be sufficiently large to allow for the constant narrowing of the gap between those two voices. The next two examples illustrate the problem. The first is correct. In the second, not enough initial space between tenor and bass was allowed, leading to difficulties that cannot be overcome:

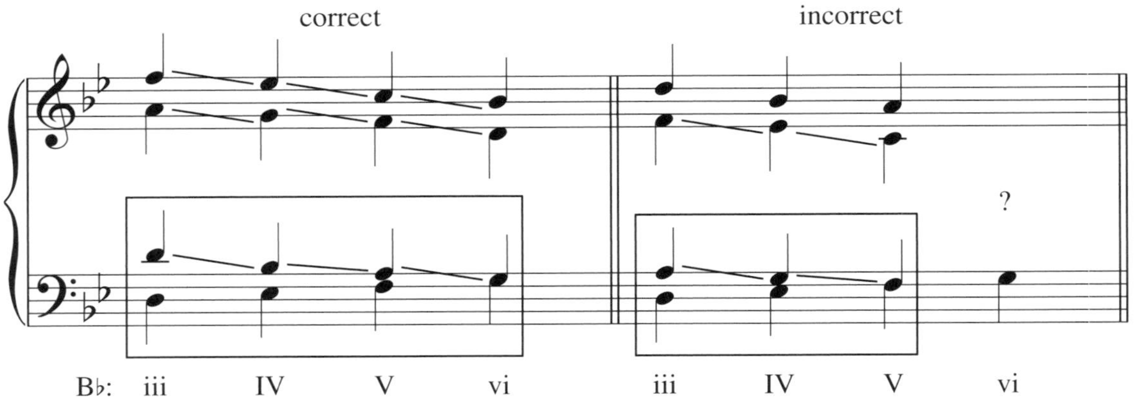

If we add eighth-note movement in the bass line, an easy solution to the problem emerges. Drop the bass line one octave; this opens up the space between tenor and bass, allowing a continuation of the proper movement of the upper voices:

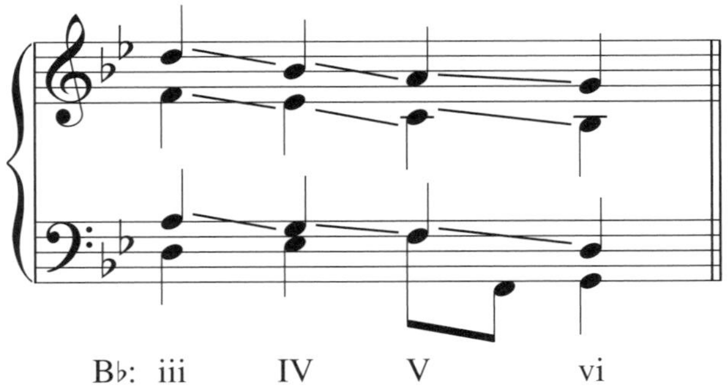

Several correct examples for study:

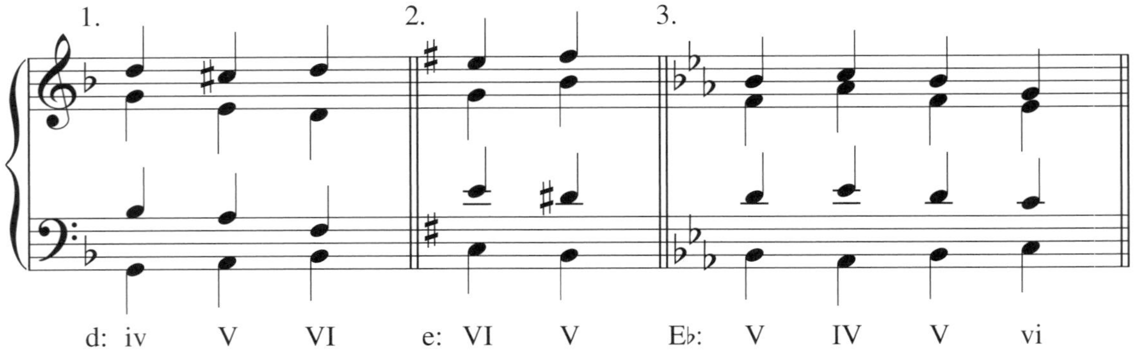

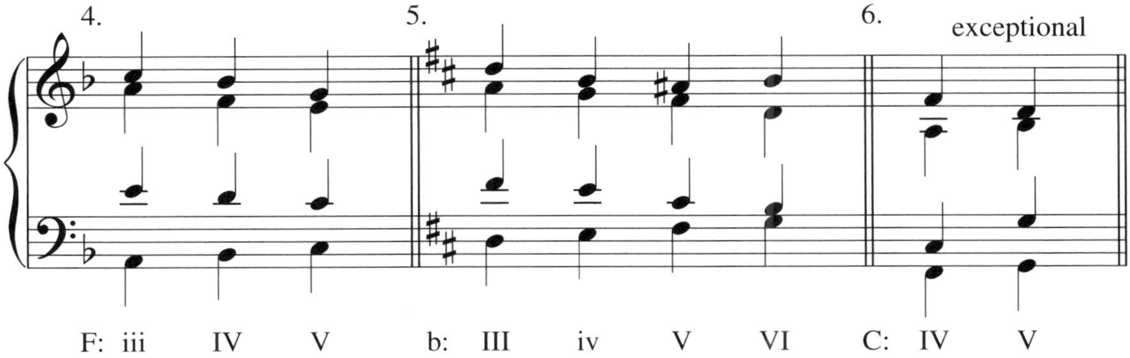

Notice the doubled third of VI in #1 and #2 above. In #3, the progression V–IV is considered "backward," but it may be used if there is an immediate return to the V chord. This progression is not advisable when the LT is in the top voice, however:

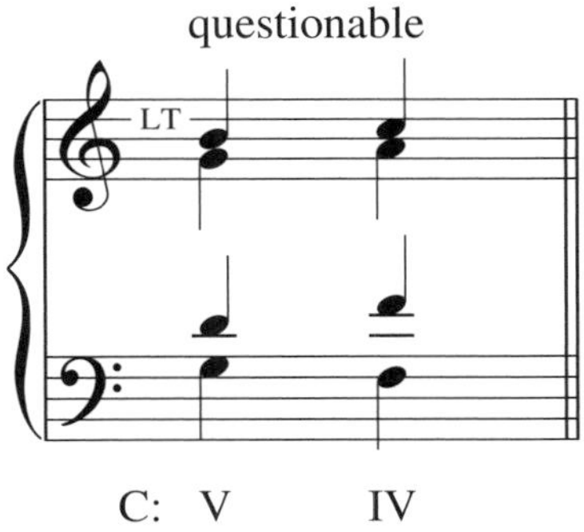

Below are some typical errors found in a student's work. Do your best to avoid such mistakes!

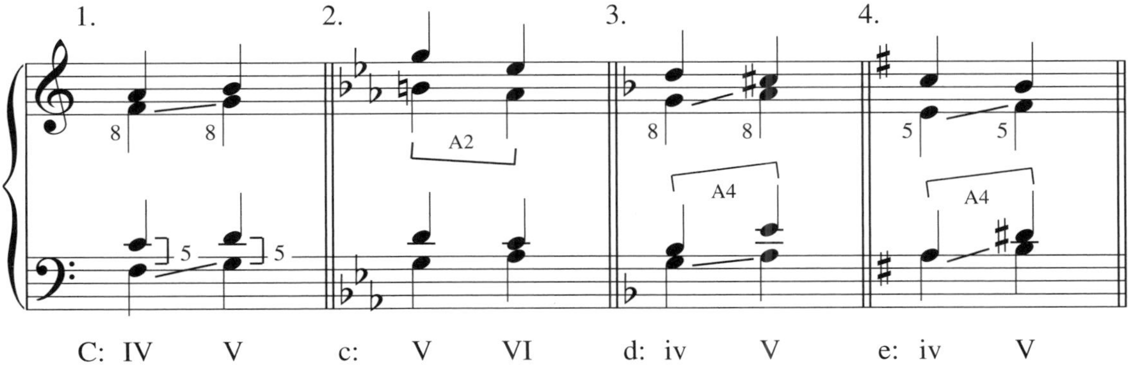

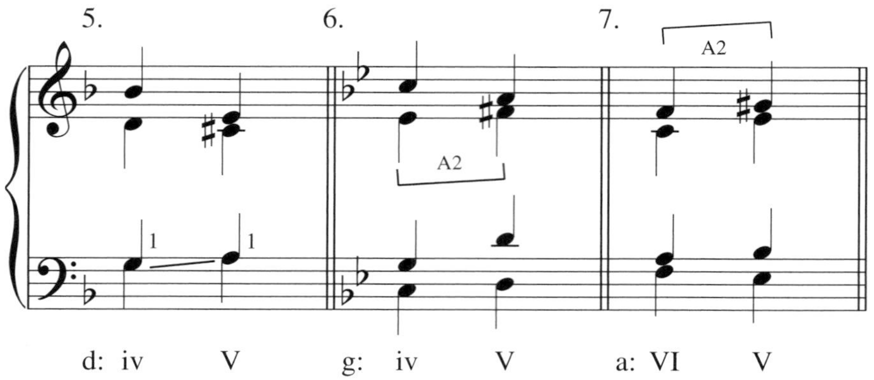

In #1, we have the most common trap of all. All four voices move up by step, creating both parallel fifths and octaves. In #2, the attempt to double the root of VI leads to the A2. Remember to double the third of the submediant triad to avoid these problems!

We are now ready to examine root position progressions in which the roots are apart by the interval of a third.

CONNECTING CHORDS WHOSE ROOTS ARE A THIRD APART

Chords whose roots are a third apart have two tones in common. Therefore the simplest, but by no means the only, way to connect the chords is to hold over both common tones. The remaining voice moves by step to the nearest chord tone. When the roots move down a third, the progression is strong and very frequent in music. Roots that move up are considered weak progressions and must be handled with caution. Compare the first example below, in which the roots move downward, with the second example, in which they move up. The first example has forward, goal-directed motion, while the second seems static and directionless:

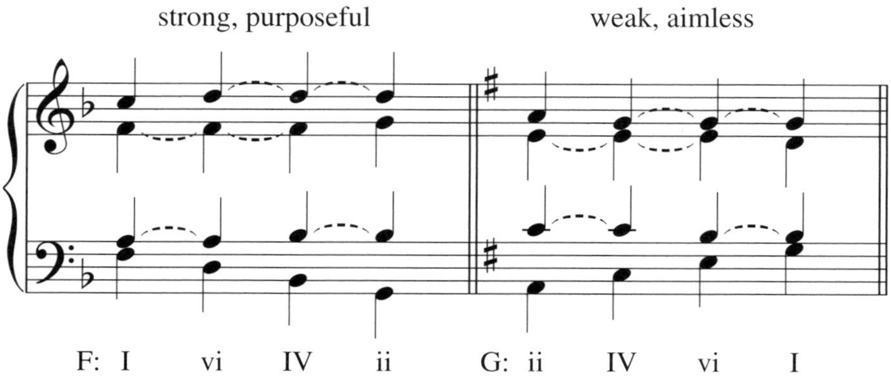

Notice how in every instance two common tones are held over and the remaining part moves by step to the nearest chord tone. Moving down a third is always good. Moving up by a third, though a weak progression, is usable if treated with caution. What matters is what follows. Movement up by a third should be followed by a strong progression, such as up a second or down a fifth (up a fourth). An excellent example is the progression I–iii. This may be followed by IV or vi, as shown in the following:

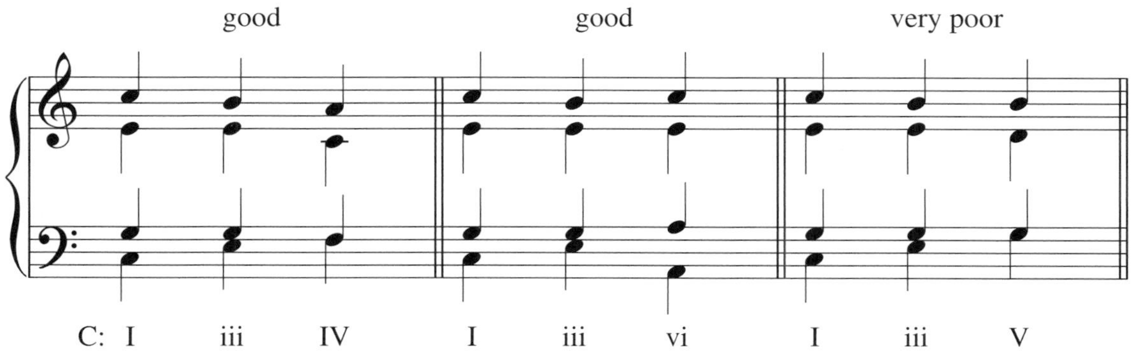

As mentioned earlier, holding over the two common tones is by no means the only way of connecting root position chords whose roots are a third apart. Without reverting to a whole set of rules, we can observe that the upper parts may move in contrary motion with the bass and result in a balanced chord, while avoiding any awkward melodic intervals or any parallels. Also, a mixture of contrary motion and similar motion can produce other good results. The example below illustrates:

Instead of the bass line always moving down a third, it is also possible for it to move up a sixth from time to time:

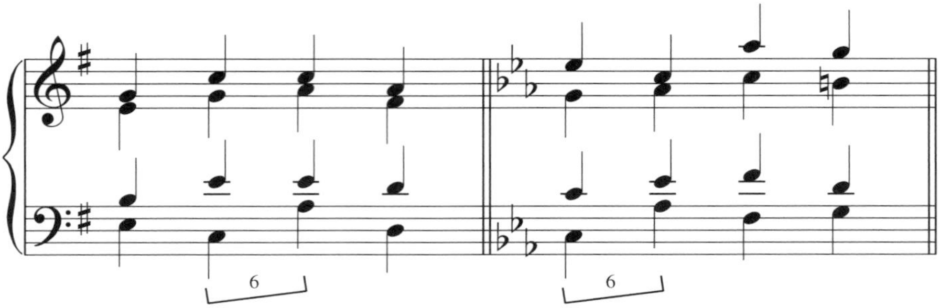

G: vi IV ii V c: i VI iv V

It should be evident that methods other than holding over the two common tones can lead to more interesting musical results, but the student must be ever mindful of the dangers of parallels and the possibility of problematic melodic intervals. Holding over the two common tones is, at any rate, a fail-safe procedure.

We have now reached the point where we may connect any chord to any chord in root position, combining all of the root movements we have learned to deal with. Let us assemble a few progressions, each of four measures duration (four-measure phrases). We'll begin with the tonic chord (or an upbeat V chord) and end with the tonic chord preceded by V. In doing so we will remember that down a fifth (or up a fourth) is very common, as is up second and down a third. Other types of movement will be used, but much less often. As we near the end, prepare for the V chord with IV or ii; vi and I are also possible but less frequent. In minor, remember always to provide an accidental when you write the V chord. You have to create the LT with the accidental. Providing necessary accidentals is a constant obligation in the business of writing harmony, so it will be well to establish this good habit at the outset. Below are several four-measure phrases, which should be studied thoroughly:

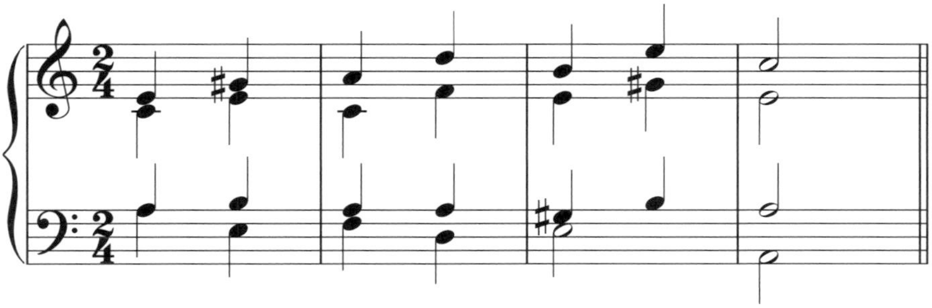

a: i V VI iv V _____ i

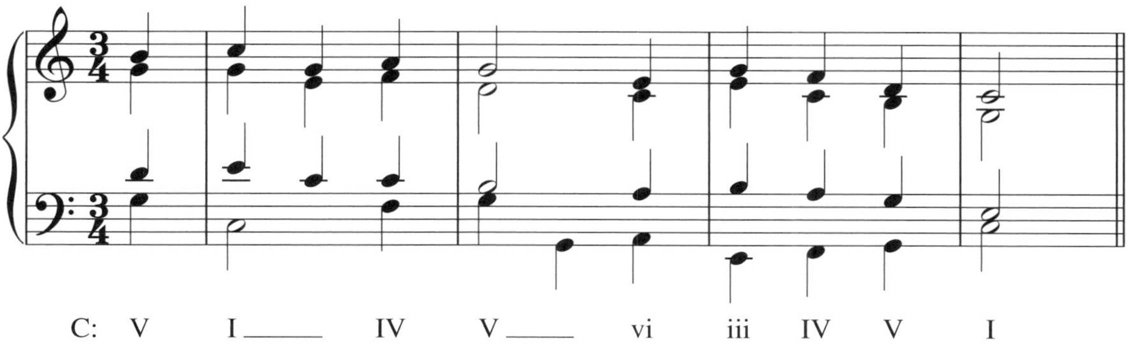
C: V I ___ IV V ___ vi iii IV V I

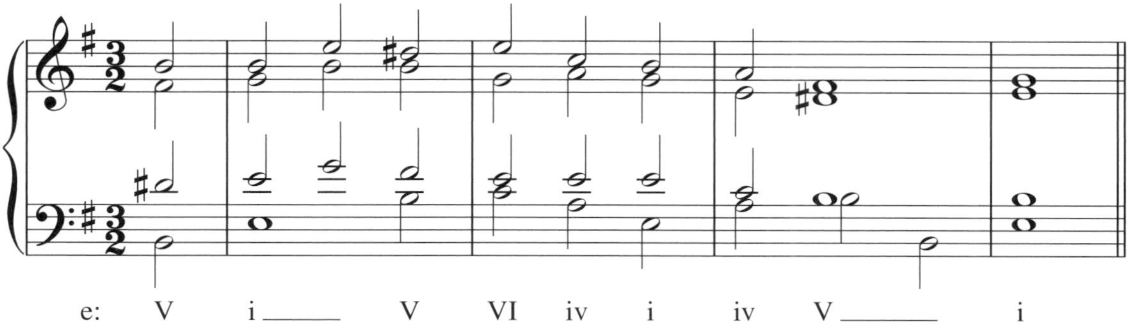
e: V i ___ V VI iv i iv V ___ i

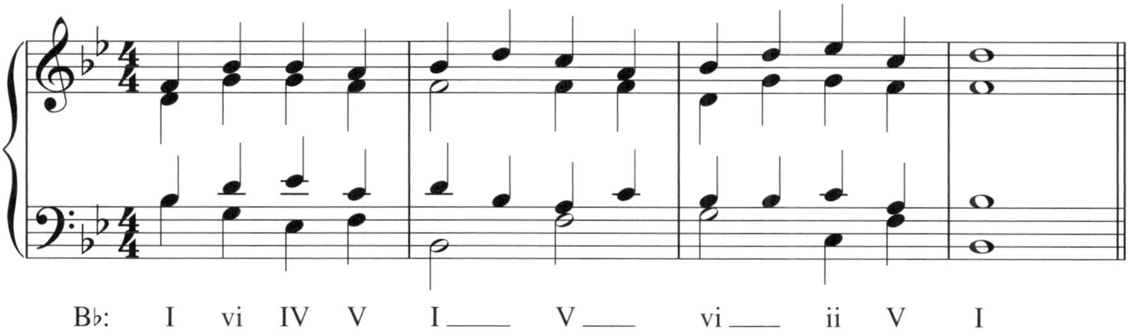
B♭: I vi IV V I ___ V ___ vi ___ ii V I

HARMONIZING A MELODY USING ONLY ROOT POSITION TRIADS

Harmonizing bass lines using only root position harmonies is relatively easy, since the chords are unambiguously determined by each bass note. But if only a soprano line is given, many decisions have to be made, and the best of many possible solutions can be achieved only by much consideration. Foremost is the choice of convincing harmonies that should progress in a logical, goal-oriented manner. Let us take, for example, the following melody in F major:

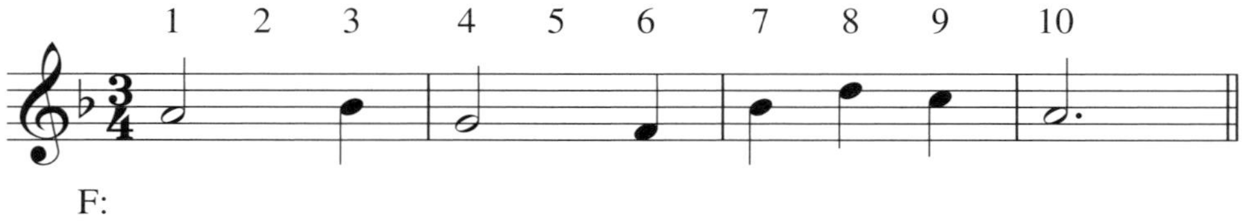

Consider these possibilities: chord repetition, a change of harmony during held tones, starting and ending on I, finishing with V–I, leading nicely into that V with IV or ii, looking for strong progressions rather than weak ones, choosing a bass line that does not form parallel fifths or octaves with the melody at any point. With all these aspects guiding us, there emerges a number of possible harmonizations of our melody. On the following page, the melody is shown with five possible bass lines. The simplest of these are #1 and #5. Number 2, #3, and #4 take advantage of a change in harmony on beat 2 of measure 1. Number 3 and #4 use a change of harmony on beat 2 of measure 3. Certain chords were not possible because of parallels; for example, on the last beat of measure 2, I, followed by IV on the next chord, would create parallel octaves with the melody. For a full realization, #2 was selected.

Adding alto and tenor to #2, we have:

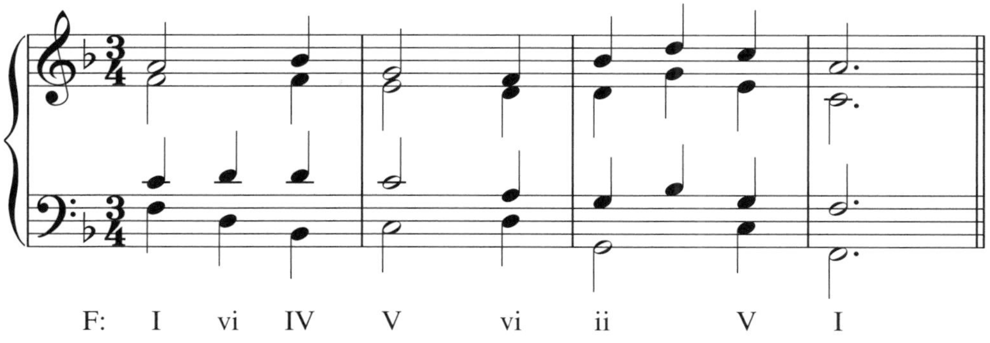

Before reading the next chapter, work out the exercises that follow.

EXERCISES

1. Analyze the harmony:

e:

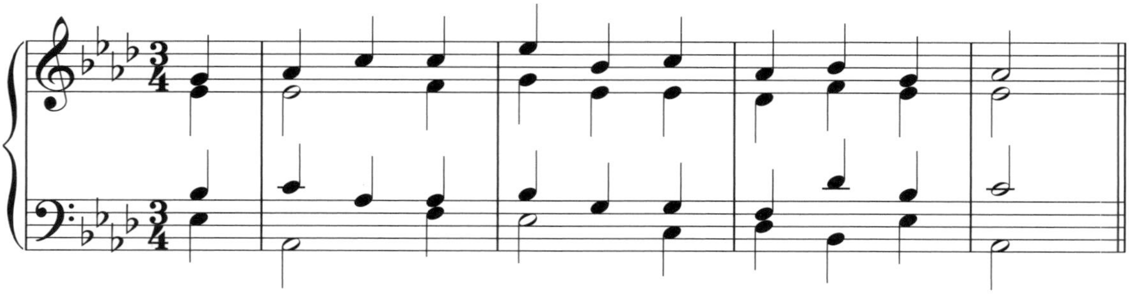

A♭:

2. Add three upper voices. Analyze the harmony:

D:

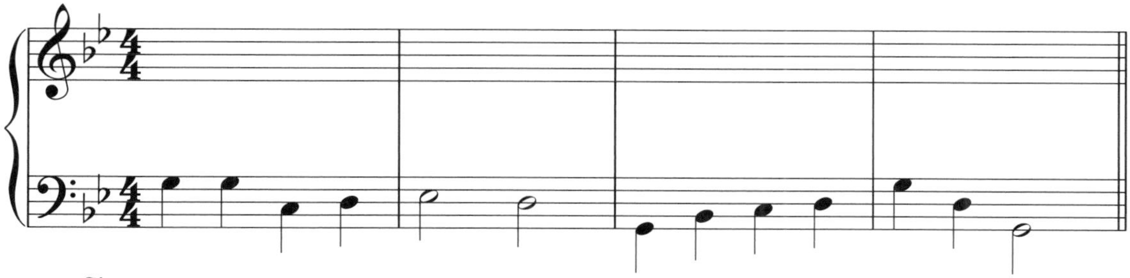

g:

C:

3. Add three lower voices. Analyze the harmony:

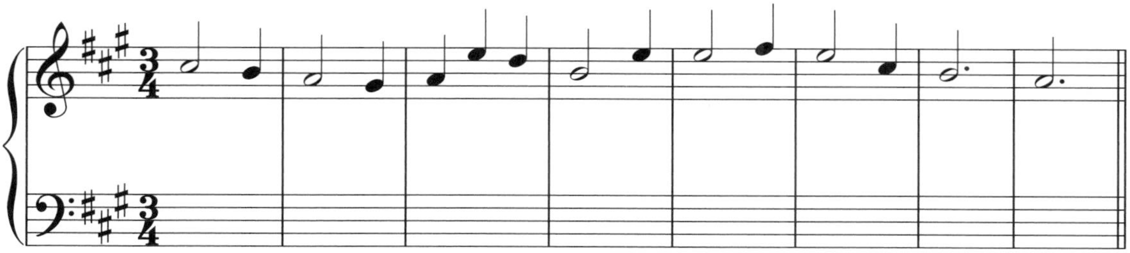

A:

c:

4. Root position progressions between chords whose roots are a fourth or fifth apart.
In all the examples below, provide a Roman numeral analysis.

Add alto and tenor. Show method used (#1, #2, or #3) between each chord.

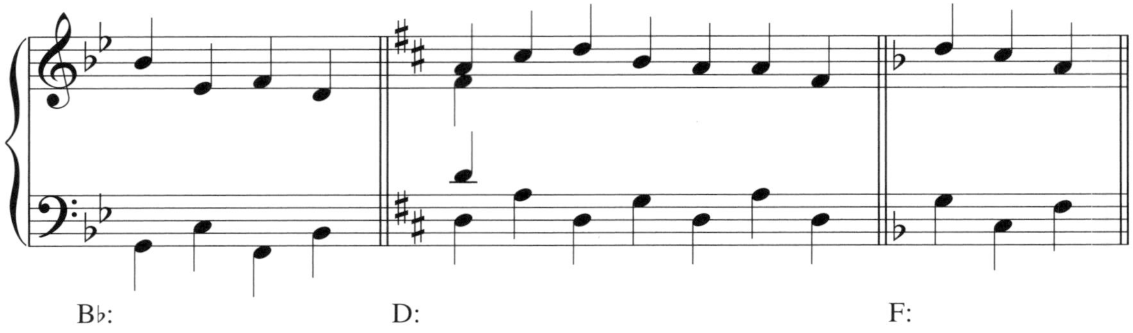

Add soprano, alto, and tenor. Use the methods indicated:

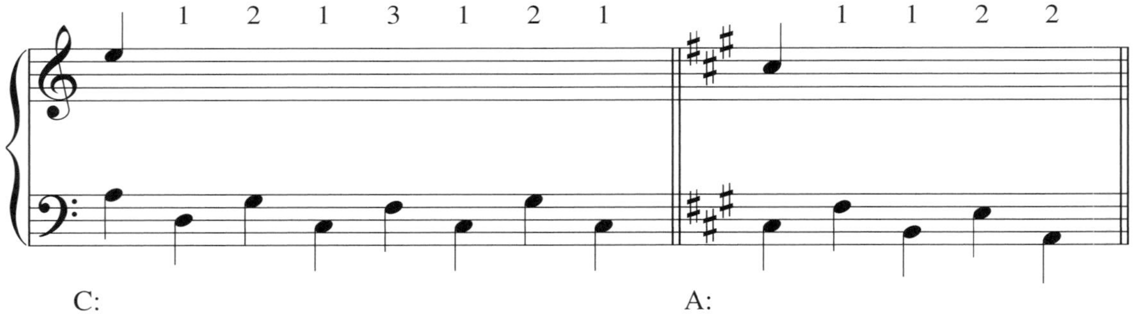

Add upper voices. Show the methods used:

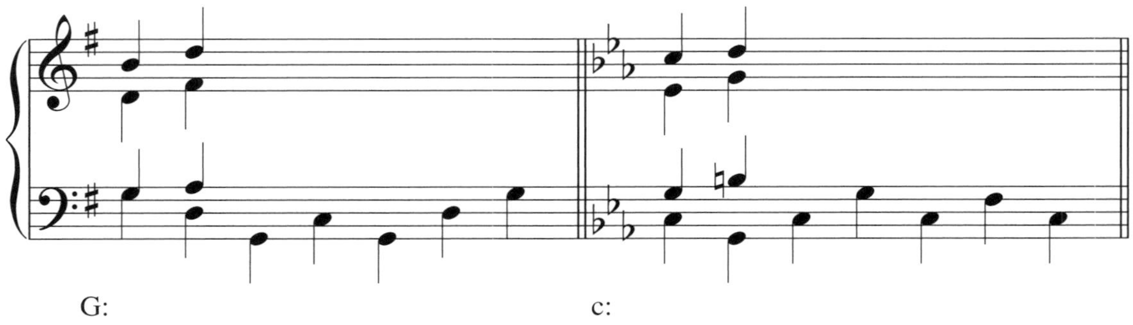

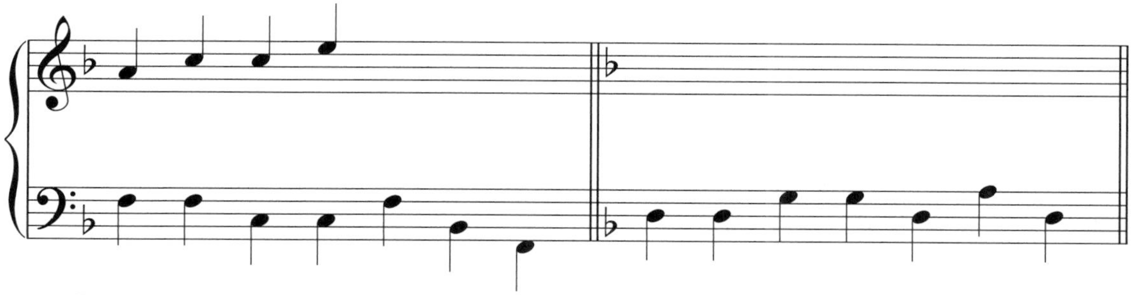

F: d:

5. Fill out in four-part harmony. Use correct doubling and spacing, avoid parallel fifths and octaves, etc.

F: IV V I G: I vi V I B♭: IV ii V vi

6. Provide a Roman numeral analysis and fill out in four-part harmony. In the last example, work out good root position harmonies, analyze, and add alto, tenor, and bass.

b: III iv V c: e:

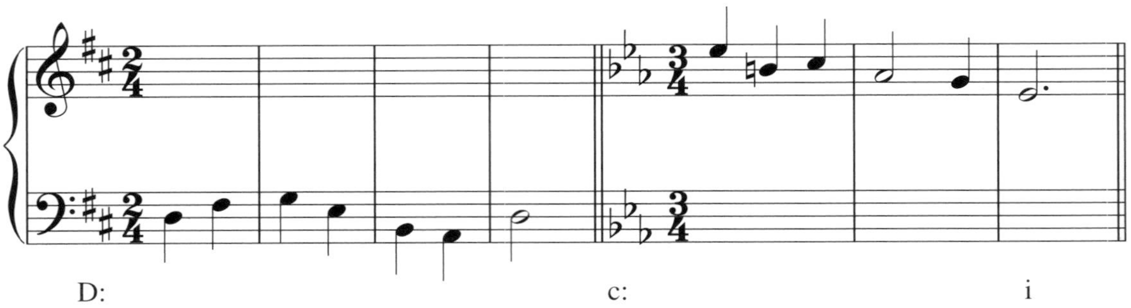
D:
c:
i

CHAPTER 4 TRIADS IN FIRST INVERSION

In **first inversion**, the third of the chord is in the lowest voice (the bass line). The root and fifth are among the upper voices. While popular music limits itself almost exclusively to root position triads (and seventh and ninth chords as well), for hundreds of years composers in the classic tradition have made ample use of inversions. In the music of the masters you will find a healthy mixture of both root position and first inversion chords; indeed, they are the most often employed chord forms in music. Major and minor triads in root position are stable chords; so indeed are first inversion triads, but less so than in root position. (As we will discover in the next chapter, second inversion triads are unstable, much less often used, and require careful handling.) Like root position triads, first inversion triads may be approached freely and therefore allow for a more interesting bass line and a wider variety of harmonies to choose from.

How do we indicate first inversion chords? We know that in root position the upper tones form intervals of a third and fifth above the root. In first inversion, the intervals formed above the bass note are a third and a sixth:

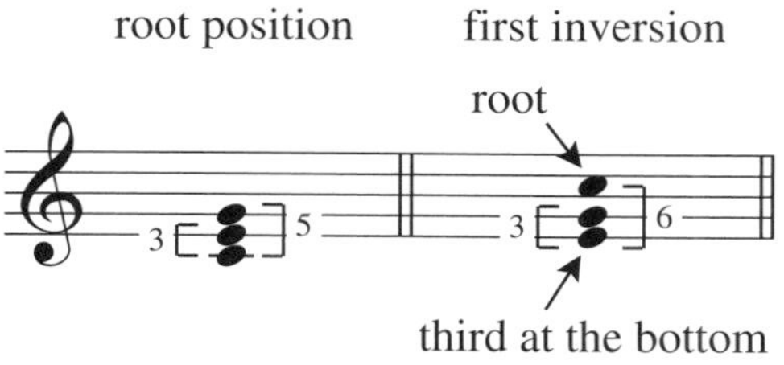

SIXTH CHORDS

First inversion triads are referred to as **sixth chords** because of this key interval of a sixth above the bass note. In Roman numeral analysis, the number 6 is written after the Roman numeral. Some older texts use both the numbers 6 and 3, but this has been simplified to a single number:

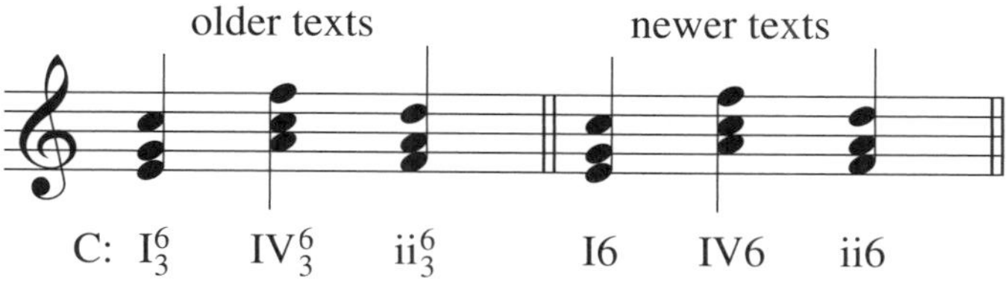

However, it is always understood that, along with a sixth, a third above the bass is present in the chord. In simplified form, here are the first inversion chords with their Roman numeral labeling in both major and minor tonalities:

first inversion triads in major and minor keys

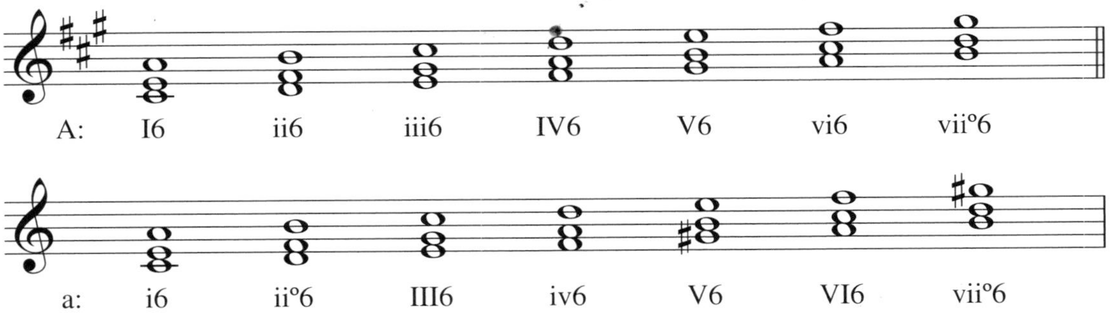

One distinct advantage in employing first inversion chords is flexibility in doubling. We have previously restricted ourselves to doubling the root of triads when writing in root position, except for the doubling of the third in the progression V–vi (V–VI in minor). Doubling of any member of the chord may be possible in first inversion. There is one note, however, that should not be doubled when writing any form of the V or vii° chords: **Do not double the leading tone.** So there are two important matters to keep in mind when you write these two chords:

1. In minor, you must always write an accidental to create the LT.
2. Don't double the LT.

Let us now examine each chord in turn, in four-part layout, with particular emphasis on doubling possibilities. In a major key:

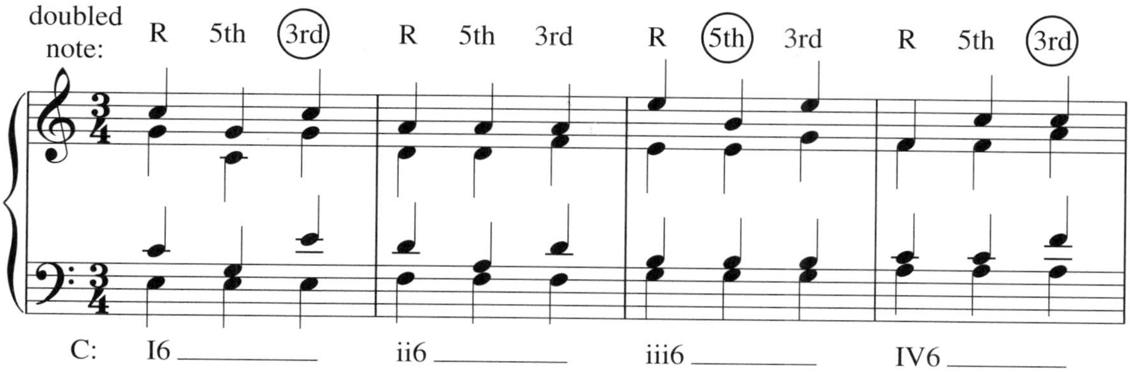

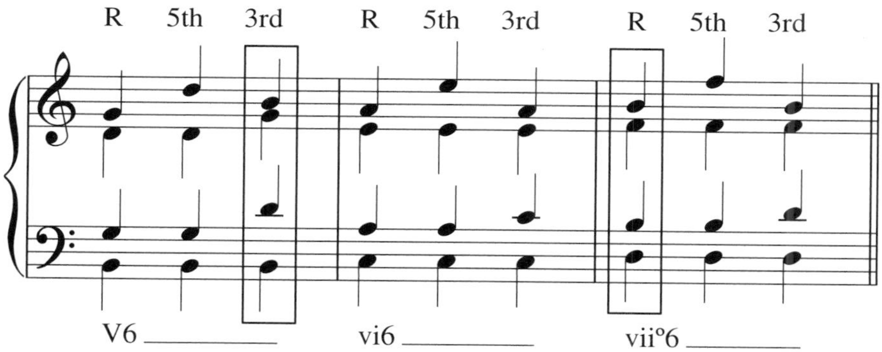

And in minor:

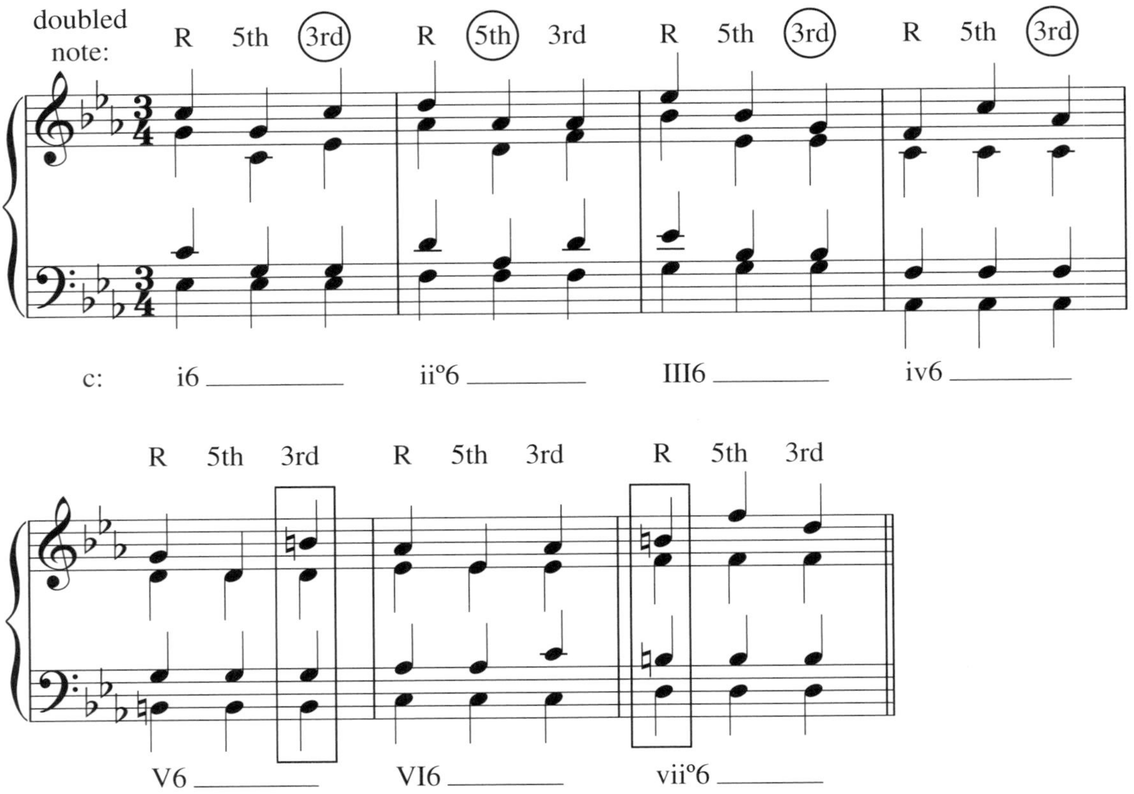

All of the chords shown are usable except those that are boxed; these contain doubled LTs and should be avoided. The circled chords contain the least-used doublings; they usually come into play as a result of voice leading necessities. The diminished triads are now very much in the picture and take a significant place in harmonic progressions. In general, double the third (the bass note) of vii°6. However, if the fifth of the chord is in the soprano part, it is often best to double the fifth, as in #3 that follows.

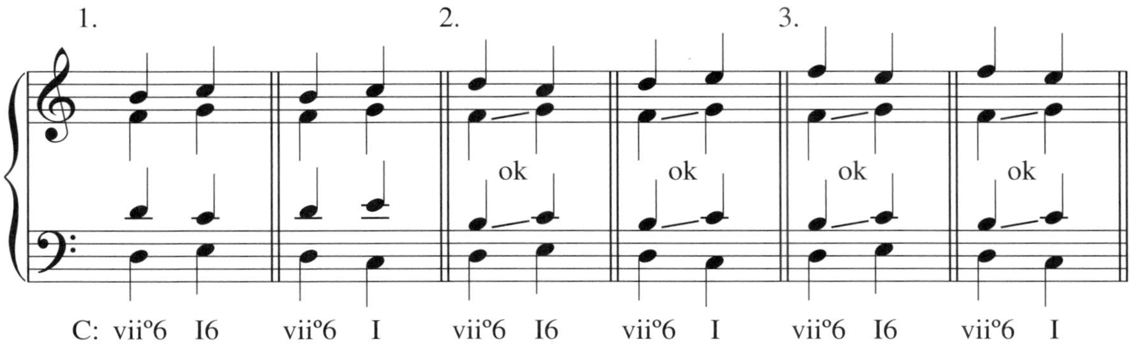

Functioning very much like the dominant chord, the leading tone chord has a strong pull toward the tonic note, resolving to either root position or first inversion, as seen in the example above. Notice the voice leading in #2 and #3 above. What appear to be parallel fifths are perfectly acceptable! Why? Because one of each pair is a diminished fifth. Only parallel perfect fifths are objectionable. Diminished to perfect, or vice versa, is always allowable, except in a single circumstance. This will be discussed in a later chapter. Parallel diminished fifths are also no problem.

Root position triads may be freely mixed with first inversion chords, as a glance at any page of the masters will soon reveal. In making chord connections, it is better not to lay down another set of rules, but rather to be conscious of your doubling liberties and to be mindful of the ever-present "dangers" of parallel fifths or octaves. Further, be particularly cautious in writing a succession of sixth chords; careless work can all too easily result in both kinds of parallels. Some correct examples of successive sixth chords:

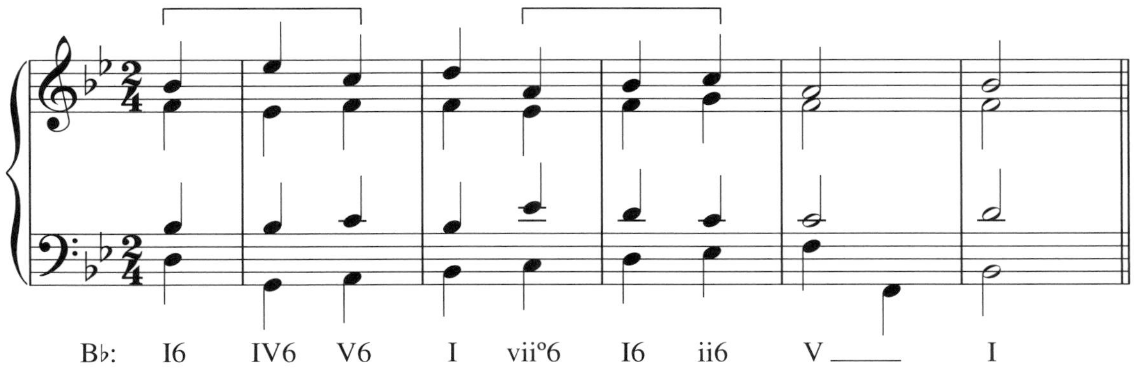

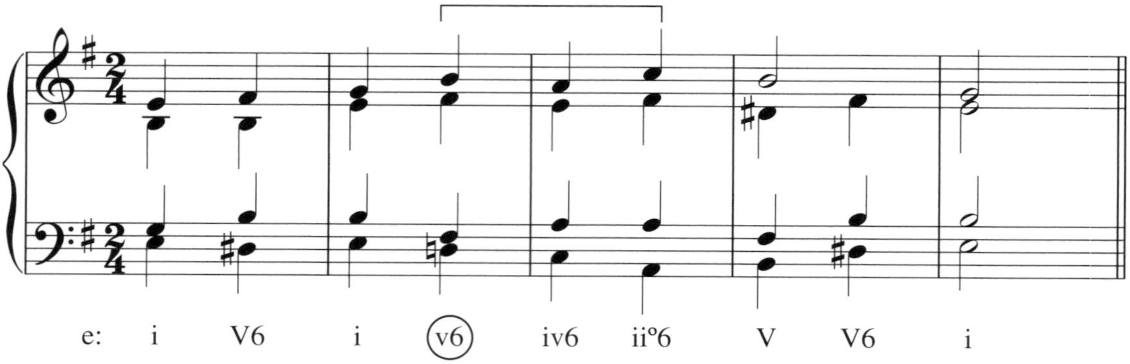

Brackets denote successive sixth chords. Observe how the octave relationships shift from part to part to avoid parallel octaves. In the second example above, the chord encircled is the natural dominant chord in minor in first inversion. In minor, the progression I–v6–iv6–V is not at all uncommon. The descent of the bass line down from the tonic through the natural seventh degree in this fashion is the usual way in which the natural dominant chord is used.

Some typical examples of student errors follow. Study them carefully:

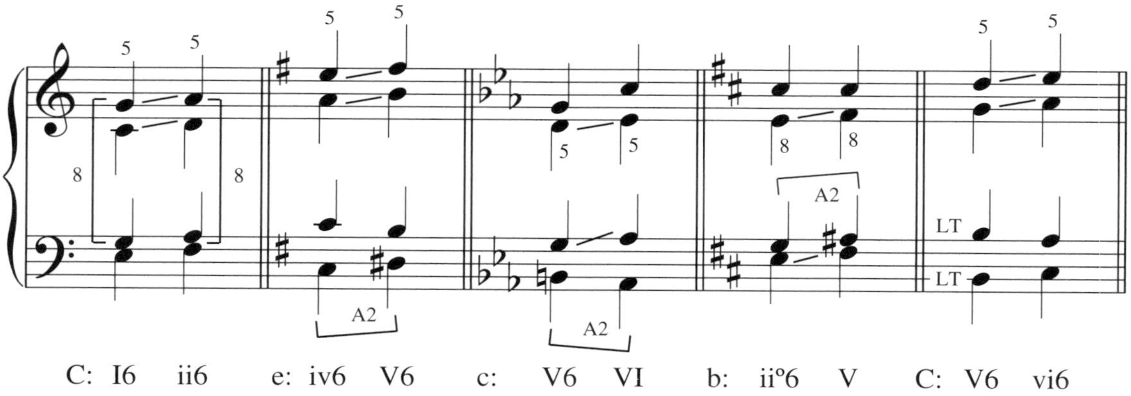

In minor keys, ii°6–V is easily abused by writing A2s or A4s in the voice leading. This progression should be treated much as in iv–V, with the upper voices moving down to the nearest chord tones of V:

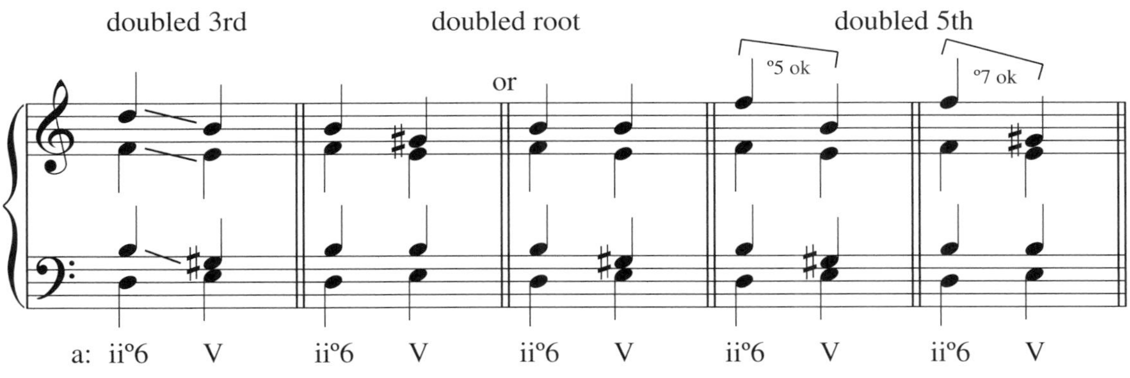

Most usual is the doubled third. Doubled root is also possible. The doubled fifth is rare. Used as in the foregoing example, it is just manageable. The melodic intervals in the soprano of d5 and d7 are not objectionable.

Two examples follow, one in major, one in minor. Notice the use of strong progressions most of the time (down a fifth, up a second, down a third). V and vii°6 in minor must have accidentals to make sure the LT, root position, and first inversion are mixed freely, successive first inversion chords are free of parallels, and both soprano and bass have good melodic contours:

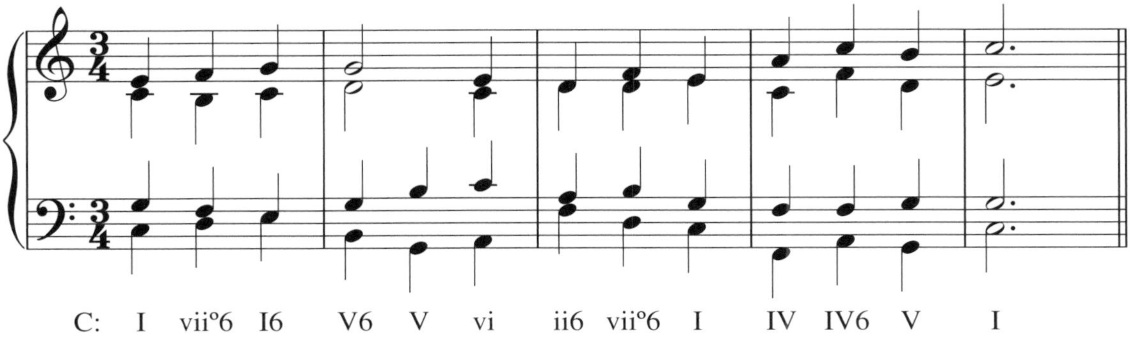

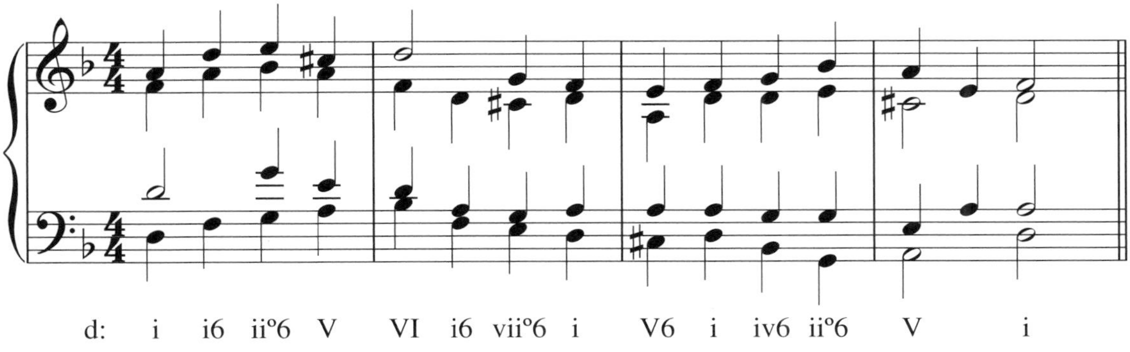

THE RAISED SIXTH DEGREE IN MINOR

Among the 13 possible chords in minor are three that have the raised sixth degree. In A minor, for example:

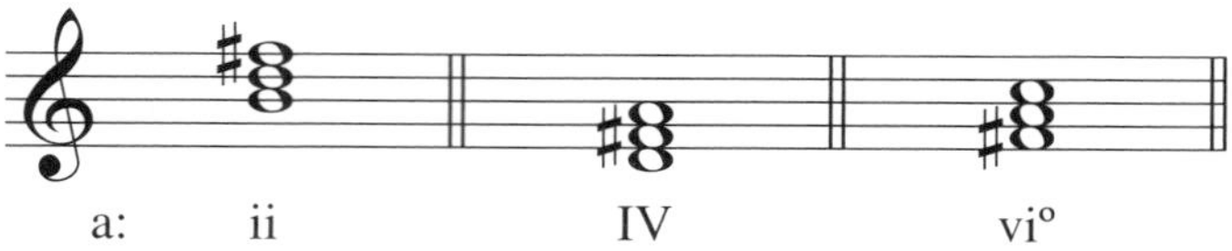

Supertonic becomes minor, subdominant becomes major, and the submediant becomes diminished. How are they introduced, and where do they move? They are usually preceded by a form of tonic and move to either V or vii°6. Examples below illustrate. Notice that, in every case, the raised sixth moves to the raised seventh degree, in conformity with the ascending melodic minor scale:

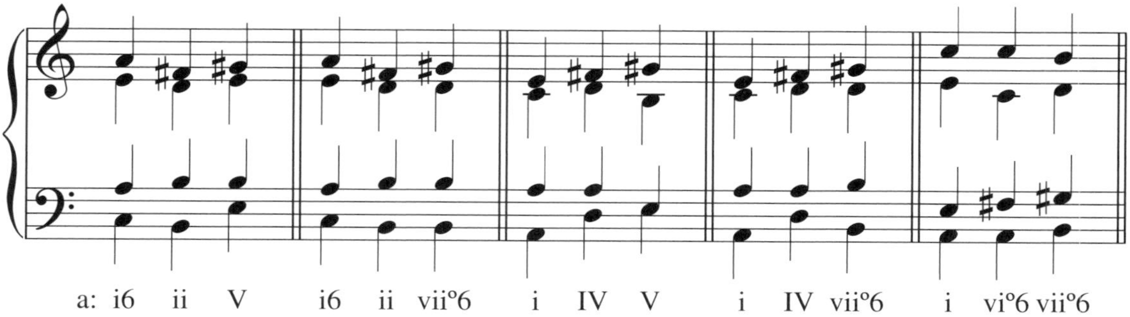

When it comes to harmonizing a given bass line, we must now consider that each bass note might be either a root or a third of a chord. Take the following bass line as an example:

Understanding that the passage should begin on I and end with V–I, the choices of harmonies become:

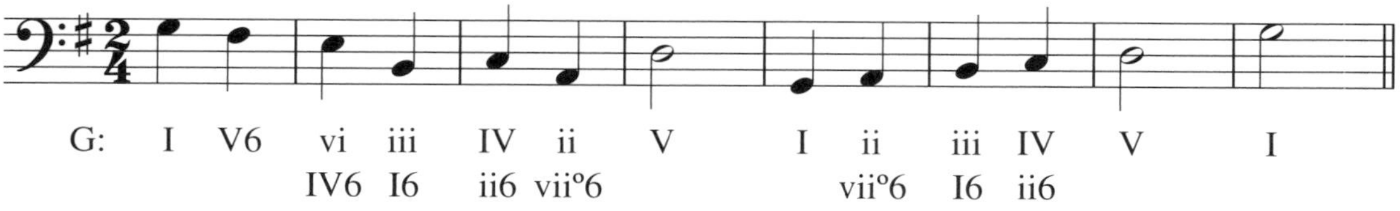

The sorting out process involves the desirability of strong progressions and harmonic variety, a mix of root position and first inversion chords, and the strong tendency of V and vii°6 to move to I. The following realization emerged, although it is by no means the only workable one. The next challenge was to shape a good soprano line and work the alto and tenor into the picture so that they also have melodic interest. After examining the passage to ensure that it has good spacing, doubling, voice leading, and no objectionable parallels, we have:

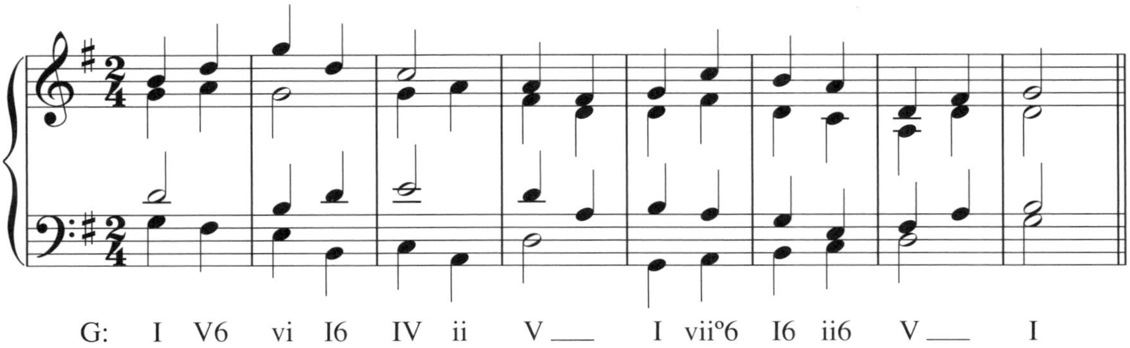

Always the most challenging assignment is to harmonize a given soprano line. Here each soprano note might be root, third, or fifth of either a root position or first inversion chord—a staggering array of choices! Let us explore a melody in G minor and see how it may be harmonized.

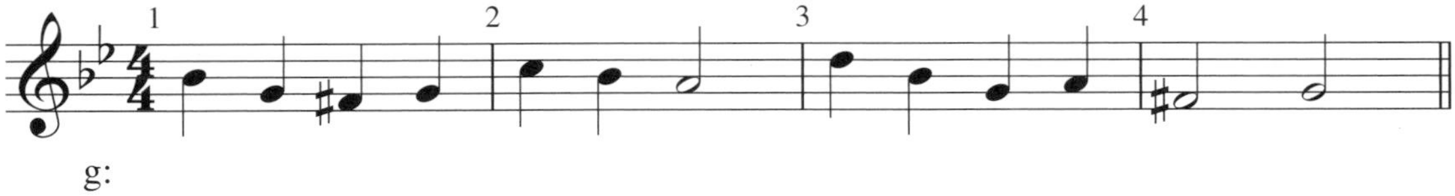

Certain decisions can be made immediately: we will begin and end on the tonic chord. The first chord of the measure 4 should be V, which makes a more convincing ending than vii°6. The middle of measure 2 appears to come to a rest on V, and the first beat of measure 3 calls for another tonic chord. Thus far, then:

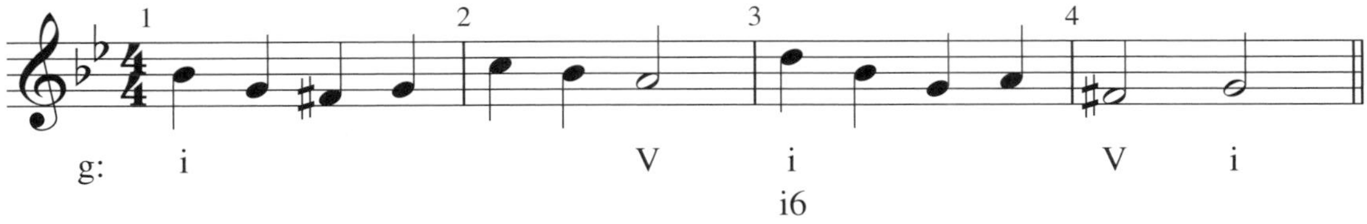

To give you an idea of the variety of possibilities for harmonization, let us look only at the remaining notes of measure 1:

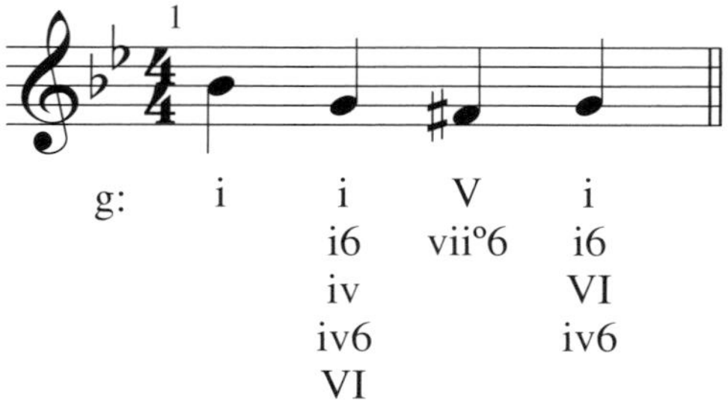

There are actually 40 different solutions for this one measure. The simplest of these is #1; this is followed by other, more interesting solutions. The ten possibilities shown here were chosen for their bass line properties and their harmonic potential. There is no single best answer, rather, many good answers:

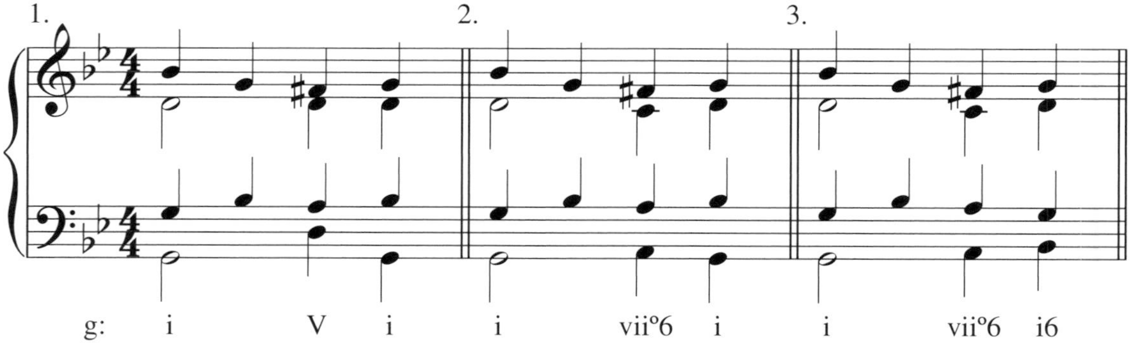

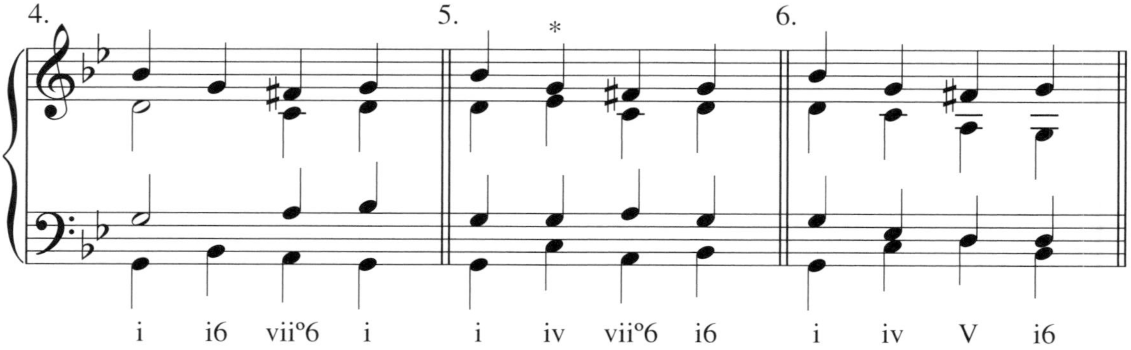

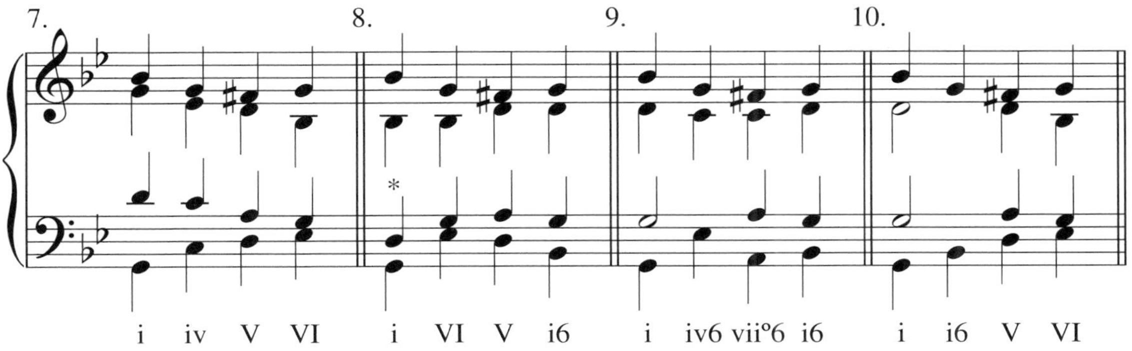

The asterisks in #5 and #8 indicate where departures from "normal" doubling in root position were needed in order to avoid parallels, either before or after the chords. Whichever of the above measures is selected will depend largely upon the choices to be made in the continuation, according to how they shape the bass line, the harmonic strength they express, and the variety of chords and chord progressions desired. Here are the chord form possibilities:

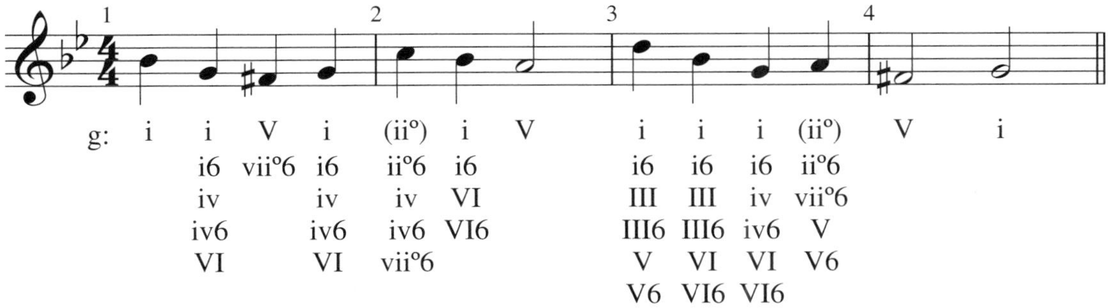

The last chord of measure three is very important. Since V comes on the next beat, it is much wiser to use a different, non-dominant type chord to precede it. The best choice here is ii°6. The supertonic chord in minor is occasionally used in root position, and is included, with parentheses, as an outside choice, but ii°6 is always a better way to go. Before ii°6, then, are a number of chords, perhaps the strongest of which is a form of VI. The first two beats of measure 3 can both easily be harmonized as tonic chords, giving us a good series of chords in measures 3 and 4. In measure 2, vii°6 works well on beat 1, resolving to the tonic chord on beat 2.

One of several good solutions is shown below. It should be studied in terms of strength of harmony, melodic shape of the bass line, spacing, doubling, and voice leading. Typically, the alto and tenor are not exciting, but they each have acceptable contours:

g: i iv V i6 vii°6 i V i6 i VI ii°6 V I

Notice that the final chord has been made into a major triad with the use of an accidental. Ending a minor piece with a major chord happens frequently in music. The raised third of the chord is called the **Picardy third**. The chord is labeled "I" instead of "i."

FIGURED BASS

This is an appropriate time to introduce the concept of **figured bass**. Developed during the Baroque era, figured bass is a shorthand method of indicating harmonies over a given bass line. Compare the two examples below, in C major. Directly below the Roman numeral progression is a figured bass line that expresses precisely the same harmonies:

Roman numeral

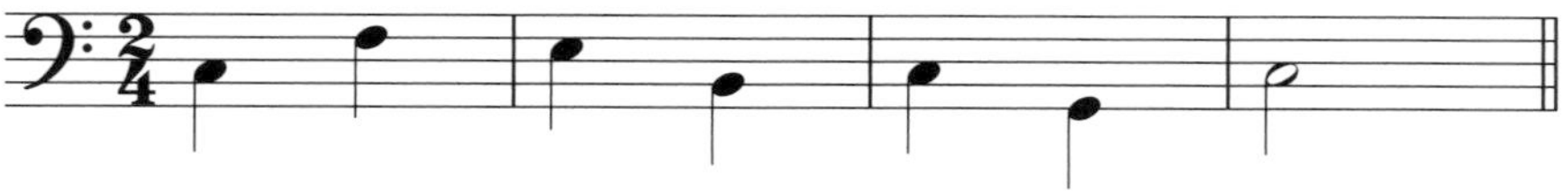

C: I ii6 I6 V6 I V I

figured bass

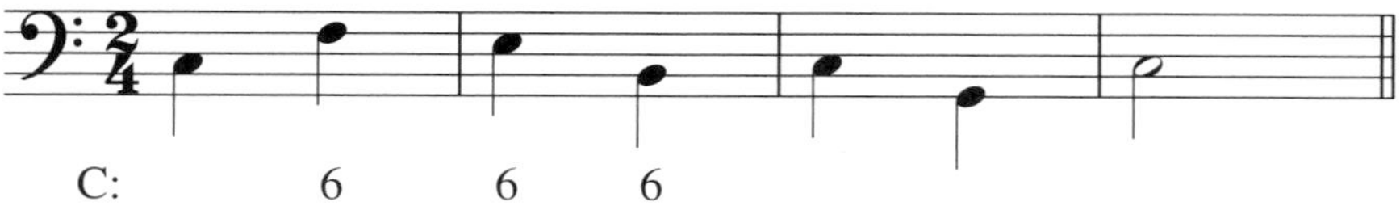

C: 6 6 6

We may observe that:

1. If there is no number, a root position triad is intended.
2. If the number "6" is present, a first inversion triad is intended.

So far, simple enough for major keys. Now look at this passage in E minor:

Roman numeral

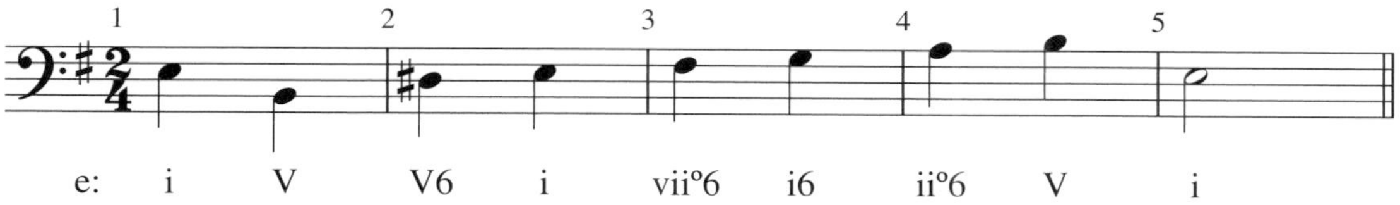

figured bass

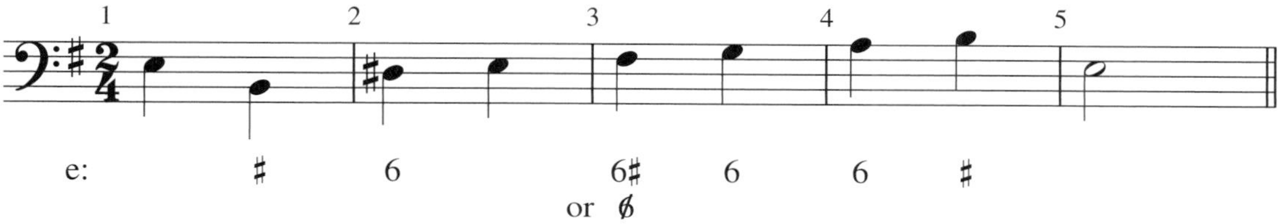

When accidentals outside the key are brought in, things get a little more complicated. We observe that:

1. A lone accidental, not associated with any number, indicates that the interval of a third above the bass has the accidental. (Note: intervals above the bass might be compound, but they are expressed in their shorter form.)
2. If a number has an accidental associated with it, the note above the bass represented by that interval has the accidental.
3. If a number has a line diagonally through it, the interval above the bass represented by the number is raised one half-step by an appropriate accidental.

In our example, the lone sharp in measures one and four must be D# (a third above the bass). In measure three, the sharp associated with the number 6 is applied to the note D (a sixth above the bass) to make D#, the LT of E minor.

It takes a little while to get the hang of it, but some study of the foregoing examples should put you on the right track. As more chord forms are introduced, their notation in figured bass will be discussed. Before you read Chapter Five, do the exercises that follow. Also, read thoroughly the following summary of principles that have been dealt with thus far in this book.

EXERCISES

1. Analyze the harmony:

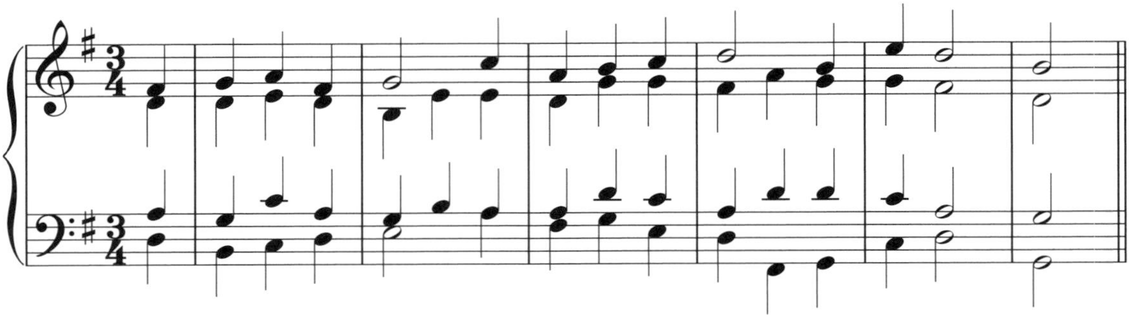

G:

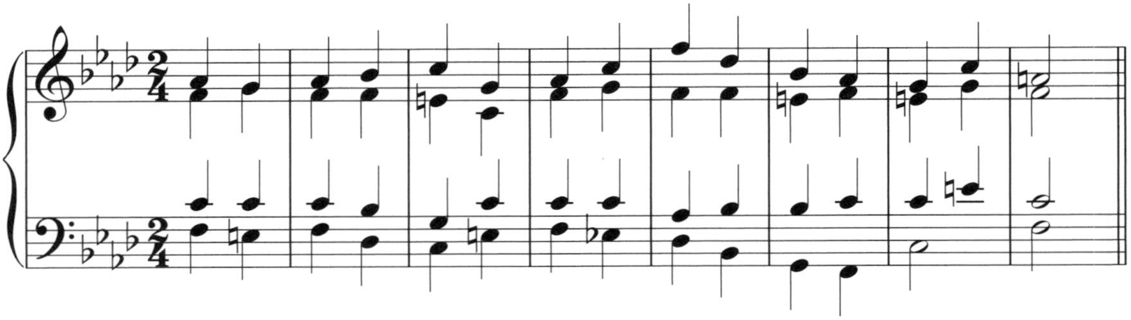

f:

2. Fill out in four-part harmony:

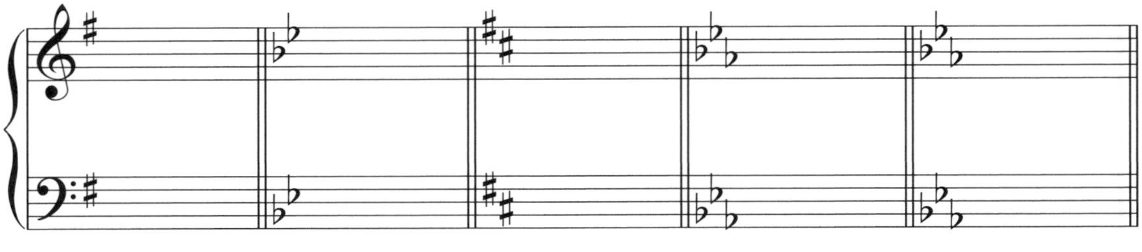

e: VI V   B♭: I6 IV6   D: IV6 V6   c: V6 i   E♭: ii6 V

3. Add three upper voices:

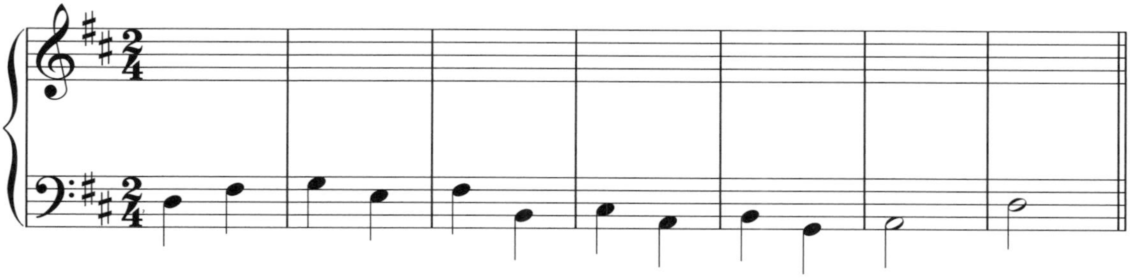

D: I I6 IV vii°6 I6 IV6 V6 V vi ii6 V I

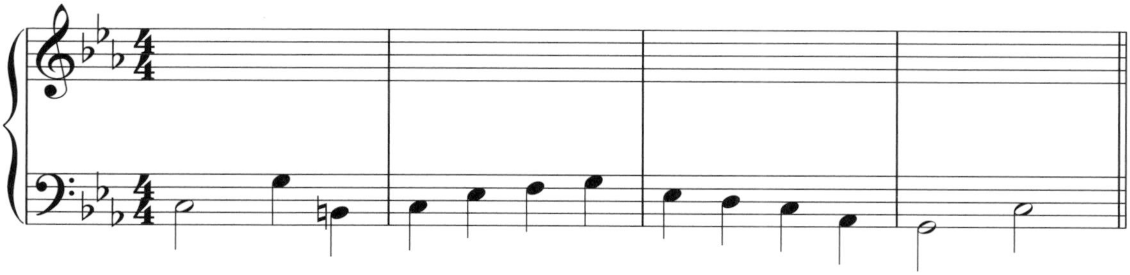

c: i V V6 i III iv V i6 vii°6 i iv6 V i

4. Realize these progressions in four-part harmony. Where there is a figured bass line, provide a Roman numeral analysis below the figured bass symbols:

C: 6 6 D: 6 6 6

R.N.: ___ ___ ___ ___ ___ ___ ___ ___ ___ ___ ___ ___ ___

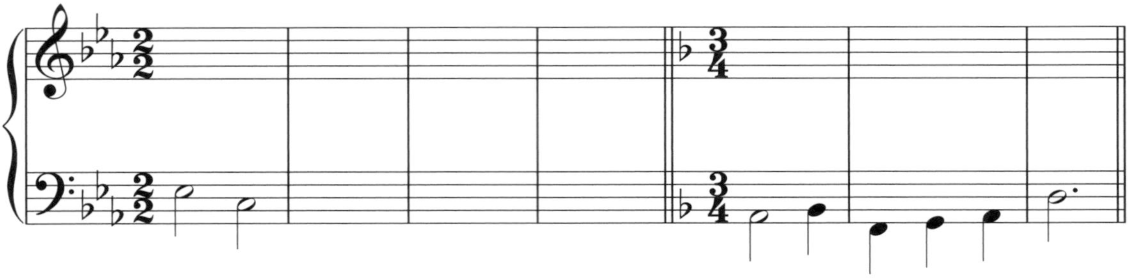

E♭: I IV6 ii6 V I vi6 V6 I d: ♯ 6 6 ♯ ♯

R.N.: ___ ___ ___ ___ ___ ___

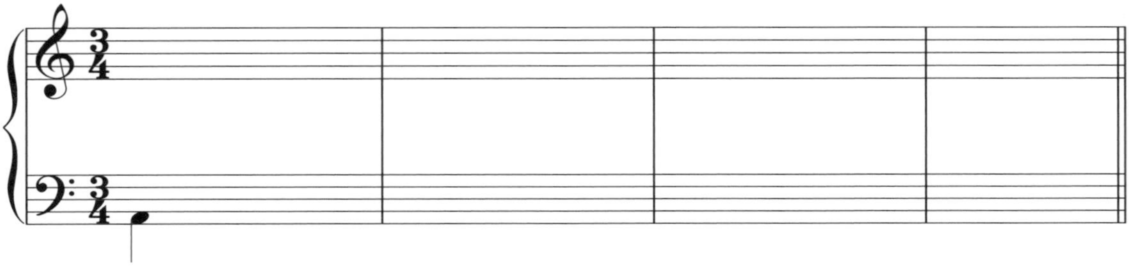

a: i vii°6 i6 ii°6 V VI iv ii°6 V6 I

5. Add three upper voices. Provide Roman numeral analysis:

a:

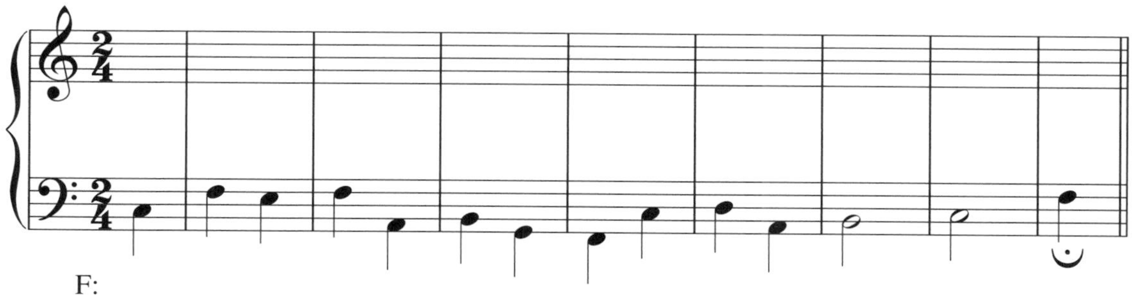

F:

6. Add three lower voices. Provide Roman numeral analysis:

e:

C:

7. Provide the Roman numeral equivalent for this figured bass line:

8. Add soprano, alto, and tenor lines above the following bass lines. Try to shape interesting melodic lines in the soprano parts. Play your work on the keyboard before handing it in! Avoid parallels, poor spacing, doubling, and so forth.

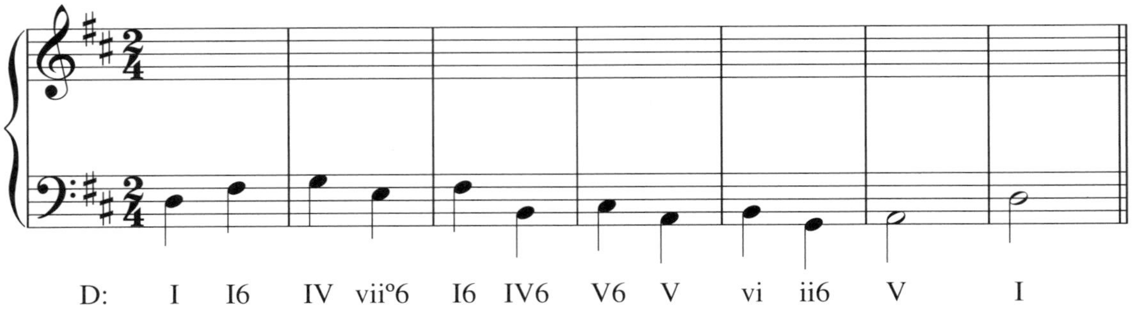

GUIDELINES FOR WRITING FOUR-PART HARMONY IN ROOT POSITION AND FIRST INVERSION

1. Remain within the ranges of the four voices.
2. Soprano and alto are written on the top staff in treble clef; tenor and bass are written on the bottom staff in bass clef.
3. Write stems up for S and T, stems down for A and B.
4. Do not exceed one octave between soprano and alto or between alto and tenor. The spacing between alto and tenor is more difficult to perceive, so be watchful here.
5. There is no restriction regarding the space between tenor and bass.
6. In general, use normal doubling in root position. This means double the root in root position.

   Exception: V–vi, V–VI.
7. Chord repetition is best when upper parts move.
8. Avoid parallel perfect fifths and octaves. d5 to P5 and P5 to d5 are okay. d5 to d5 is okay. Avoid parallel unisons, or any combination of unison and octave.
9. Avoid awkward melodic intervals in all voices: A2, A4, A5, sevenths and ninths. (d7 is okay.)
10. Don't cross parts. If there is a very good melodic reason to do so, crossed parts between alto and tenor may happen, but only very briefly.
11. Overlap of more than the interval of a second should be avoided. Remember, overlap occurs only between adjacent voices.
12. If in any melodic line there are two (or more) skips in the same direction, the pitches concerned should be all or part of a triad (except augmented), or a dominant seventh or supertonic seventh chord. For example, avoid two fourths in a row, two fifths in a row, etc.
13. Begin by establishing the tonic key, and end well with V–I, both in root position.
14. Use sensible harmonic progressions, mostly down a fifth (up a fourth), down a third, up a second, etc.
15. Strive for an interesting soprano line and bass line. Alto and tenor do not have to be as good.
16. In progressions that move up or down a fifth or fourth in root position, use Methods #1, #2, or #3 to be safe.
17. In minor keys, V and vii°6 require the seventh degree of the scale to be raised with the appropriate accidental.
18. Progressions that move up a step in root position require the upper voices to move up to the nearest chord tones.

19. Progressions that move down a second in root position require the upper voices to move up to the nearest chord tones.

20. In the progression V–vi (major key), you may either

    1) double the third by resolving the LT up, or

    2) move the LT down a step to double the root of vi, if the LT is in an inner voice, or, if in the soprano, it moves down by step from the tonic tone.

21. In a minor key, the progression V–VI requires resolution of the LT up. Other voices move down. The third is doubled.

22. Root position progressions that move down a third may be treated in a number of ways successfully. The safest way is to hold over the two common tones. This is the least interesting method, however.

23. Look for the possibility of a single high note in the soprano. This may appear anywhere in the line.

24. Do not double the LT.

25. In first inversion, use the freedom in doubling.

26. In vii°6 double the third (the bass note). If the fifth of the chord is in the soprano, it may be doubled.

27. The vii°6 chord is a very fine one, and may be used freely. For now, do not use in root position.

28. When sixth chords follow one another, be careful with your voice leading and doubling in order to avoid parallels.

29. Feel free to use unison doubling in your work. This is common.

30. When resolving V or vii°6, be aware of where the LT is and treat its resolution properly. If the LT is in the soprano, resolve up by step. If it is in alto or tenor, it may move up, or it might move down a third to provide the fifth of the tonic chord.

31. In chord repetition of V, the LT may move from voice to voice freely. Pay close attention to the LT when the chord resolves. The same applies to vii°6.

CHAPTER 5 TRIADS IN SECOND INVERSION

In second inversion, the fifth of the chord is in the bass; the root and third are among the upper voices:

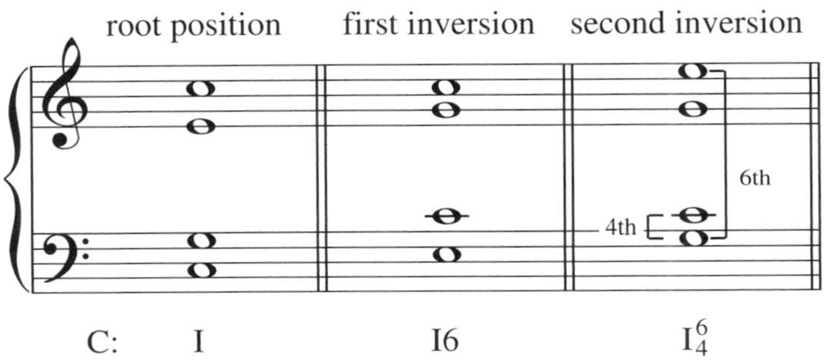

SIX-FOUR CHORDS

The intervals formed by the upper voices with the bass are a sixth and a fourth, which explains why these chords are called **six-four chords**. The interval of a perfect fourth above the bass is the cause for the unstable character of all six-four chords. Accordingly, they are used only in special well-defined ways. They may not be approached or left freely, as is true of root position and first inversion chords. There are four ways to use six-four chords. Learn them well and be able to recognize when they are applicable and to identify them by their specific type. The four types of six-four chords are:

1. cadential tonic six-four (I^6_4, i^6_4)
2. passing six-four
3. pedal (or stationary) six-four
4. arpeggiated six-four

The Cadential Tonic Six-four Chord

In the next chapter, we will examine cadences in detail. Suffice it to say here that cadences occur at the ends of phrases, denoting a momentary (or final) halt in the musical flow, much as periods, semi-colons and commas in grammar. A typical harmonic approach to a cadence is by way of the **cadential tonic six-four chord** (I^6_4, i^6_4). Here is how it is used:

1. It precedes the V chord.
2. It always occurs on a strong beat, stronger than the V that follows.

3. It is approached by step or by leap, most often by some form of subdominant or supertonic harmony, although submediant and tonic are possible.
4. The fifth of the chord is doubled.
5. It may occur in a part of the phrase that is not necessarily the actual cadence.
6. The voice leading into the V chord is flexible.

Some examples:

In triple meter, the cadential six-four chord may occur either on beat one or beat two:

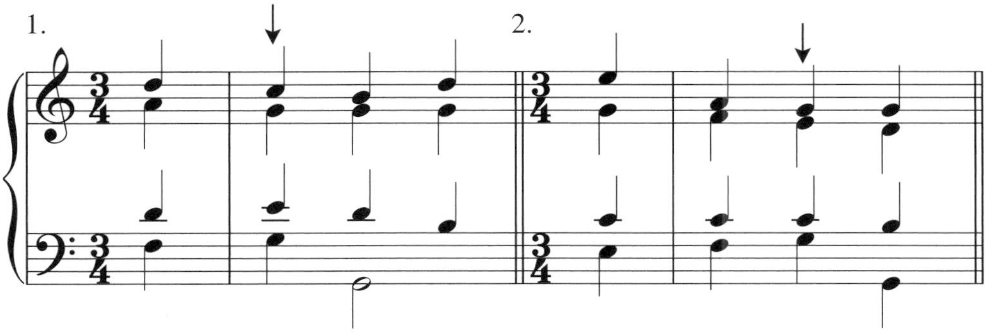

C: ii6 I^6_4 V ______ C: I6 IV I^6_4 V

The Passing Six-four Chord

Here are the characteristics of the **passing six-four chord**:

1. Three chords are involved.
2. The middle chord is a six-four chord.
3. The bass moves by step in one direction (up or down).
4. Any chord may be a passing six-four chord.
5. It occurs on a weak beat (more usual) or strong beat.
6. The outer chords must both be stable chords; they usually are forms of the same chord.
7. It follows from #6 that six-four chords cannot appear in succession.
8. The most common passing six-four chords are V^6_4 and I^6_4.
9. The fifth of the chord is doubled.

Some examples:

a: i V^6_4 i6 C: IV6 I^6_4 IV F: IV I^6_4 IV6 c: vii°6 iv^6_4 V6

The Pedal (Stationary) Six-four Chord

What is **stationary** here is the bass line. The characteristics:

1. There are three chords involved.
2. The bass line remains on the same pitch in all three chords (octave skips are possible).
3. The middle chord is a six-four chord.
4. The outer chords are stable chords.
5. Usually the outer chords are the same chord, but this is not absolutely necessary.
6. The six-four may appear on a weak beat (more usual) or a strong beat.
7. Voice leading is flexible. The simplest solution is the least interesting. See #1 and #2 below.
8. The fifth of the chord is doubled.

Some examples:

Notice that all three types of six-four chords discussed so far call for doubling of the fifth of the triad. The same indeed is true for the fourth type, the arpeggiated six-four chord.

The Arpeggiated Six-four Chord

What is involved here is chord repetition.

1. Two or more chords are needed.
2. The six-four chord must be preceded by one or more stable forms of the same chord.
3. The six-four chord is usually on a weak beat.
4. The chord may be left freely.
5. Any chord may be an arpeggiated six-four chord.
6. The fifth of the chord is doubled.

Some examples:

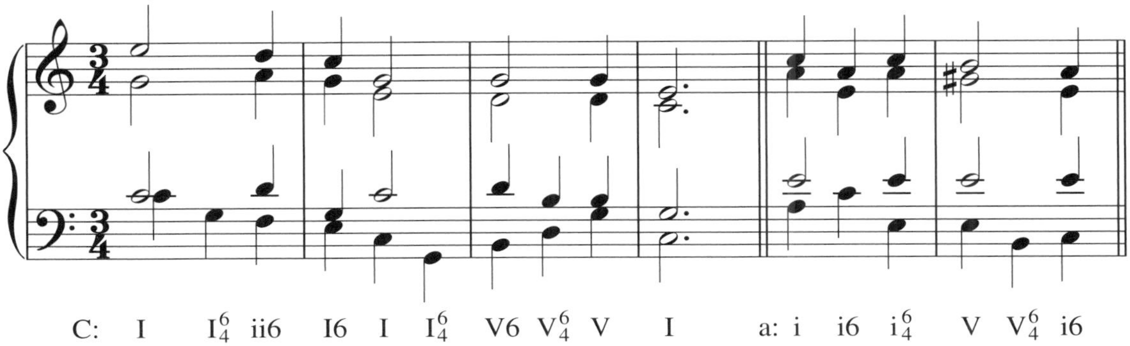

Passages incorporating all four types of six-four chords:

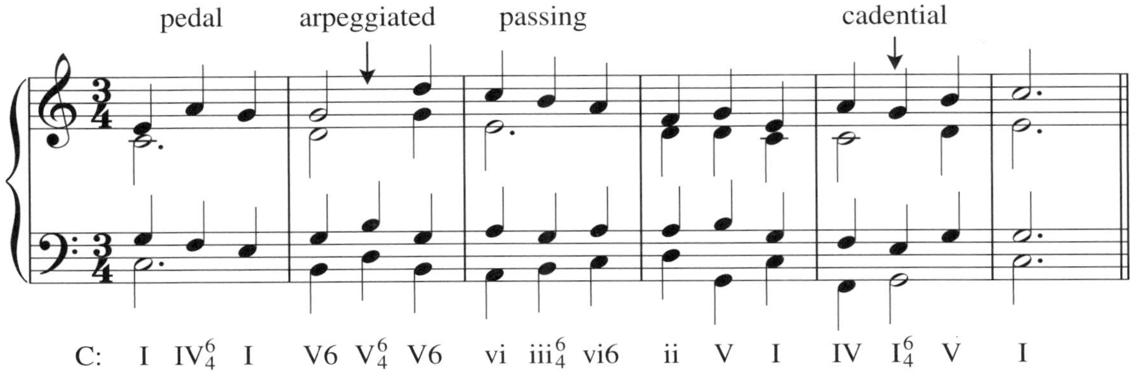

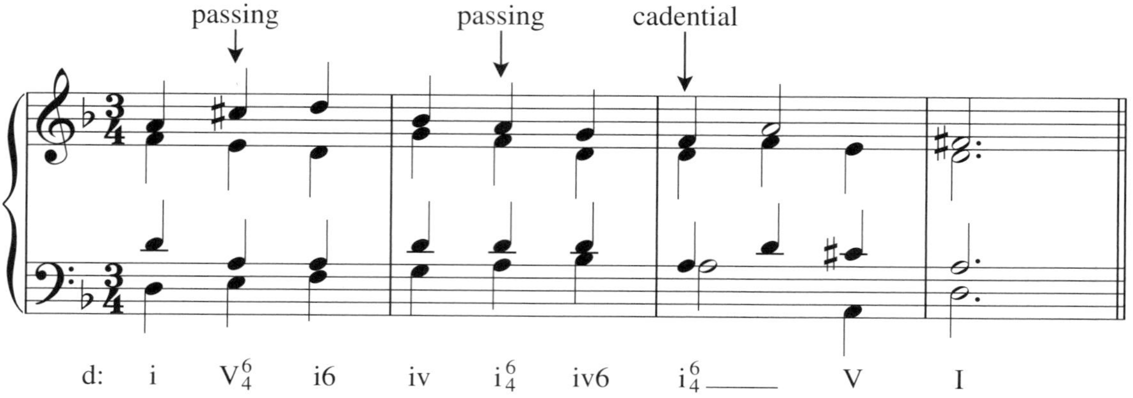

FIGURED BASS AND THE SIX-FOUR CHORD

Both numbers are used in figured bass, so there is a direct correspondence between Roman numeral analysis and figured bass numbers. However, in minor keys, any accidentals that appear in the music outside the key signature are taken into account. For example, the V^6_4 chord would have an accidental (or slanted line) associated with the number six:

Compare the following two passages:

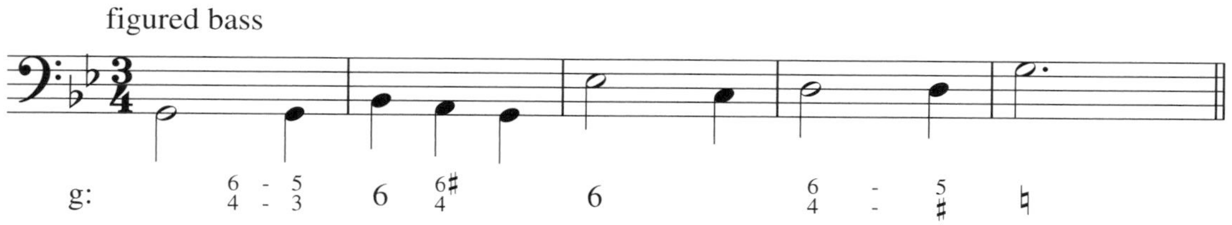

Roman numeral

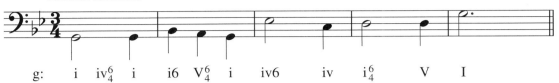

g: i iv^6_4 i i6 V^6_4 i iv6 iv i^6_4 V I

Notice that in measure 1 of the figured bass line, the numbers 6–5 and 4–3 are shown. Why? On beat 2, a six-four chord sounds. On beat 3, a root position triad is intended. If there were no number at all, the tendency would be to continue the six-four chord into beat 3; since there is no change of bass note, one might think that the six-four should be prolonged. To ensure that a root position triad sounds on beat 3, the numbers $^5_3$ are written in to guarantee that the intended chord will take place. This is a common procedure in figured bass.

When harmonizing a given bass line, look now for the occasional opportunity to bring in any of the six-four chords. Ask yourself:

1. Does the bass line move up (or down) by step through three chords (possible passing six-four)?
2. Is the bass note held through three beats or more (possible pedal six-four)?
3. Does the bass note hold the dominant tone for at least two beats, the first tone being on a strong beat (possible cadential six-four)?
4. Does the bass note move through tones of the same chord (possible arpeggiated six-four)?

Things to remember:

1. There are only four ways in which six-four chords are usually used.
2. Six-four chords are never used in succession.
3. Do not treat six-four chords with the same freedom as root position or first inversion triads.
4. Use six-four chords sparingly.
5. Double the fifth or all six-four chords.

Problems in harmonization of a bass line and harmonizing a given soprano line will be taken up once again at the end of the next chapter. Before moving on, do the exercises that follow.

EXERCISES

1. Provide Roman numeral analysis and identify six-four chord types:

G:

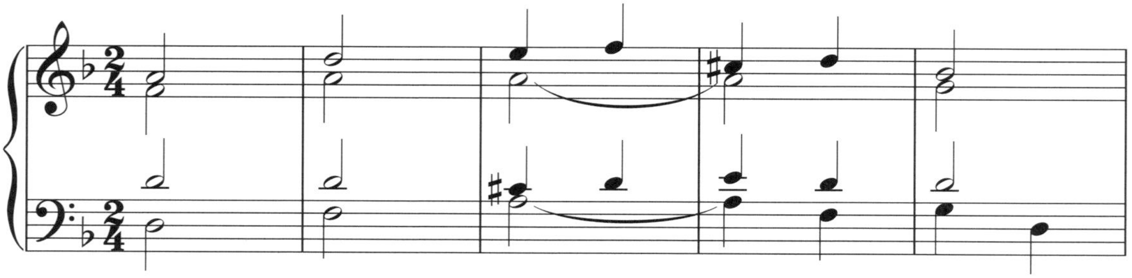

d:

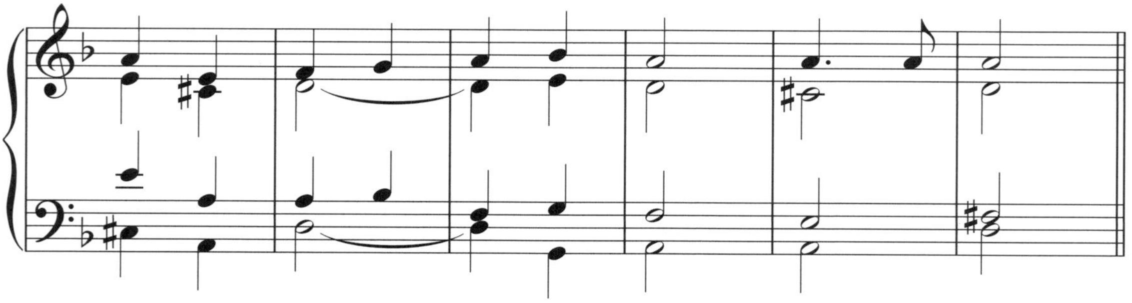

2. Using three chords, write the required six-four types. Choose your own meter and provide any necessary barline:

cadential passing

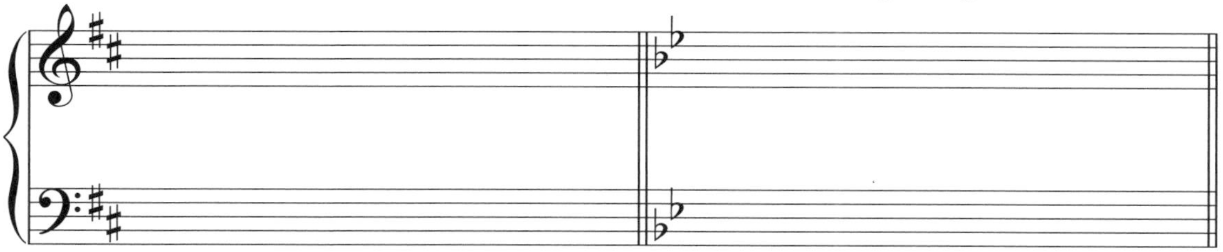

b: g:

pedal arpeggiated

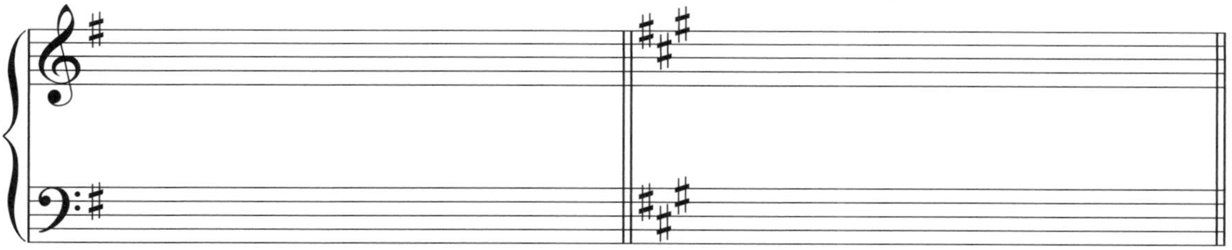

e: A:

3. Add three upper voices and identify the six-four types used:

A: V I6 I I^6_4 ii6 ii V6 I IV^6_4 I V^6_4 I6 ii6 I^6_4 V I

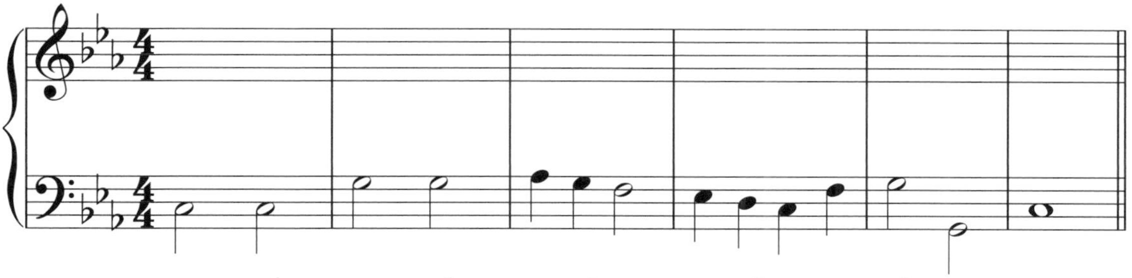

c: i iv^6_4 i V i^6_4 V VI i^6_4 iv i6 V^6_4 i iiº6 i^6_4 V I

4. Fill out in four-part harmony. Where there is a figured bass line, provide a Roman numeral analysis on a separate line below the figured bass line:

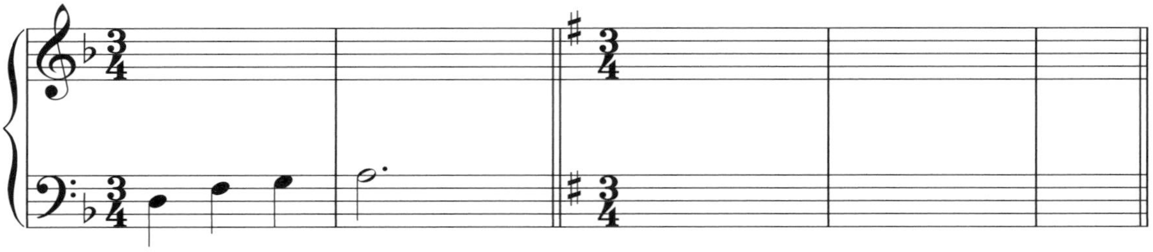

d: 6 6 ♯ $^{6}_{4}$ $^{-}_{-}$ $^{5}_{\sharp}$ G: IV vi$^{6}_{4}$ vii°6 I6 V$^{6}_{4}$ I V

R.N.: ___ ___ ___ ___ ___ ___

c: 6 $^{6}_{4}$ ♮ 6 $^{6\!\!\!/}_{4}$ ♮

R.N.: ___ ___ ___ ___ ___ ___ ___

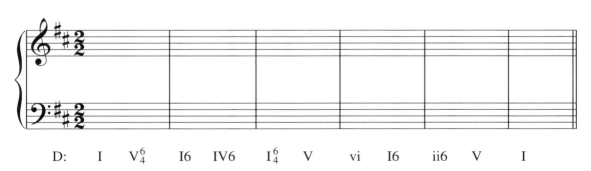

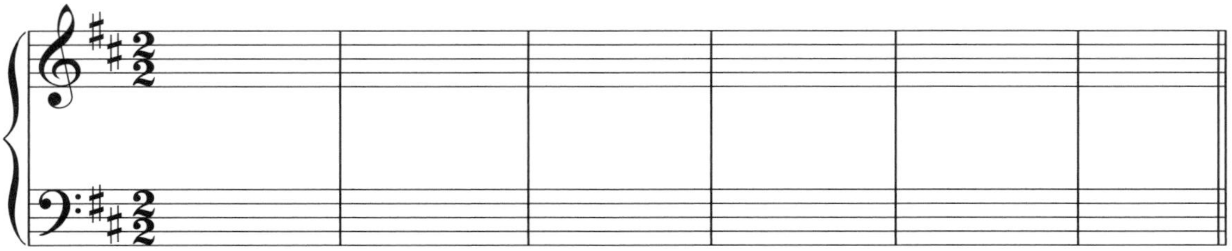

D: I V$^{6}_{4}$ I6 IV6 I$^{6}_{4}$ V vi I6 ii6 V I

CHAPTER 6 CADENCES

A **cadence** is a pause in the musical discourse, as mentioned briefly in Chapter Five (p. 75). The pauses signal the ends of phrases. These endings are shaped by certain harmonic progressions. Each type of progression, which requires only two chords, defines a particular kind of cadence. The various cadences have the following names and will be examined in the order given:

1. Authentic Cadence
    a. Perfect Authentic Cadence (PAC)
    b. Imperfect Authentic Cadence (IAC)
        1. Leading Tone IAC
2. Half Cadence (HC)
    a. Phrygian Half Cadence (Phr.HC)
    b. Plagal Half Cadence (Pl.HC)
3. Deceptive Cadence (DC)
4. Plagal Cadence (Pl. C)

THE AUTHENTIC CADENCE

This is a general term defined by the progression dominant to tonic, irrespective of inversions—any form of V moving to any form of I (i). Authentic cadences are always further refined into either a **perfect authentic cadence** (PAC) or an **imperfect authentic cadence** (IAC).

The Perfect Authentic Cadence

There are three conditions that must be met to satisfy the requirements for this type of cadence:

1. The V chord must be in root position.
2. The I (i) chord must also be in root position.
3. The tonic note must be in the highest voice of the I (i) chord.

If any of these three conditions is not present in the cadence, no perfect authentic cadence exists, but rather one of the forms of imperfect authentic cadence.

Examples of the PAC:

Perfect Authentic Cadence
tonic note in soprano

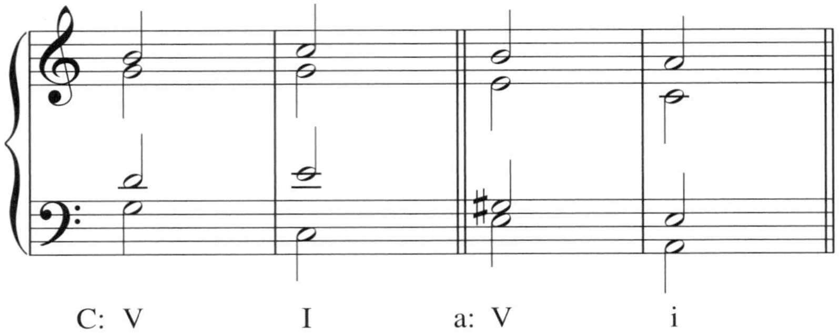

dominant and tonic in root position

The Imperfect Authentic Cadence

Taking our cue from the definition of a PAC, we need only to create any kind of situation that differs from the three requirements for a PAC:

1. The tonic note is not in the soprano, or
2. Either or both of the chords are not in root position.

Clearly, several possibilities exist for making an IAC. All of the following are examples of the IAC:

Imperfect Authentic Cadence

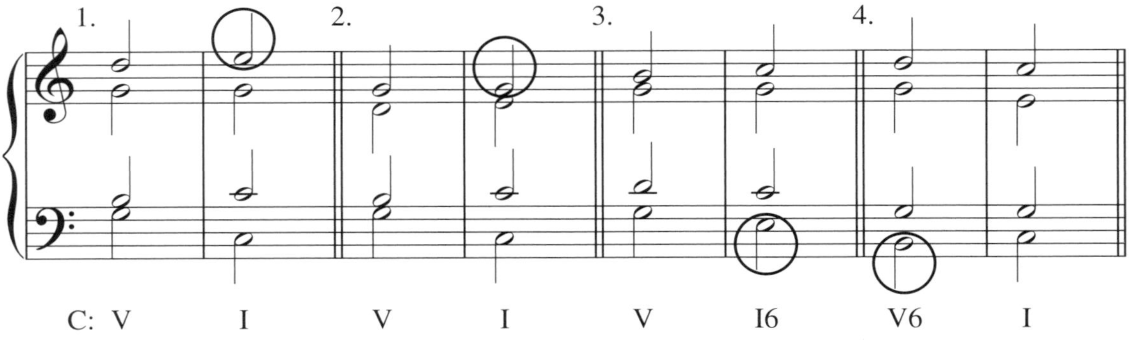

In #1 and #2, the tonic note is not in the soprano; although V and I are in root position, it is an IAC. In #3, I6 makes it an IAC. In #4, V6 makes it an IAC.

When vii°6 is used instead of a form of V, the cadence is called a **leading tone imperfect authentic cadence**:

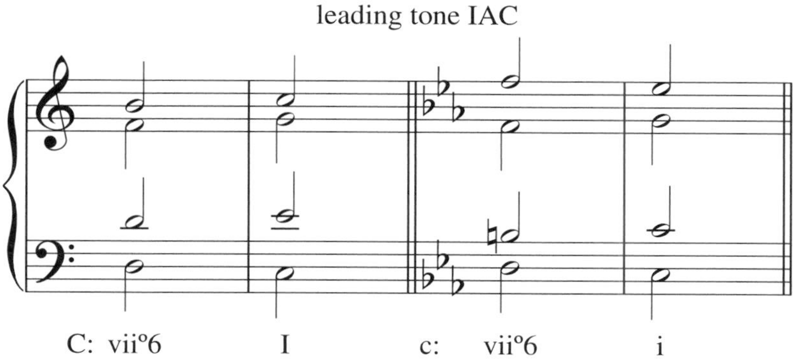

Since vii°6 is closely related in function to dominant chords, it qualifies as a form of **authentic cadence.**

THE HALF CADENCE

The **half cadence** ends with the V chord, almost always in root position. The V chord is preceded by any chord that leads nicely into V: IV, IV6, ii, ii6, vi, I, I6.

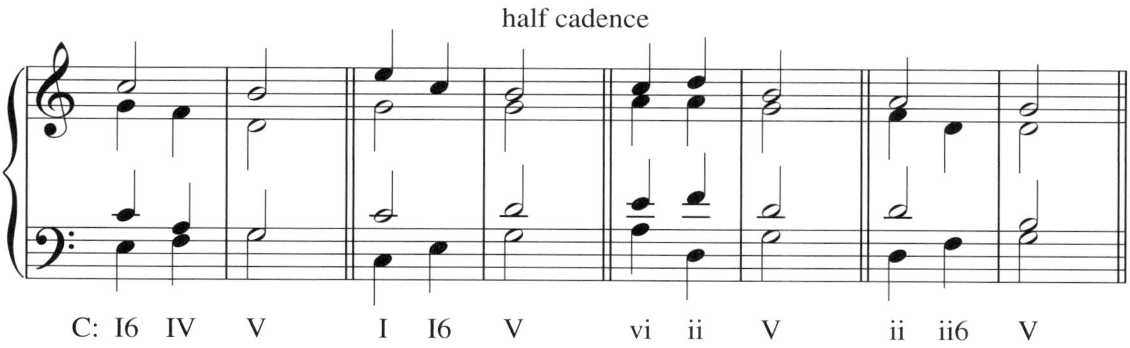

The Phrygian Half Cadence

In minor, the progression iv6–V is given a special name, the **Phrygian half cadence**, so-called because the movement down a half-step in the bass line is reminiscent of the first two steps of the Phrygian mode. An example in G minor:

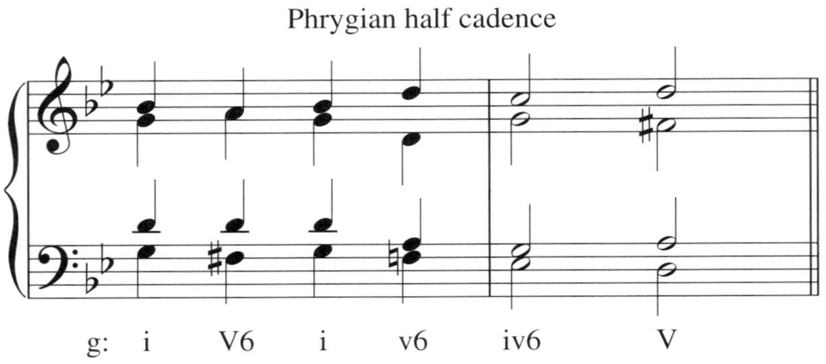

The Plagal Half Cadence

A half cadence ending in IV instead of V. It is very rare. The first phrase of "Auld Lang Syne" ends with a **plagal half cadence**:

THE DECEPTIVE CADENCE

When V resolves to some chord other than the tonic chord, we have a **deceptive cadence**. The most common progression is to the submediant: V–vi, (V–VI in minor), occasionally V–IV6 (V–vi6). As our harmonic vocabulary increases, we will encounter other types of deceptive cadences.

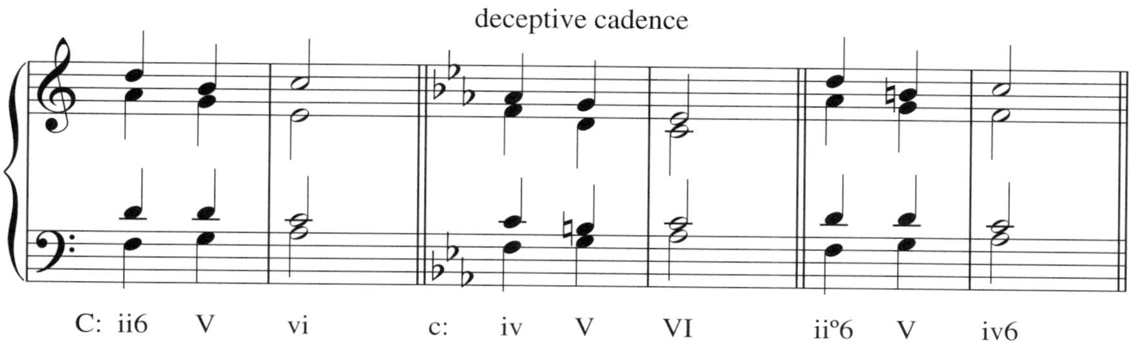

THE PLAGAL CADENCE

The **plagal cadence** is usually added as an afterthought following an authentic cadence. The progression is IV–I (iv–i), both chords usually in root position. It is common at the ends of church hymns.

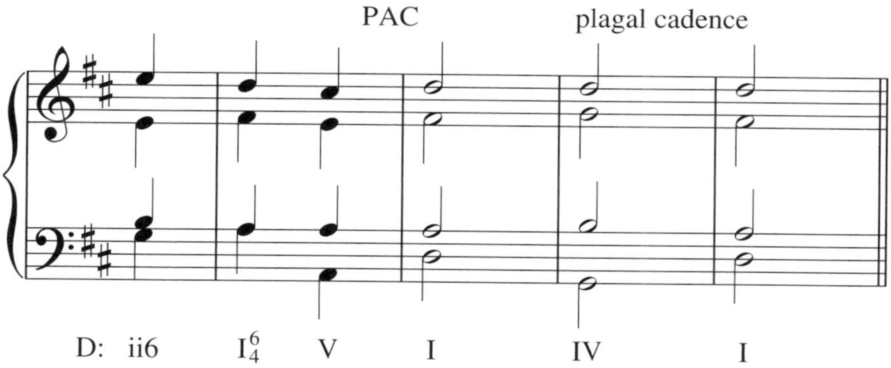

Several examples of cadences are shown below, as they appear in a church-style hymn, with four-measure phrases following one another in regular succession. Each phrase ends with a particular kind of cadence:

HARMONIZING A BASS LINE

Using all the material we've learned thus far—root position, first and second inversion, cadences—let us **harmonize a bass line**. We music consider that a bass note might be the root, third, or fifth of a triad. (Remember, if it is to be the fifth of a triad, it must fulfill the requirements for six-four chords. Review Chapter Five!). Let us see how the following bass line may be harmonized:

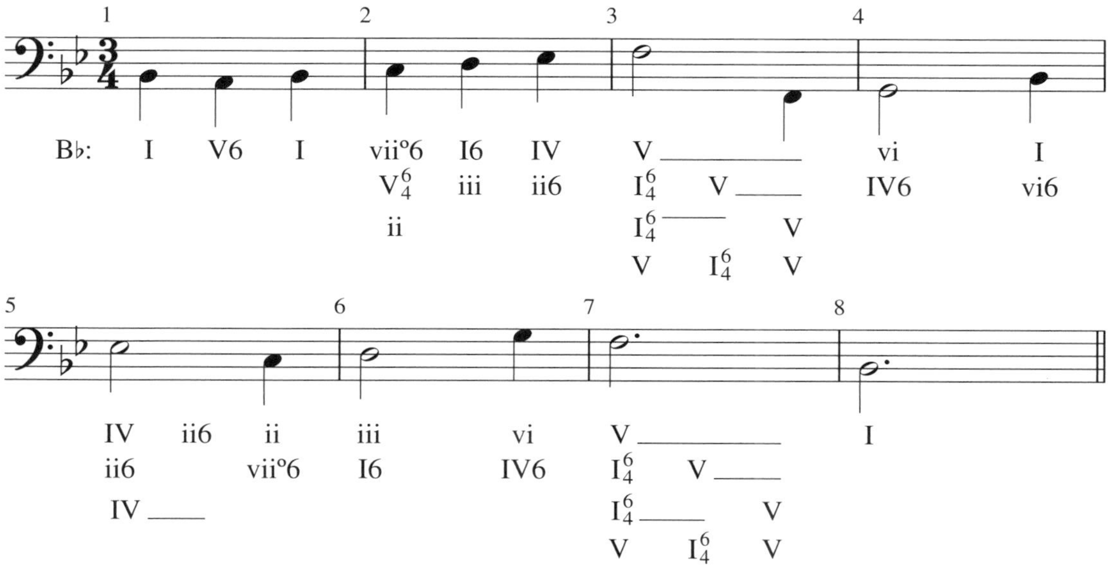

Measure 1 clearly establishes the tonality with I–V6–I; no other solution is reasonable here. The first beat of measure 2 could be ii, vii, or V^6_4, but vii°6 here is generally the best-sounding chord. Beat 2: I6 is the preferred choice. iii is not a frequently used chord. Beat 3 calls for either IV or ii6; both are equally good. Measures 3 and 7 offer the same possibilities, and there are many. Measure 4: vi is the best choice for the deceptive cadence. Instead of I on beat 3 of measure 4, it would be better to continue submediant harmony with vi6. Measure 5: IV or ii6. Beat 3 could be either ii or vii°6. The latter is good, moving nicely to I6 in measure 6. Beat 3 of measure 6 may be either vi or IV6; measure 7 offers several choices. One possible solution follows. The only six-four chords used were cadential six-four chords in measures 3 and 7:

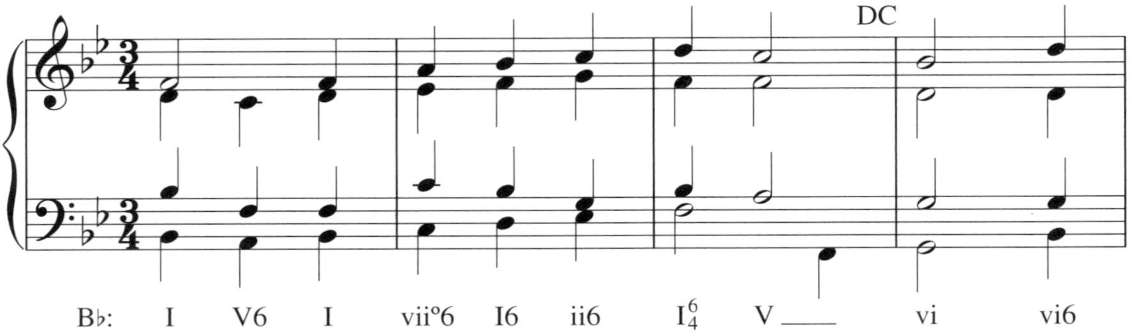

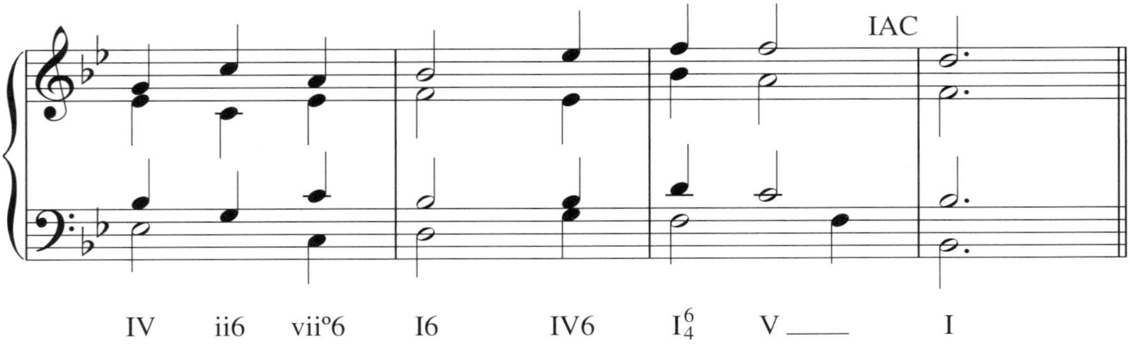

HARMONIZING A MELODY

Now let us **harmonize a melody** using all the resources we've learned. Much more searching is required to find workable results. With only the soprano line given, it is far more difficult, for instance, to determine whether a six-four chord can come into play. Of course, it is possible to harmonize a melody without the use of any six-four chords, but that would be a needless limitation of our harmonic resources. Let us explore the following four-measure melody:

Beginning and ending on the tonic chord, establishing a good sense of the home key, preparing for the return home at the end, looking for good harmonic progressions, shaping a convincing bass line—all considerations must somehow work together to produce a result. In terms of where we might place a six-four chord, there are four possibilities:

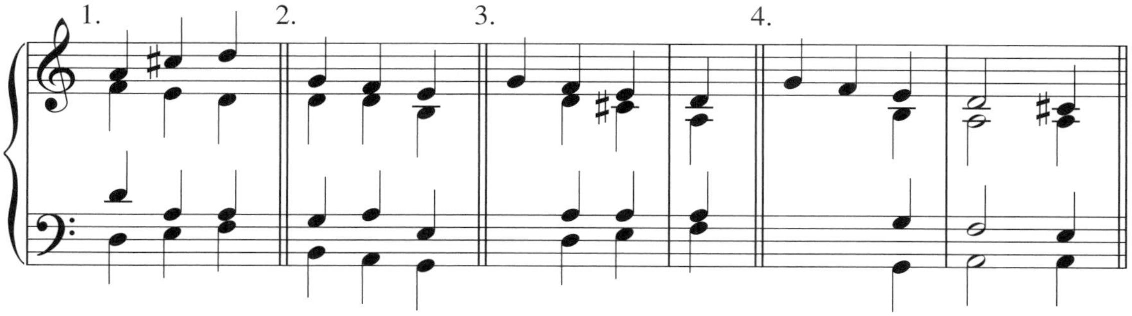

d: i V^6_4 i6 iv6 i^6_4 ii°6 i V^6_4 i6 ii°6 i^6_4 V

The seven realizations that follow are by no means the only respectable harmonizations of our melody; they should be examined in terms of bass line, harmonic progressions, mixture of first and second inversion chords, occasional six-four chords, convincing beginning and conclusion, and degree of interest in alto and tenor parts.

1.

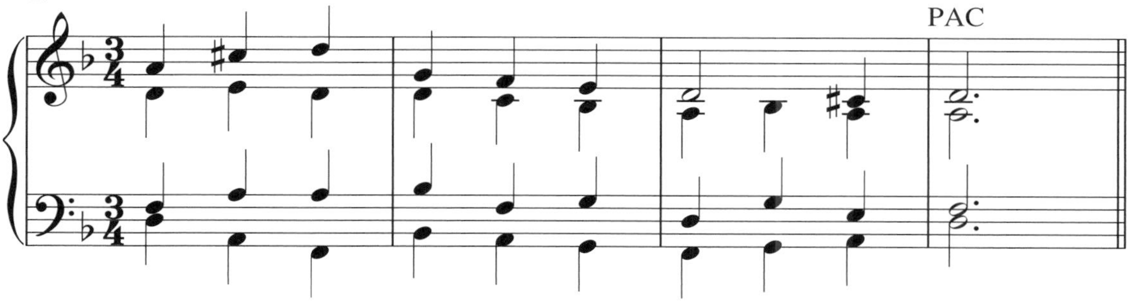

d: i V i6 iv6 III6 ii°6 i6 iv V i

2.

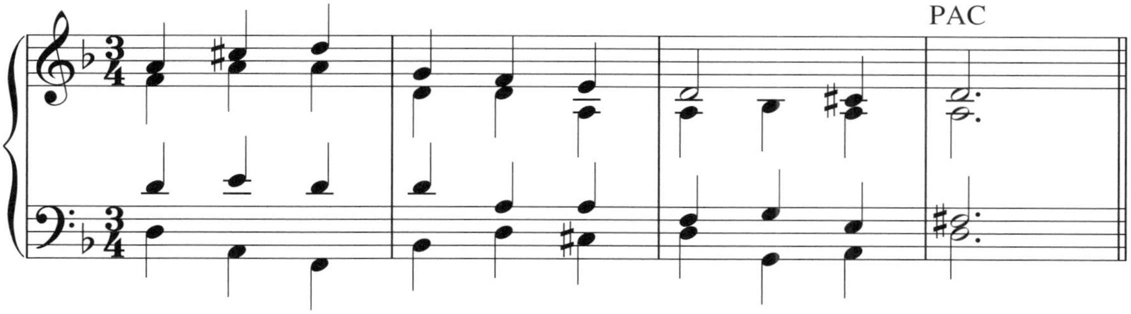

d: i V i6 iv6 i V6 i iv V I

3.

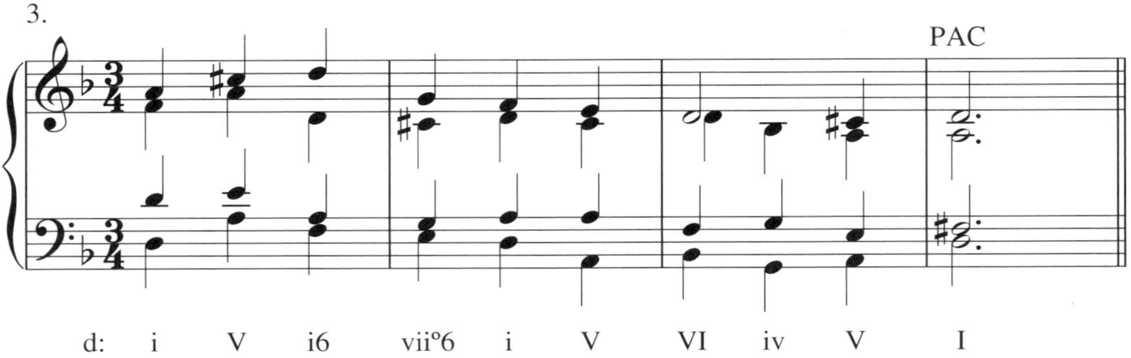
PAC
d: i V i6 vii°6 i V VI iv V I

4.

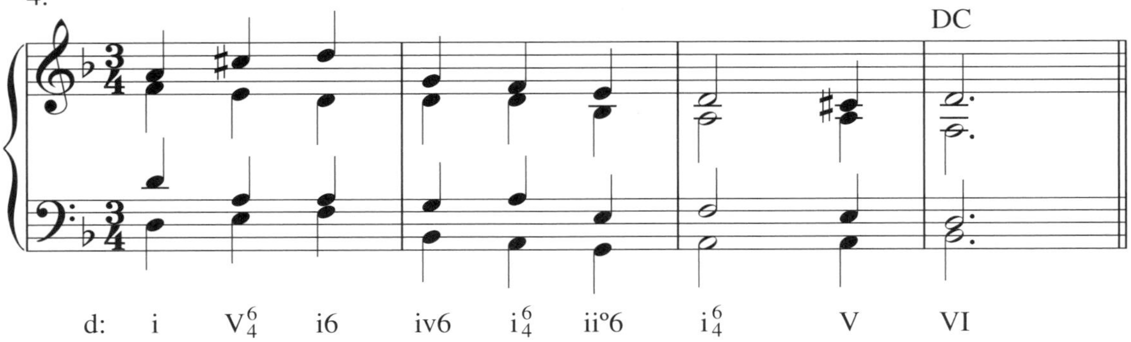
DC
d: i V$^6_4$ i6 iv6 i$^6_4$ ii°6 i$^6_4$ V VI

5.

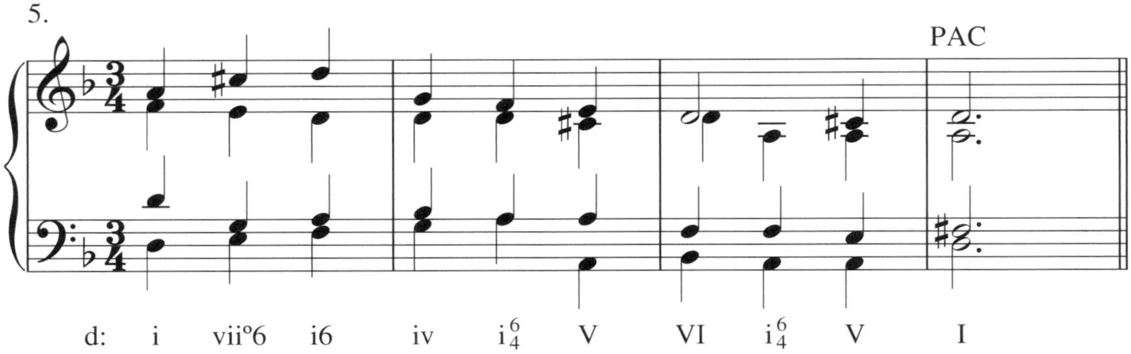
PAC
d: i vii°6 i6 iv i$^6_4$ V VI i$^6_4$ V I

6.

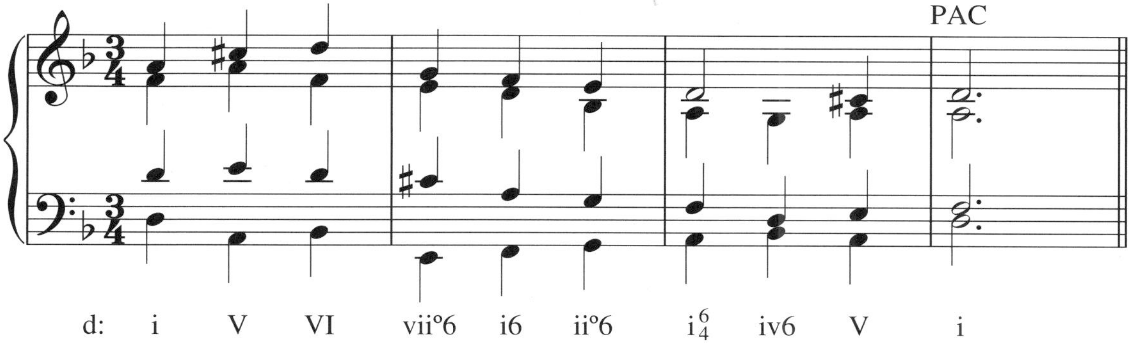

7.

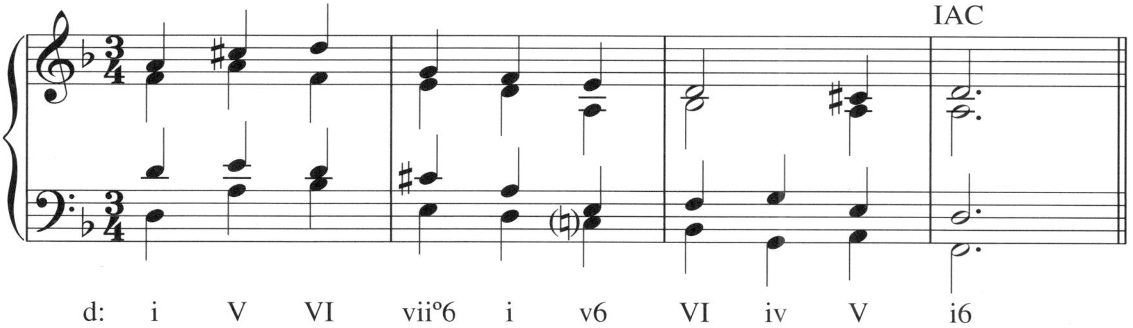

The next chapter introduces new and extremely important material: **non-harmonic tones**. Before moving ahead, however, review thoroughly the contents of this and previous chapters, and work out the following exercises for Chapter Six.

EXERCISES

1. Provide a Roman numeral analysis, and identify all six-four chords and all cadences.

2. Using three chords in each Example, write the required cadences. Choose your own meter and provide barlines.

perfect authentic cadence | imperfect authentic cadence

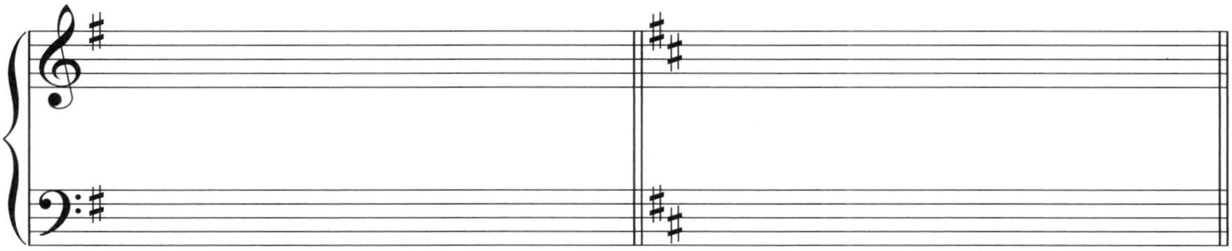

G: | b:

deceptive cadence | half cadence

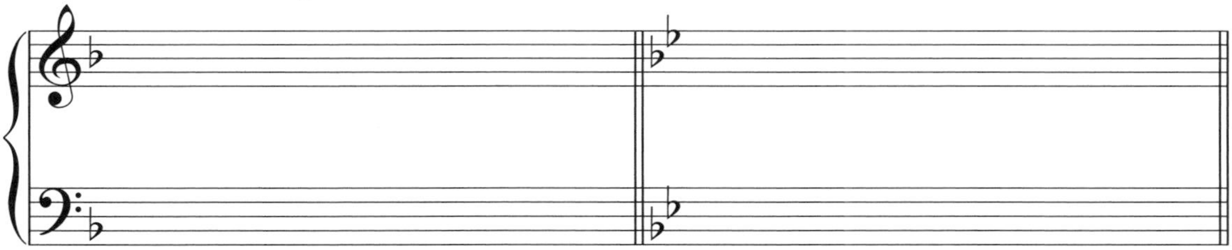

F: | g:

3. Add three upper voices. Identify six-four chords and cadences.

D: I IV$^6_4$ I V I$^6_4$ V I6 vii°6 I V

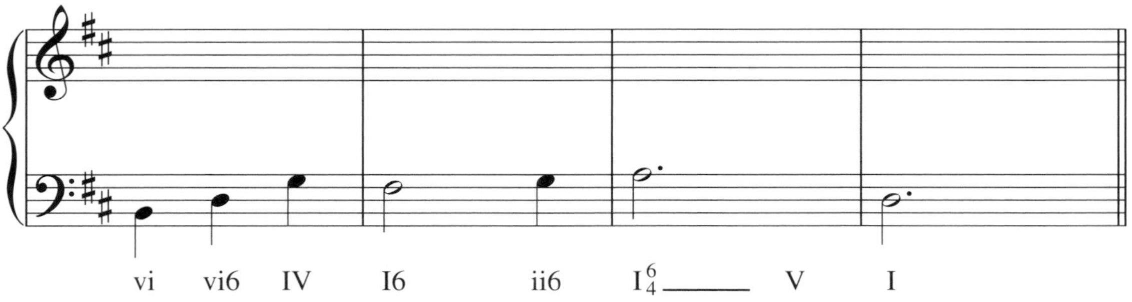

4. Add three upper voices. Use at least two six-four chords. Analyze the harmony and identify six-four chords and cadences.

5. Add three lower voices. Use two six-four chords. Analyze the harmony and identify six-four chords and cadences.

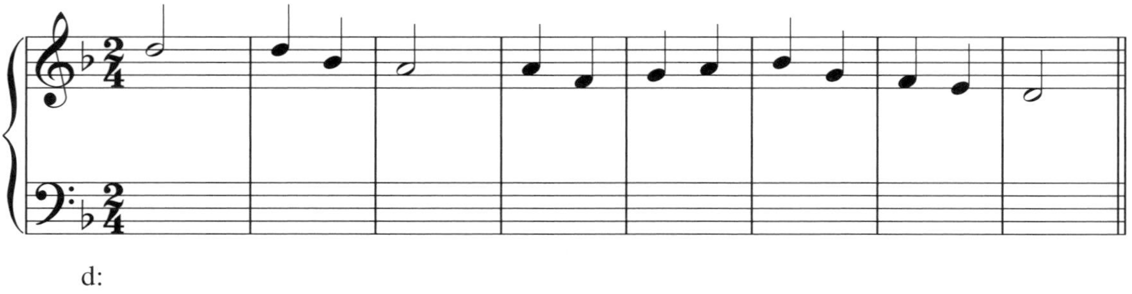

CHAPTER 7 NON-HARMONIC TONES

So far, all our attention has been given to chords and the tones that make up chords. It is time now to look at another kind of tone in music: the **non-harmonic tone**. These are produced by certain types of melodic motion in one or more voices and create dissonances as they move through given chords. Non-harmonic tones do not change the prevailing harmony; they add melodic interest and provide welcome dissonance in a musical discourse. Composers have long recognized the great value of these tones and have treated them in a number of well-defined ways. The non-harmonic tones in tonal music are shown below and will be examined in the order given:

1. Passing Tone (PT)
    a. Unaccented
    b. Accented
    c. Diatonic
    d. Chromatic
2. Neighbor Tone (N)
    a. Unaccented
    b. Accented
    c. Diatonic
    d. Chromatic
3. Changing Tone (CT)
4. Appoggiatura (APP)
    a. Accented
    b. Unaccented
    c. Diatonic
    d. Chromatic
5. Escape Tone (E)
6. Anticipation (ANT)
7. Pedal Tone (PED)
8. Suspension
    a. Tied
    b. Not tied
    c. With embellished resolution
    d. Double Suspension
    e. Retardation (RET)

Non-harmonic tones are defined by the manner in which they are approached and left. The approach to and the departure from non-harmonic tones may be by 1) stepwise motion, 2) a leap, or (3) by repetition—with or without a tie. Non-harmonic tones (NHTs) may appear in any voice. They are usually flanked by chord tones, but occasionally they may follow one another in immediate succession. They may appear singly or simultaneously with other NHTs. All of these aspects will be demonstrated in the examples that follow.

PASSING TONE

The most common of all NHTs is the **passing tone**; it is approached by step and left by step in the same direction. It may appear on either the weak or strong portion of a beat and may be diatonic or chromatic. When they occur simultaneously with other passing tones, they move in parallel thirds or sixths when they move in the same direction. Contrary motion passing tones may also occur:

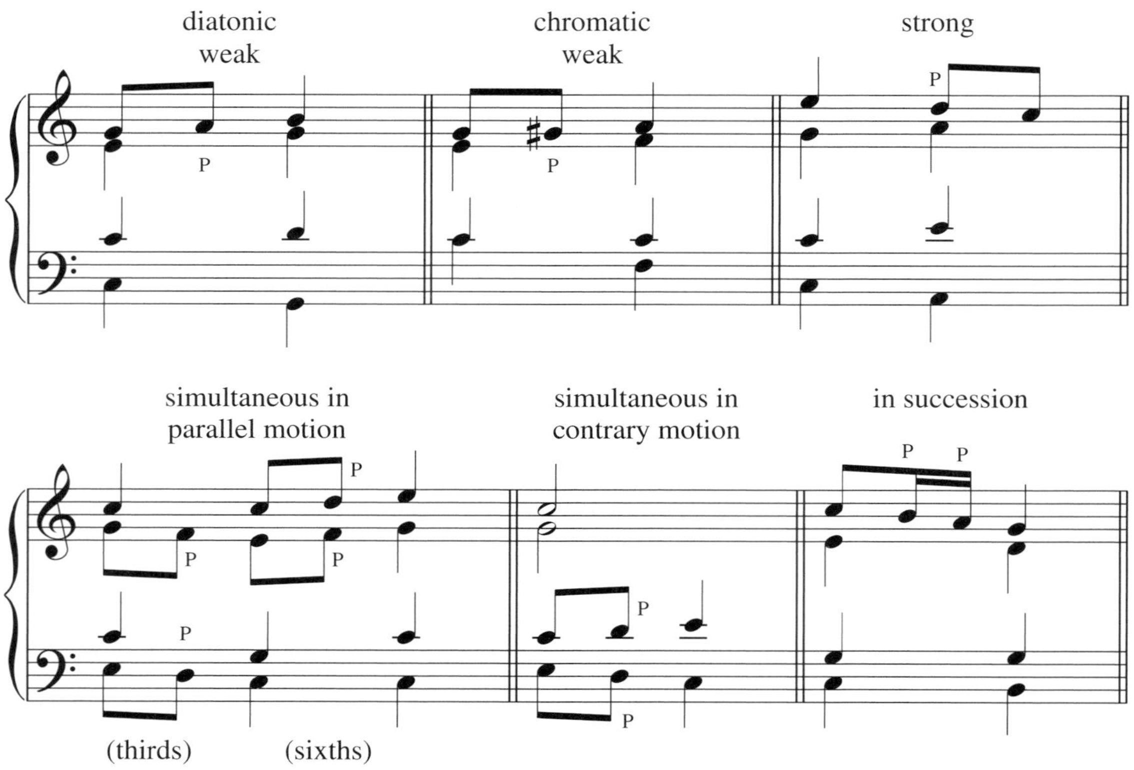

Some warnings regarding NHTs and parallel fifths and octaves: Be careful not to create parallels where they did not exist before adding NHTs. Also, NHTs do not eliminate the poor effect of parallels. The examples below illustrate:

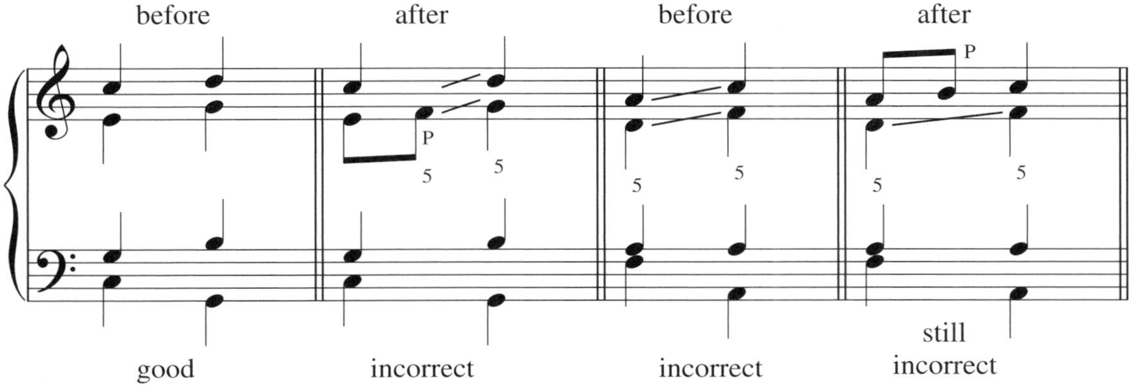

Parallel fifths arising from the use of NHTs may be usable if the second of the two fifths contains a NHT. See Example A below. In Example B, both fifths contain a NHT. In this case, both chords do not contain a perfect fifth, and the ear still perceives the formation as devoid of any fifths.

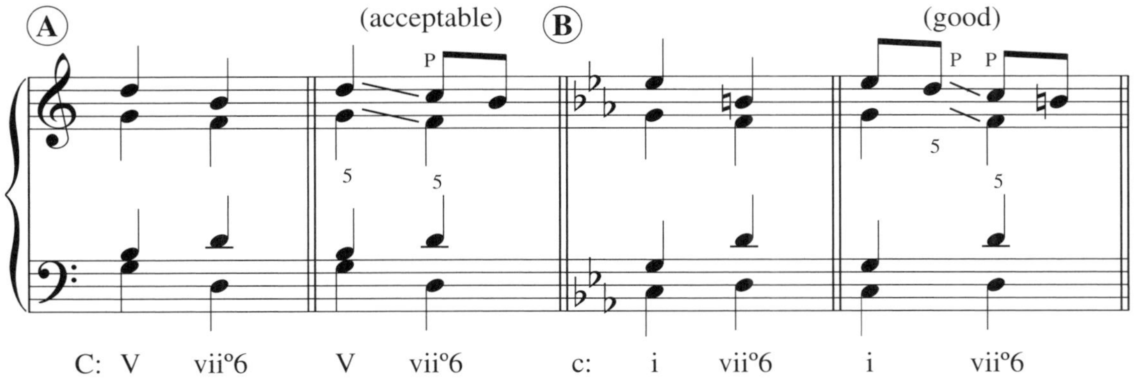

NEIGHBOR TONE

Sometimes called **auxiliary tone**, the **neighbor tone** is approached by step and left by step in the opposite direction, returning to the original pitch. The starting direction may be up or down. Neighbor tones, like passing tones, may be diatonic or chromatic, weak or strong, and they may be used simultaneously. They may also be used in combination with passing tones, and they may appear in any voice or voices.

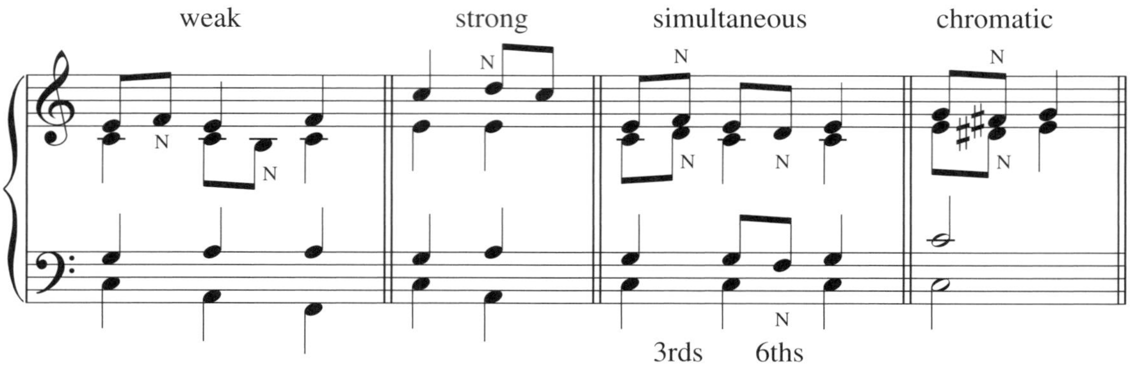

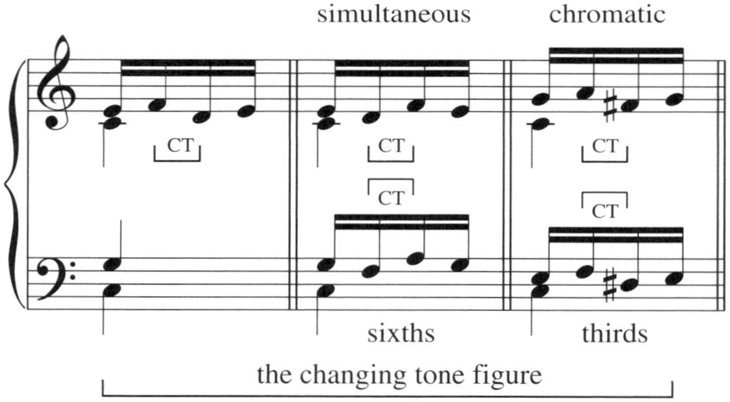

CHANGING TONE

An extension of the neighbor tone is the **changing tone** (see above). Upper neighbor is followed immediately by lower neighbor (or vice versa) before returning to the original starting point. They are diatonic or chromatic. The ear must be the final determinant when considering whether or not to use chromatic NHTs.

The changing tone may be coupled with a change of harmony, as in Example A below. Example B shows two seldom used variants. These should not be overused.

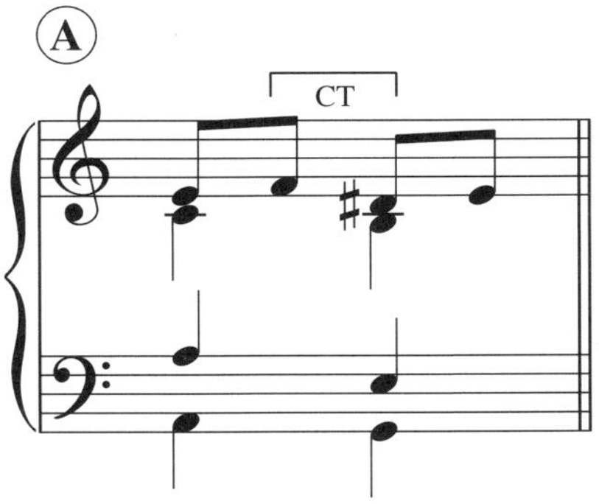

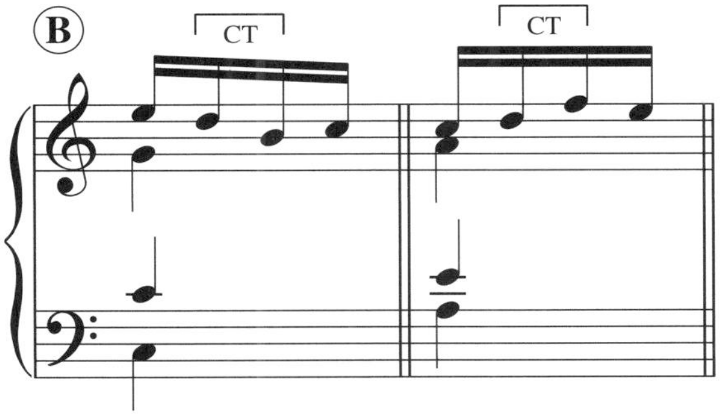

APPOGGIATURA

From the Italian meaning "to lean," the **appoggiatura** is approached by a leap of a third or more and resolved by step. It may be strong or weak, diatonic or chromatic. The weak-beat appoggiatura is not an accurate description, since this NHT evolved as a strong-beat dissonance. As a weak-beat NHT, some theorists are beginning to term it as a **reaching tone**. The direction of approach is most often up and the direction of resolution most often downward, but any combination of up or down in both approach and resolution is usable. The examples below illustrate:

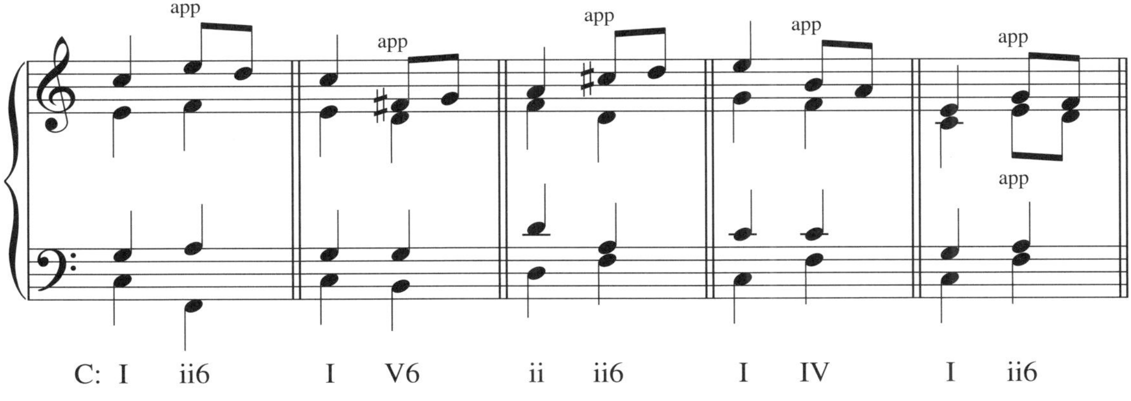

The Examples above show the strong-beat appoggiatura in various configurations. The last example is a double appoggiatura moving in thirds.

Weak-beat appoggiaturas ("reaching tones") in similar fashion are shown below. The last example is a double weak-beat appoggiatura moving in sixths. This is a very expressive dissonance; Bach and his Baroque contemporaries made use of it, but the Romantic Period composers employed this dissonance far more frequently.

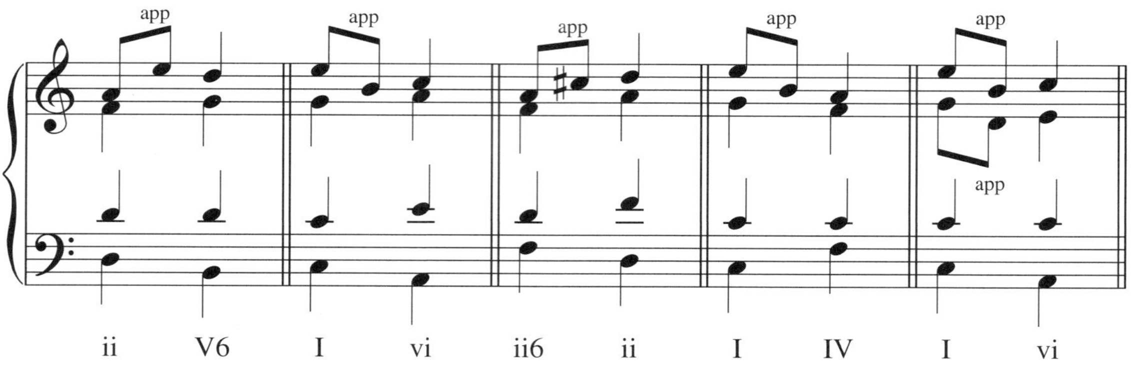

ESCAPE TONE

Also called **échappée** (French), the **escape tone** is approached by step and resolved by a skip. A word of caution: students tend to abuse this NHT more than any other. If treated in one particular way, the escape tone is quite effective and may be called upon frequently. This way is to approach the tone by a step up and resolve down by a skip of a third. It occurs only on the weak portion of a beat. Examples:

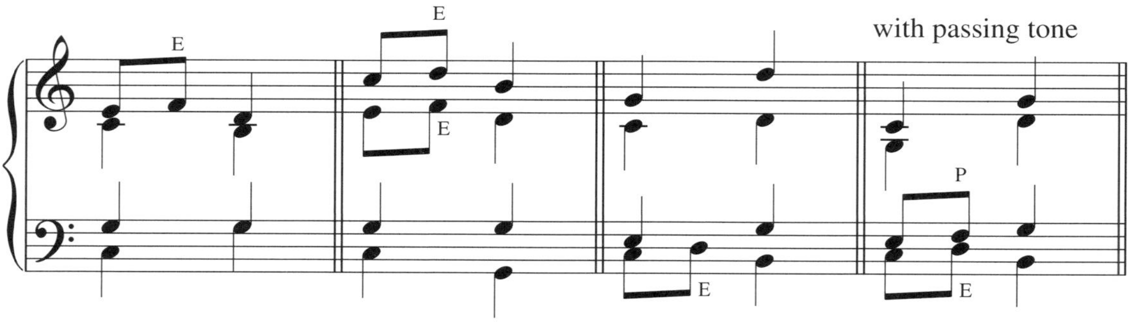

It is not easy to find in the literature of the masters examples of escape tones used other than the way shown above. Approach this NHT by a step up on a weak beat, resolve by a drop of a third. Until the student has a full grasp of all the NHTs and a sensitivity to their aural effect, it will be advisable to use this NHT in this one way.

ANTICIPATION

As its name implies, this NHT anticipates the chord tone that follows. It is approached by step or skip, and resolved by repetition. Like the escape tone, the **anticipation** is a weak-beat dissonance. It is often seen in cadences, but it may occur anywhere:

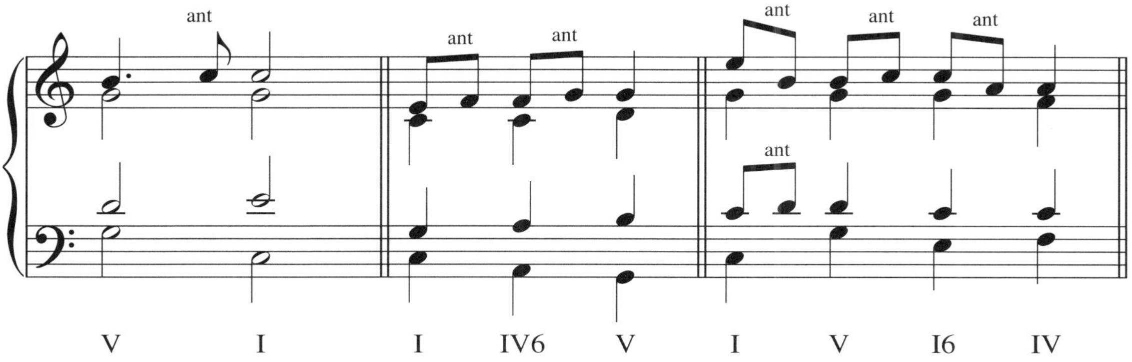

Anticipations are not as commonly used as passing tones, neighbor tones, or even escape tones; use them sparingly.

PEDAL TONE

This is a sustained tone, most often in the lowest voice, over which a series of chords moves, forming chords that are dissonant to the **pedal tone**. The tone itself is usually the dominant pitch or the tonic pitch. Both types are shown in the following examples. Chords that form dissonance with the pedal tones are indicated with an asterisk.

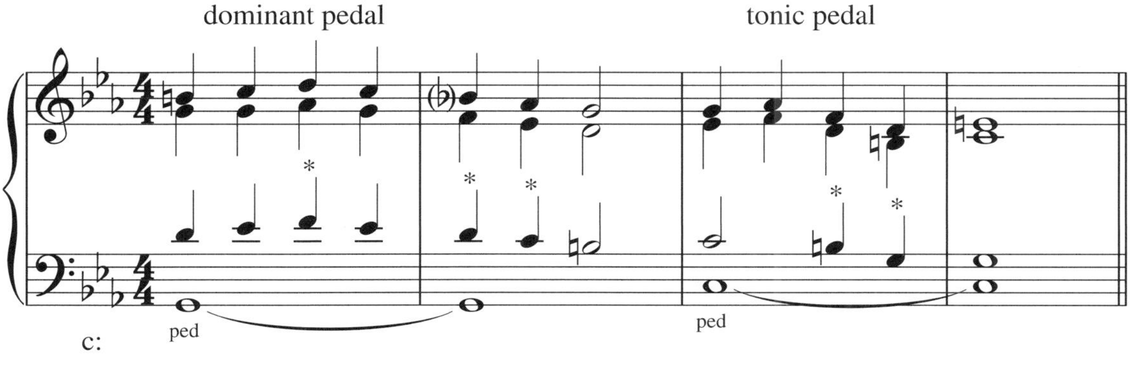

More rarely, a pedal may appear in an upper voice, as seen in the next example. Pedal tones are effective ways of producing prolonged tension in cadences.

tonic pedal in upper voice

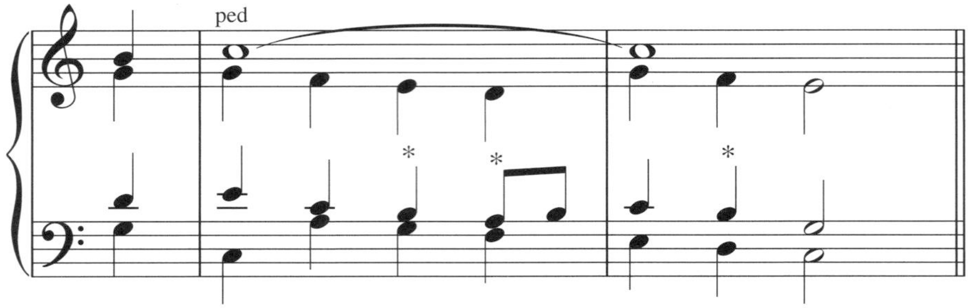

Before proceeding to a discussion of the suspension, examine the following examples for instruction in the use of the kinds of NHT tones dealt with so far. Example A is a basic progression. Example B is an elaboration of this progression with various kinds of NHTs added to enrich the music.

A

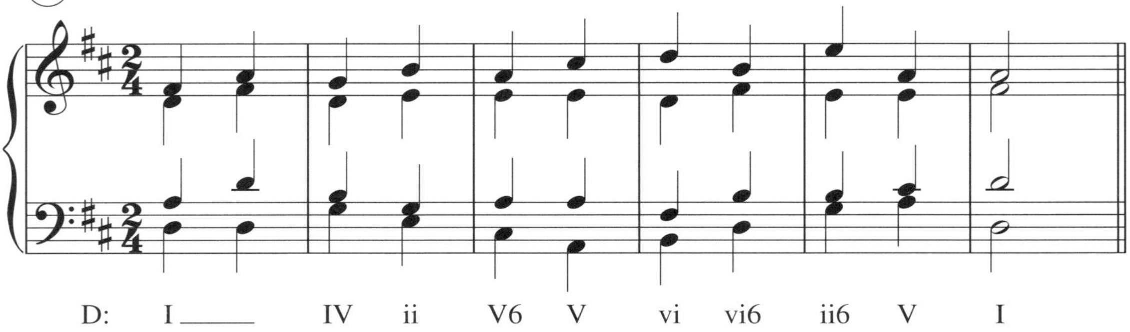

B

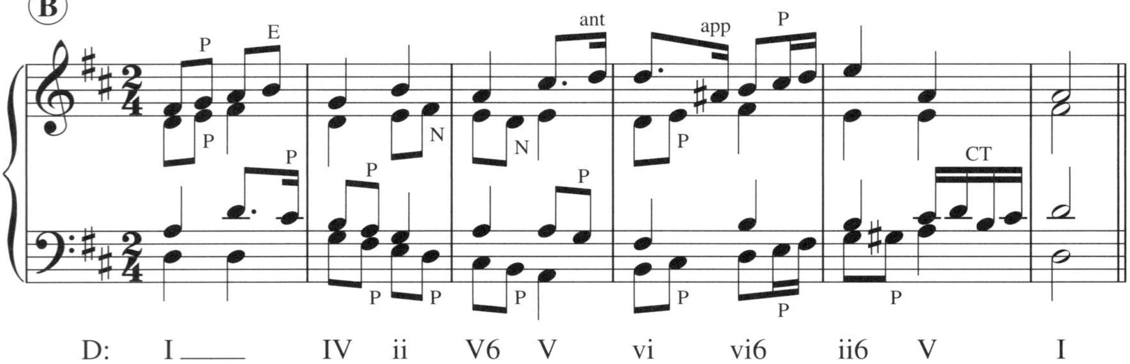

CHORD TONE SKIPS

In the above examples of NHTs, you will notice that NHTs are often coupled with chord tone movement. **Chord tone skips**, with or without NHTs, are an integral part of the musical fabric; they will hereafter be incorporated into the examples in this book. They can create parallels where parallels did not exist, so they must be handled with caution. Some illustrations follow. A very common student error is seen in the last Example (*) below, where the chord tone skip creates doubled LT (DLT) and parallel octaves, ruining an otherwise good progression! Chord tone skips are labeled as "CS."

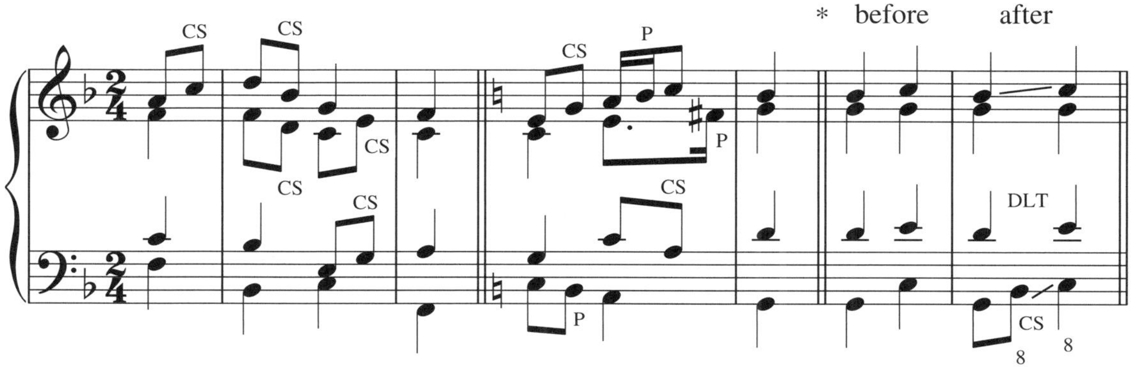

The problem above is easily corrected by adding a chord tone skip in the soprano part:

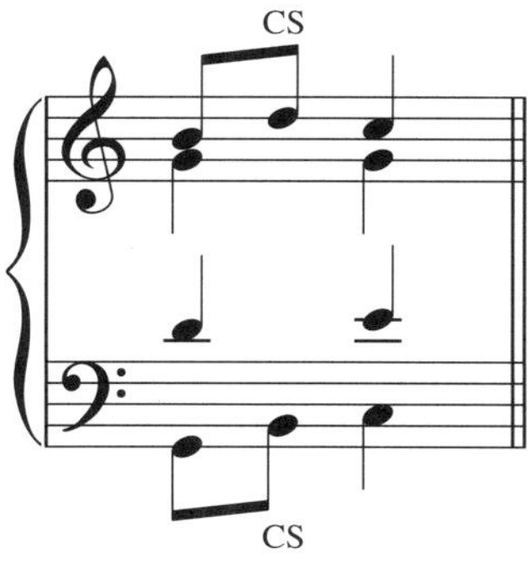

SUSPENSION

The most difficult NHT for the student is the **suspension**. It is indeed a more complicated formation, with many aspects to consider and be aware of. The suspension is a strong-beat NHT approached by a tied (or repeated) tone, and resolved down by step. The tone of resolution must be metrically weaker than the suspension tone. The suspension may occur in any part. Let us first examine this NHT as it occurs in voices above the bass. In the examples that follow, note that the preparation tone (the first of the tied or repeated tones) is a chord tone. The suspension takes place over a harmony to which it does not belong, then moves down by step to a chord tone of the intended harmony.

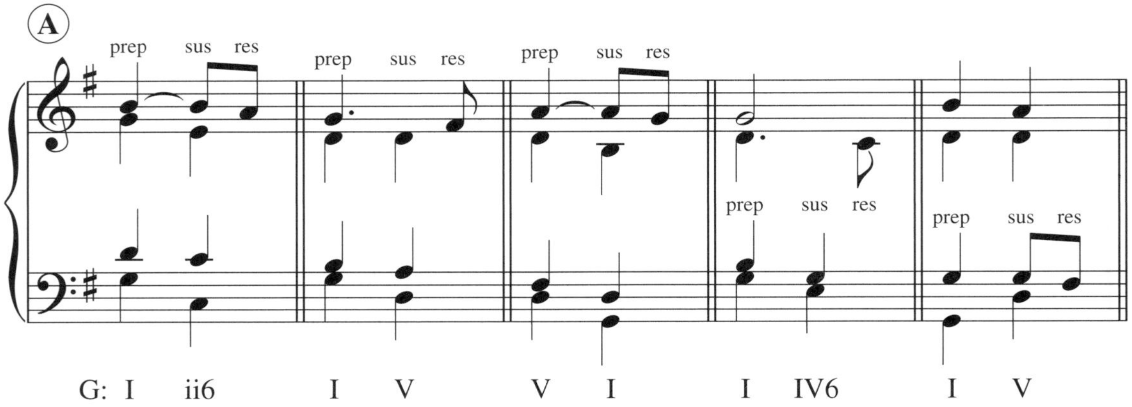

In all the above examples, the suspension takes place directly on beat two and resolves on the weak portion of that beat. In two of the examples a dotted quarter is written, eliminating any need for a tie. This is instructive in that it reminds us that there need be no tie present in the notation in a suspension. The final example shows a repeated tone instead of a tie. The rhythmic effect here is quite different, there being no syncopation, but the basic function of preparation, suspension, and resolution remains the same. Some theorists prefer to call the suspension without a tie by some other name—"prepared appoggiatura," for instance.

Taking precisely the same examples in A above, a more informative identification of the suspension can be found in Example B. Here the suspension is labeled in terms of the intervals formed between the suspended tone and the bass, as well as the resolution tone and the bass. This is how suspensions will be labeled henceforth in this text.

B

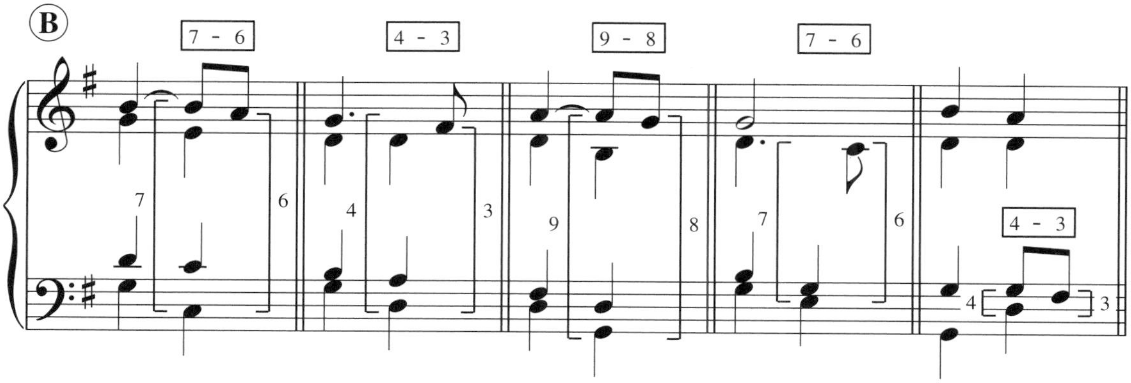

In upper voice suspensions, the most common are the 7-6 and 4-3, while the 9-8 is used less frequently. In the 9-8, the resolution tone is present in the bass. Usually, the resolution tone in the 7-6 or 4-3 suspension is not present in the other voices. Far less effective is the 6-5 suspension; there is no strong sense of dissonance. Furthermore, at the point of the suspension, a chord form can be interpreted:

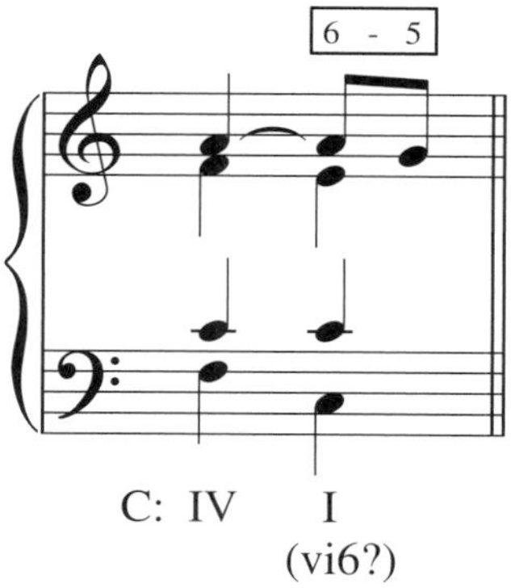

The resolution tone may function also as a preparation tone for another suspension. The process may be prolonged, forming a "chain suspension," as the following Example demonstrates.

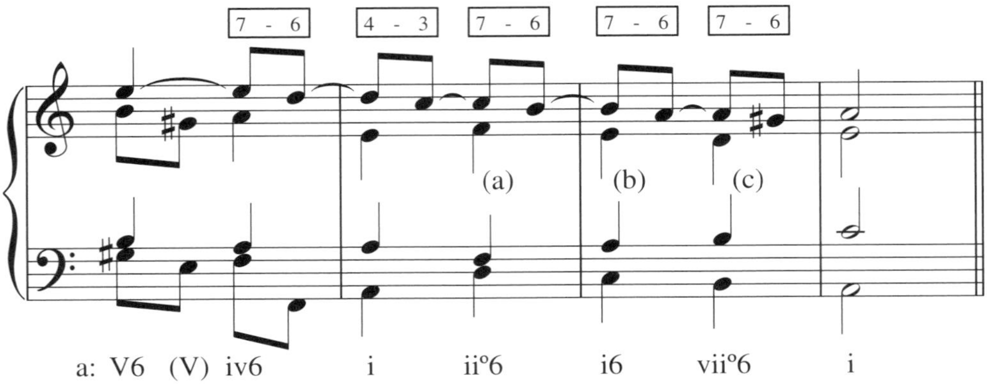

The apparent parallel fifths seen at (a), (b), and (c), are not objectionable. These fifths are not chord tone fifths and are therefore not experienced as such. Note also at (b) that the resolution tone of this suspension (A) is present in the tenor voice. In matters such as this, the ear must be the judge.

There is a situation concerning parallel fifths and the suspension that seems to break the rule that NHTs do not eliminate the poor effect of parallel fifths. Compare Example C with Example D below. Example C is obviously incorrect, but Example D is often found in the works of the masters:

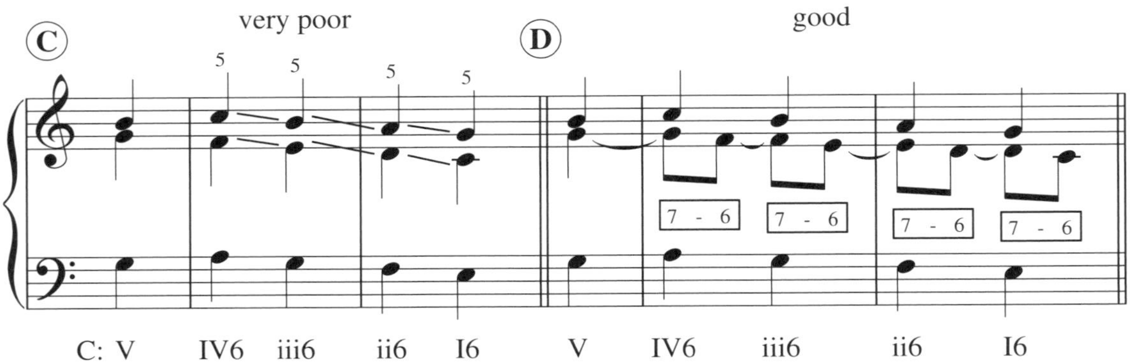

Suspension in the Bass

Suspensions in the lowest voice, though rarer than upper voice suspensions, are quite effective. The interval analysis is almost always 2-3. This label (2-3) is used regardless of the actual size of the interval. In Example A, the suspended tone forms the interval of a second with the tenor, then resolves down a step to form a third. In Example B, the interval is a ninth resolving to a tenth. Even so, the shorter form (2-3) is employed in the analysis.

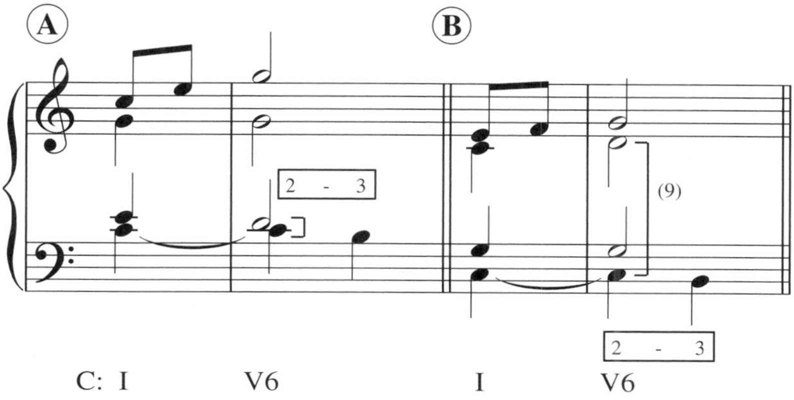

In the 2-3 suspension, the resolution tone is usually not present in the upper voices at the point of suspension. Exceptions to this rule are very rare. Example C demonstrates.

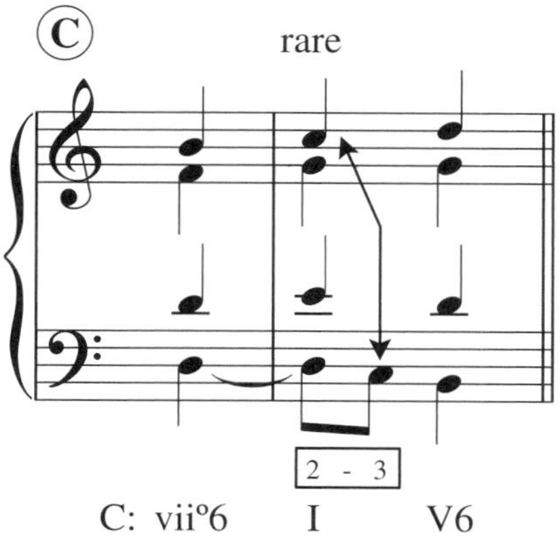

Embellished Resolution of the Suspension

The move to the resolution tone may be delayed by inserting chord tones and/or NHTs between the suspension tone and the resolution tone. One progression showing several possibilities is shown below:

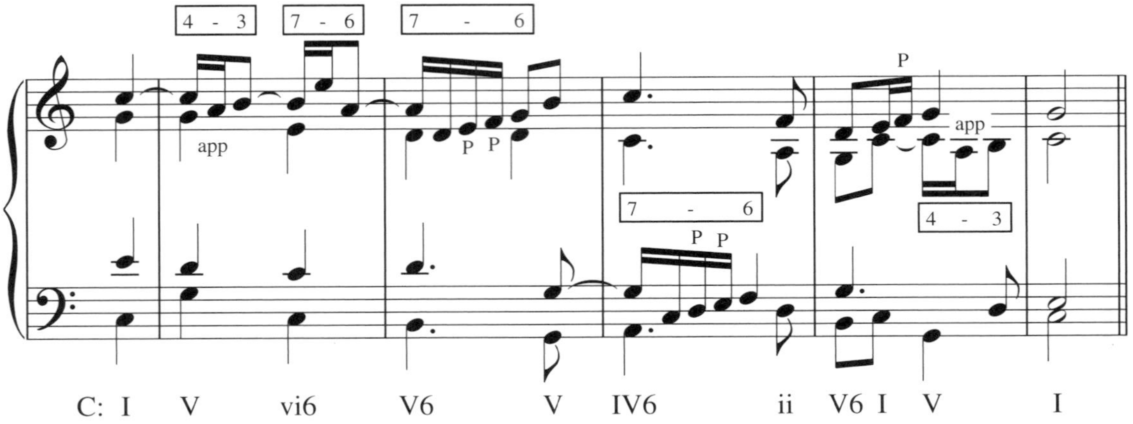

Change of Bass at Point of Resolution

In all the foregoing examples of upper voice suspensions, the bass note (and the harmony) has remained unchanged as the suspension resolved. Frequently, the bass line moves to a different pitch at the point of resolution; this may or may not involve a change of harmony. Further, the change of bass may be coupled with the delayed resolution of the suspension. Examine carefully the examples below:

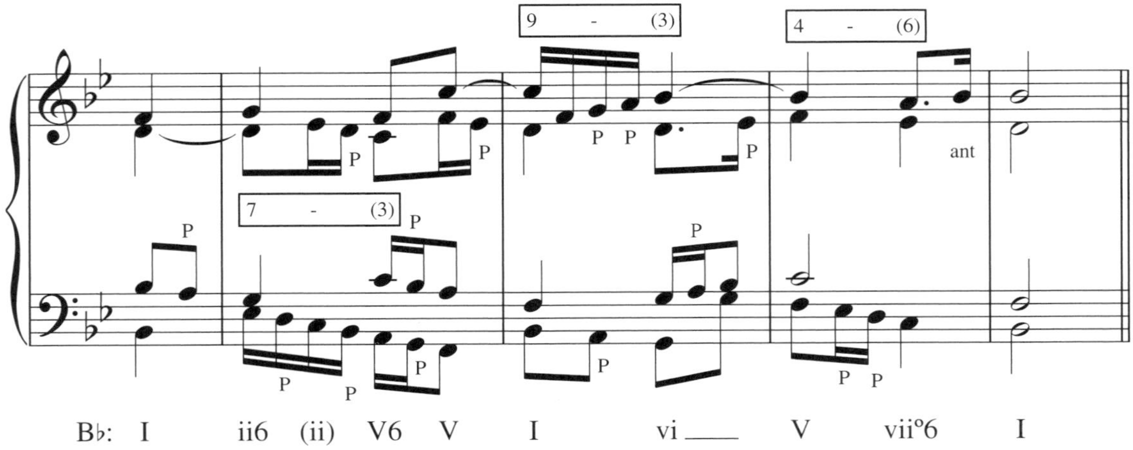

Notice the intervallic analysis. The numbers in parentheses are the actual intervals formed with the bass at the point of resolution. Instead of the expected 7-6, there is a 7-(3), instead of 9-8, there is a 9-(3), and so on. The parentheses tell us that this is not the usual form of resolution. Composers take advantage of all these variants in suspensions.

Rhythm and Suspension

With respect to the suspension with a tie, there is a principle regarding the durational relationship between the preparation tone and the suspended tone: the preparation tone may be equal to or longer than the suspended tone, but it should not be shorter. Very few exceptions to this rule are to be found in the literature of pre-20th century music. However, if there is no tie, no rhythmic restrictions apply. Observe the following examples:

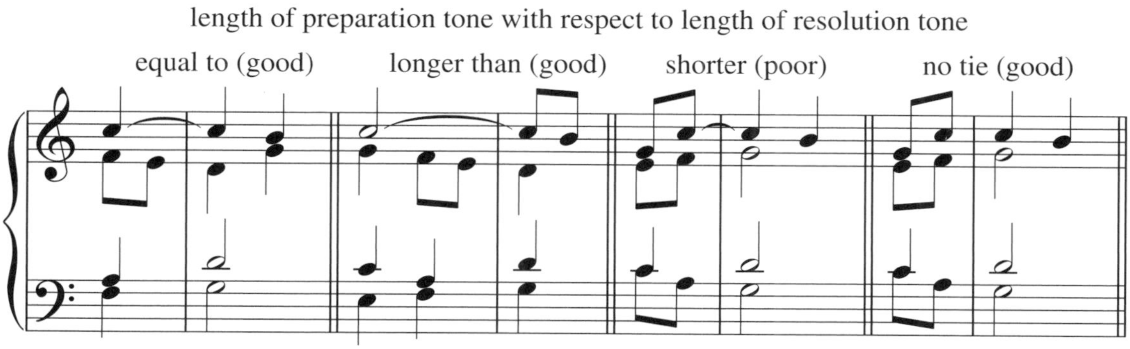

Double Suspension

Two suspensions may take place simultaneously, forming a **double suspension**. The resolutions more often than not occur simultaneously, but a staggered resolution is also possible. The interval analysis follows the same method, as the examples that follow demonstrate:

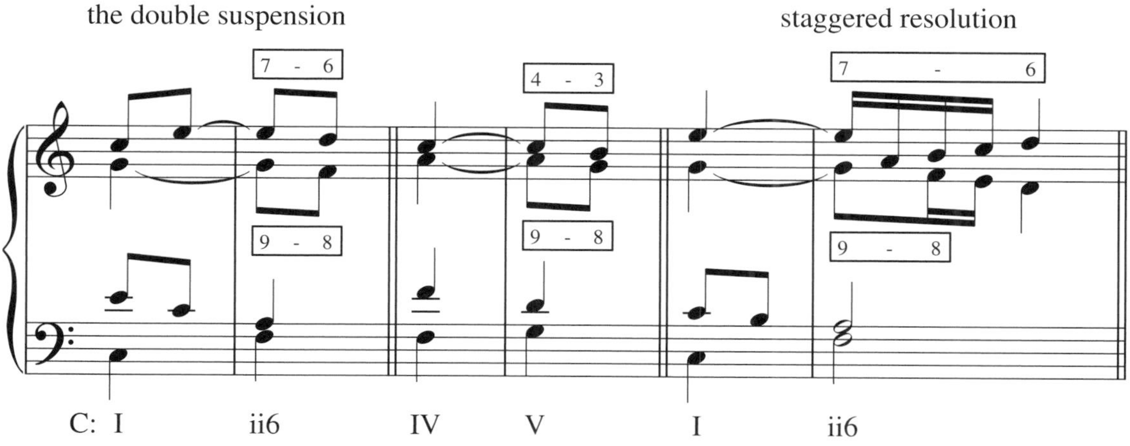

Retardation

An upward-resolving suspension is called a **retardation**. No interval structure analysis is necessary. Retardations involving the bass voice are extremely rare and usually not satisfactory in effect. Retardations may occur together with suspensions:

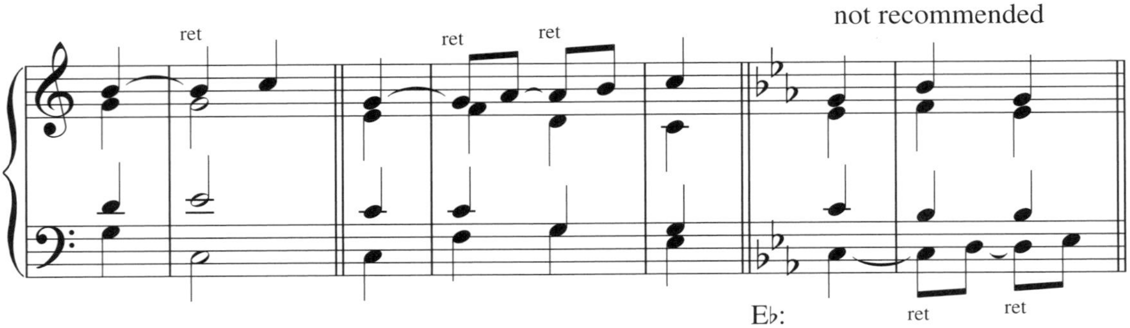

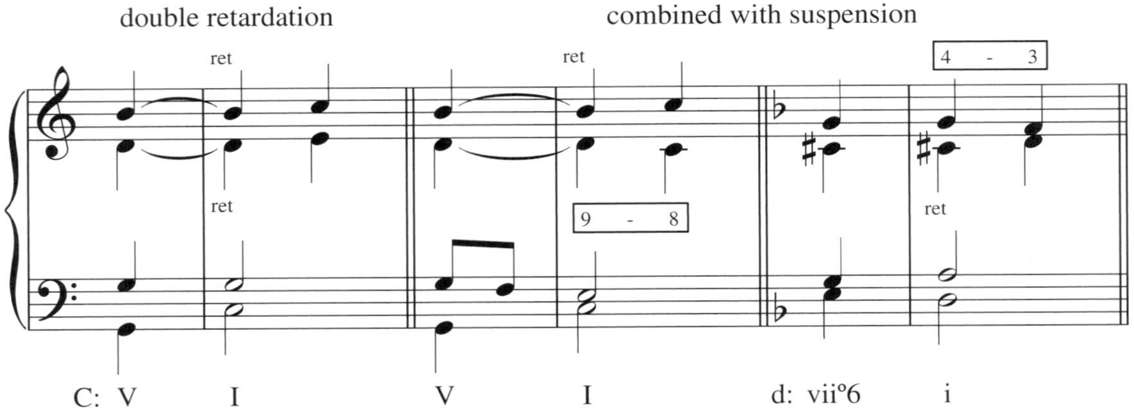

Without NHTs music would be a third-rate art form, lacking the richness and expressivity provided by the infinite variety of dissonances afforded by the judicious employment of NHTs. Among the great composers, J.S. Bach, Gustav Mahler, and Richard Strauss come to mind as the greatest models for the study of NHTs.

Example A below presents a straightforward progression in E minor. Example B is an elaboration of Example A, in which a variety of NHTs and chord skips transform the skeletal character of Example A into more convincing musical statement.

(A)

(B)

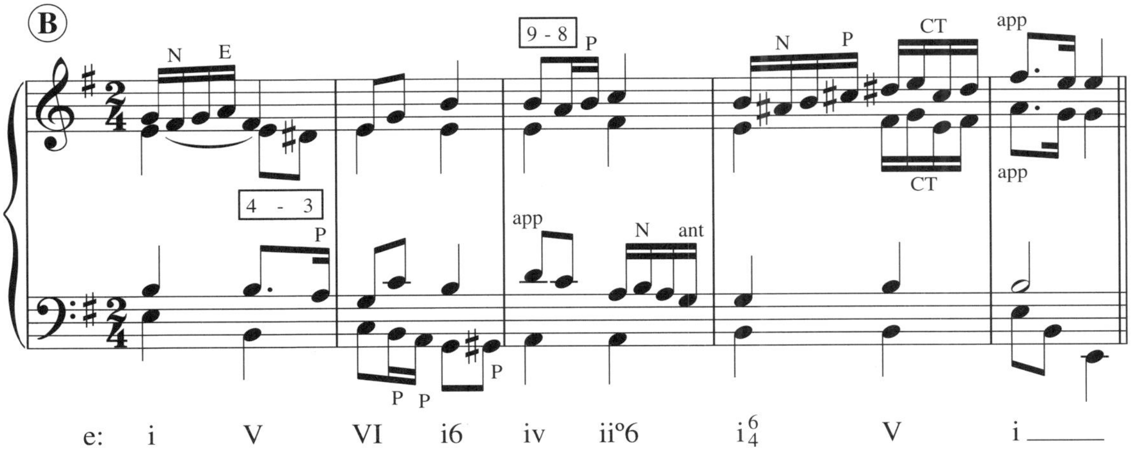

Before moving on to the next chapter, work out the exercises that follow.

EXERCISES

1. Locate and label each non-harmonic tone in the following example. Identify each NHT by its specific type using the appropriate abbreviation.

2. Analyze the harmony in this chord progression.

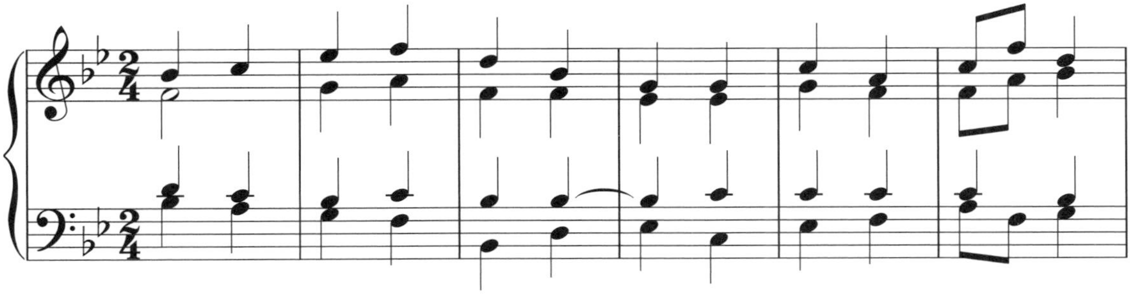

B♭: I V6

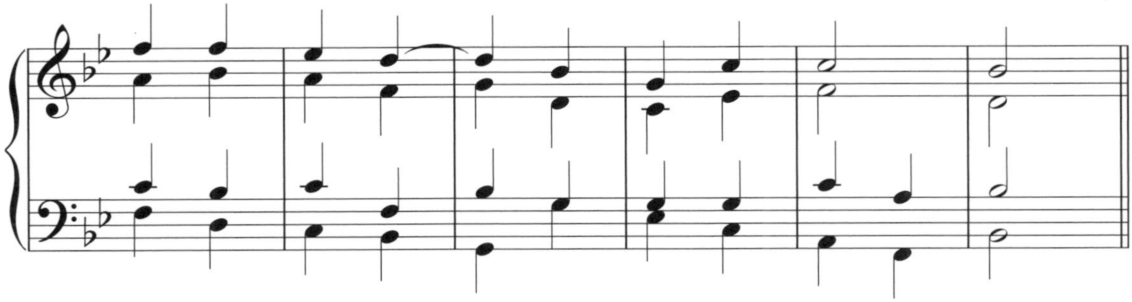

3. The harmony in this chord progression is the same as that of Exercise 2. Analyze the NHTs in this example.

4. Analyze the harmony and label all NHTs according to type.

CHAPTER 8 THE DOMINANT SEVENTH CHORD

Among the five types of seventh chords used in tonal music, by far the most common is the **dominant seventh chord**. (Review the seventh chords on page 10.) With the introduction of a seventh to a triad, a dissonance is added that must be handled with the same kind of caution as the LT. The seventh of all seventh chords is a dissonance that wants to resolve down by step. The approach to the seventh is free: it may be approached by repetition, by step in either direction, or by a leap. As with the V chord as a triad, the dominant seventh has a strong pull to the tonic triad. It may also resolve deceptively to the submediant or, more rarely, to the first inversion of the subdominant.

In root position, the dominant seventh is indicated as V7. It is of course understood that above the root (in the bass) is a third and a fifth. If all four chord members are present, it is called the "complete dominant seventh chord." Examples of the complete V7 chord and their resolutions are shown below.

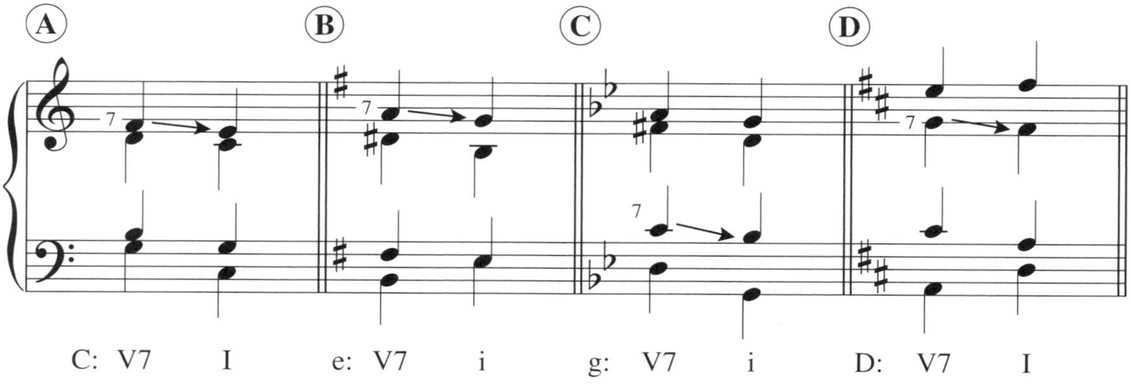

In each example above, the location of the seventh and the direction of its resolution are shown. In Examples A, B, C, and D, the LT drops down a third to help form a complete tonic triad. In Example D, a doubled third is possible in the melody line if so desired.

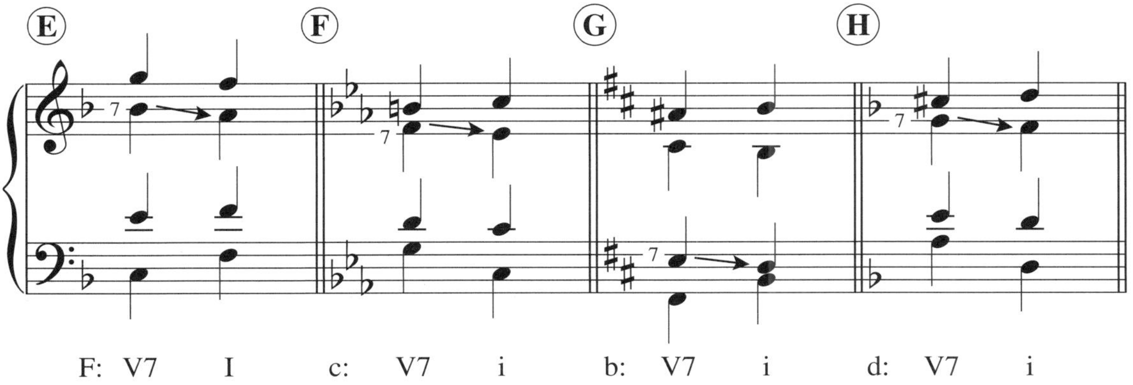

In E above, resolving the LT up to the tonic note results in the tonic chord with tripled root, which is always acceptable. In F, G, and H, where the LT is in the soprano part, the tripled root of the tonic chord is inevitable in order to avoid parallels and awkward voice leading.

Another form of the V7 chord is the "incomplete dominant seventh chord," in which the fifth is omitted and the root is doubled. The resolution of this chord gives the complete tonic triad.

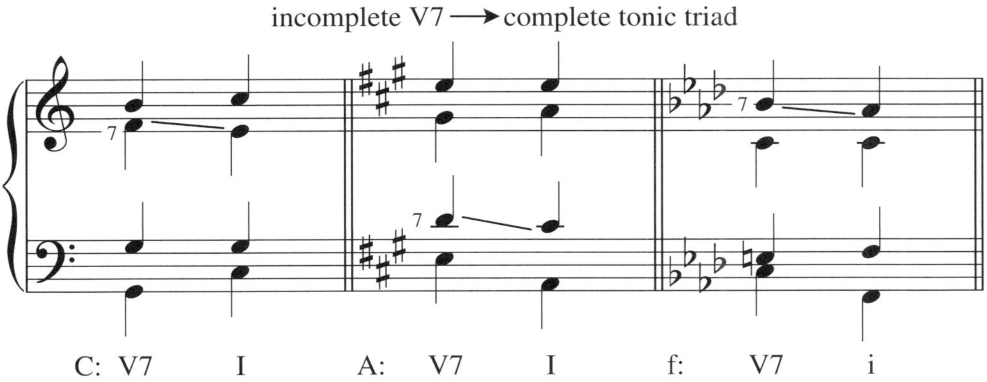

APPROACHES TO THE SEVENTH

The following examples show how the seventh may be approached either by **repetition**, by **stepwise motion**, or by **leap**. Any chord that precedes V may precede V7, so there is not much new material to learn here.

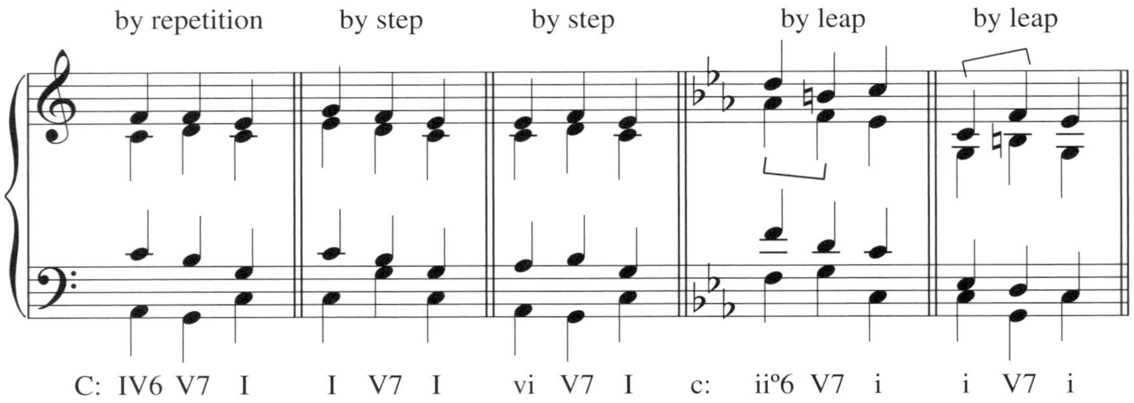

Instead of resolving to the tonic chord, V7 may resolve deceptively to vi (VI), as in Example A. In Example B, the rarer move to IV6 is seen. In the latter case, the seventh of the chord is held over:

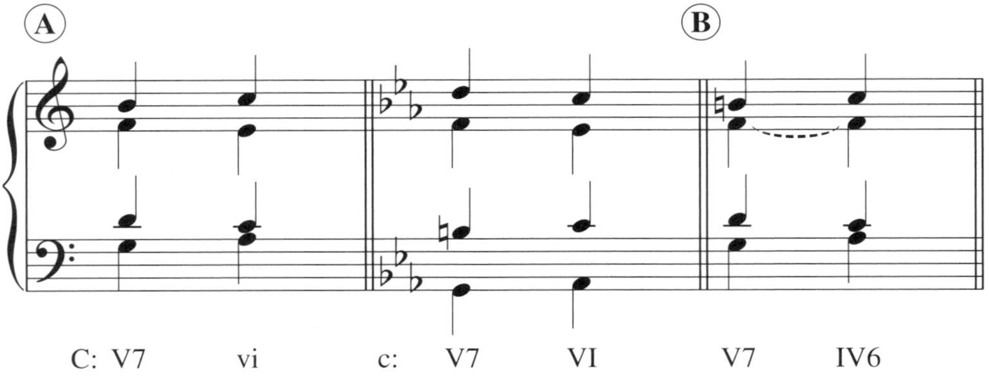

Be sure to double the third of vi (VI) in Example A above.

INVERSIONS OF THE DOMINANT SEVENTH CHORD

The V7 chord may be used in all inversions. Let us examine the interval structure above the lowest note when this chord (and any seventh chord) is subjected to inversion. It is extremely important that the student become intimately familiar with the various designations for the inversions of seventh chords. We already know that in root position, the chord is written as V7, with the understanding that a third and fifth are also present above the bass note.

When the chord is written with the third at the bottom, the intervals formed above the bottom note are a sixth, a fifth, and a third. The Roman numeral designation omits the third (although it is understood to be present), and the chord is labeled V^6_5. When the fifth is the lowest note, a sixth, fourth, and third are formed; here the sixth is omitted, and the chord is labeled V^4_3. Lastly, when the seventh is the lowest note, a sixth, fourth, and second are formed; the sixth is omitted, and the chord is labeled V^4_2. All seventh chords follow precisely the same method of labeling. Study the example below and memorize these labels as soon as possible.

inversions of the dominant seventh chord

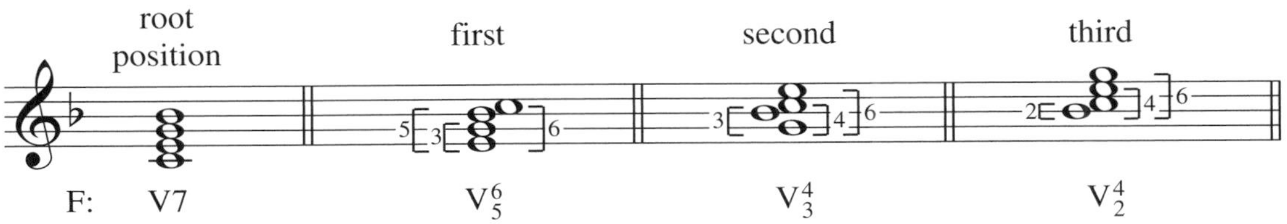

Whether in root position or in any inversion, the voice leading is straightforward: the seventh resolves down by step; the LT, if in soprano or bass, resolves up. If the LT is in alto or tenor, it might move down a third to form the fifth of the tonic chord. The V^4_3 chord is a special case. It may resolve to either I or I6. When resolving to I6, the seventh may rise (see Example C below). V^4_2, with the seventh in the bass, must resolve to I6 (Example D). Study these:

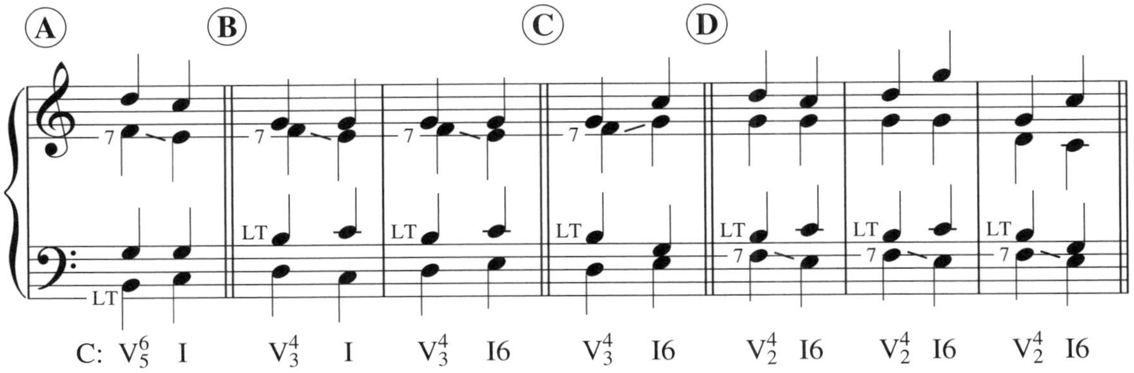

Another important instance of the rising resolution of the seventh takes place in the progression V7–I6 (i6). Here the seventh must rise (Example A below). If the seventh resolves in the usual down-by-step manner, the resulting voice leading between the bass and the part containing the seventh is awkward; the effect of the interval of a seventh moving to an octave is very similar to parallel octaves and should be avoided (Example B).

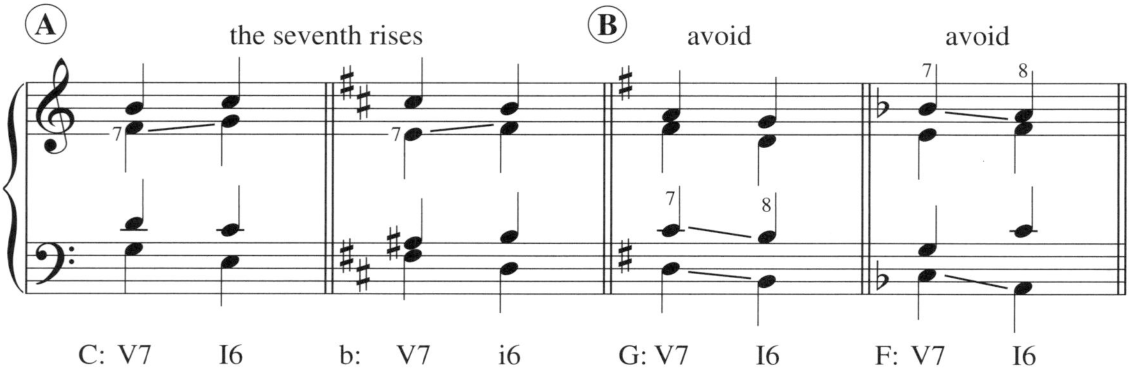

The Incomplete Dominant Seventh in Inversion

V^6_5 and V^4_2 may employ the incomplete form: two roots, third, and seventh. Examples:

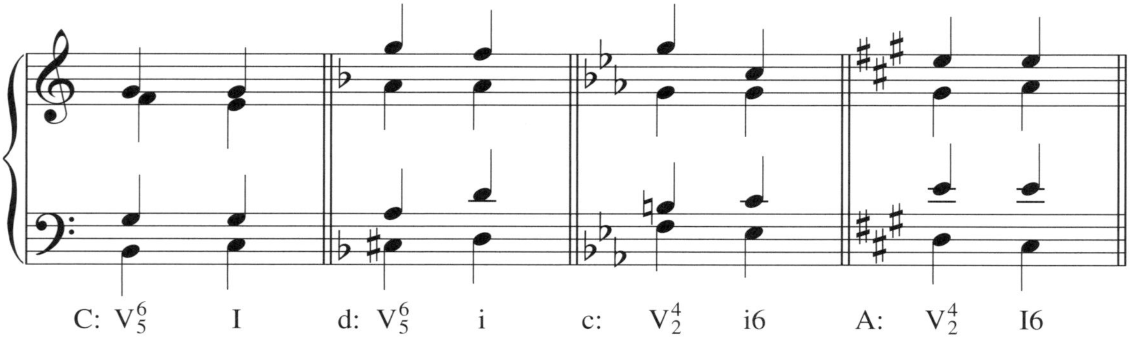

Chord Prolongation

The dominant seventh chord may, instead of resolving immediately to I or vi, be prolonged and may freely move through inversions before resolving. During **prolongation**, the LT and the seventh may transfer freely from voice to voice. But when the chord resolves, close attention must then be given to the treatment of the LT and seventh (Example A). V7 may follow V, but once introduced, it usually does not revert back to V (Example B). vii°6 is so similar to V7 in sound that it may also be involved in the prolongation (Example C):

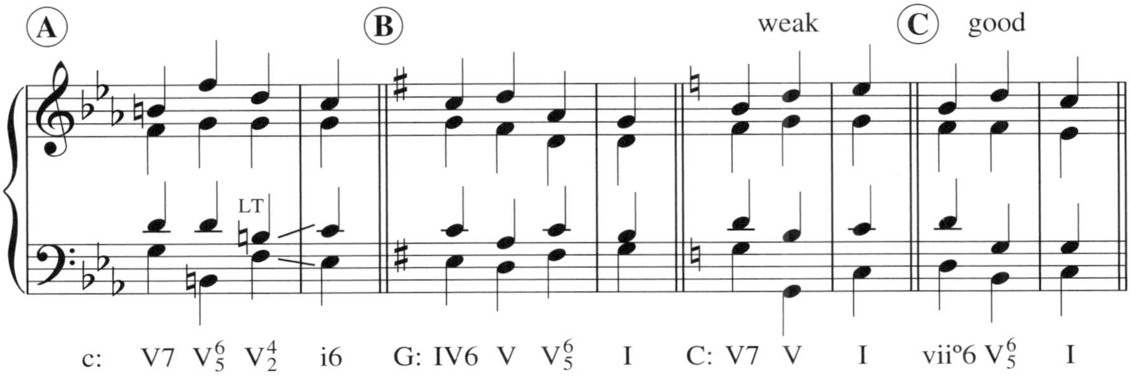

Study the following examples in the use of the dominant seventh:

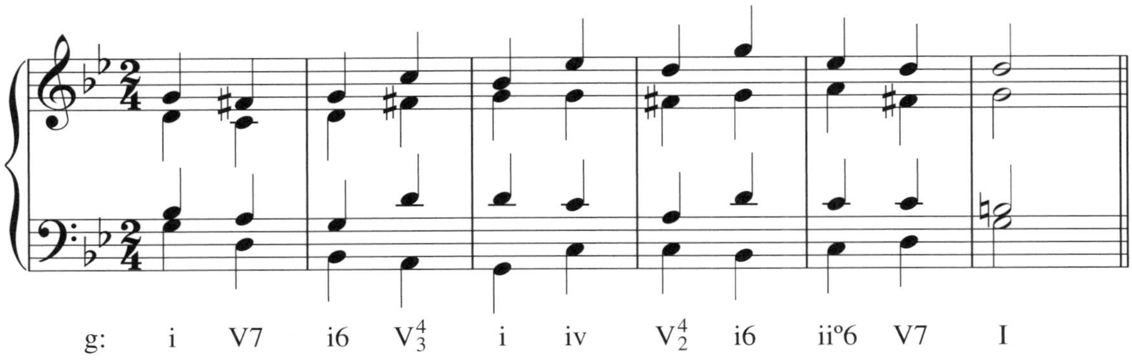

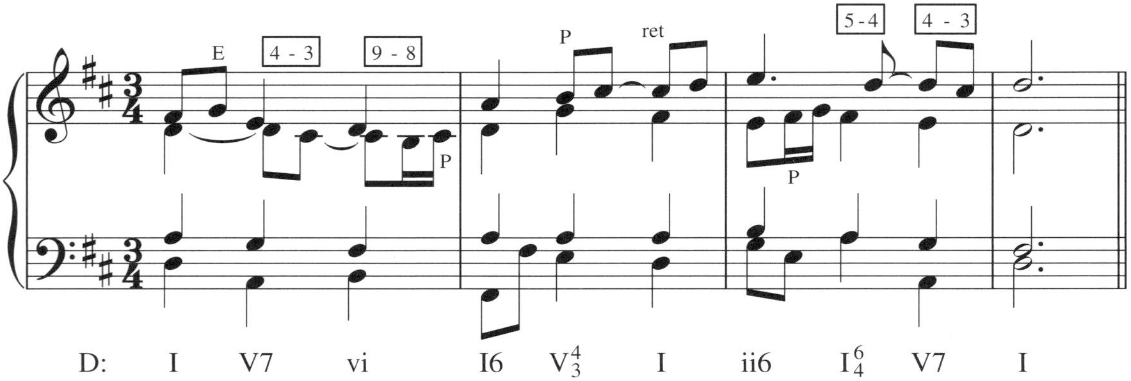

FIGURED BASS AND THE DOMINANT SEVENTH CHORD

In major keys, the figured bass symbols duplicate the Roman numeral indications exactly for the dominant seventh chord, as the example below shows:

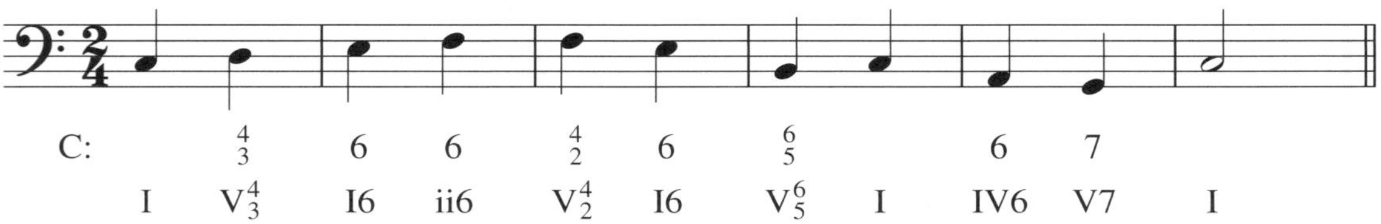

With regard to the V7 chord in minor keys, the figured bass must take into account any altered pitches above the bass note. This affects the notation in root position, second, and third inversions, as seen below:

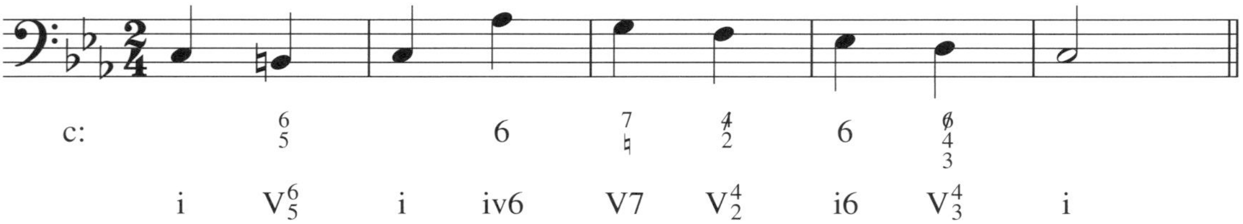

The figured bass indication for the V^4_2 chord has a slash through the 4 (4), telling us that the fourth above the bass is raised a half-step to become B♮, the leading tone. (A natural sign next to the number 4 may be used in lieu of the slash.) With the V^4_3 chord, the sixth above the bass is raised—B♮—requiring the addition of the number 6 above the $^4_3$, with a slash through the 6 (6), or a natural sign next to the number.

Work out the exercises for the chapter before moving on to Chapter Nine.

EXERCISES

1. Analyze:

2. Fill in any missing information. Complete four-part harmony.

d: E♭: b: c:

F.B.: $\begin{smallmatrix}4\!\!\!/\\2\end{smallmatrix}$ 6 6 $\begin{smallmatrix}7\\\sharp\end{smallmatrix}$

R.N.: V^6_5 V^4_3 I6 III V^4_3 i6

3. Dominant seventh chord. Provide Roman numeral analysis below the figured bass. Add upper parts (soprano, alto, tenor). Enrich with NHTs and additional chord tones.

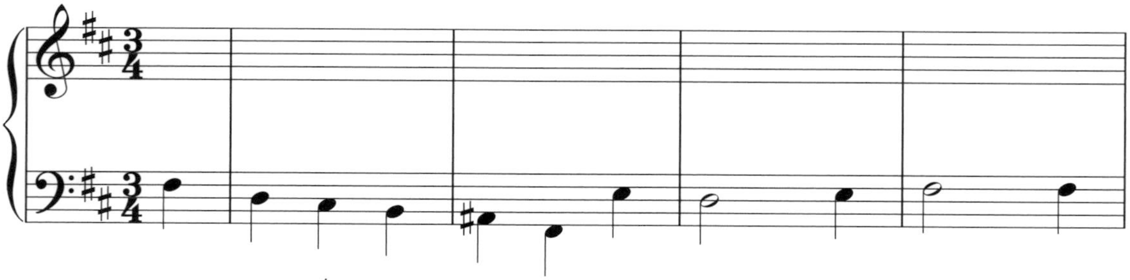

b: ♯ 6 $\begin{smallmatrix}6\!\!\!/\\4\\3\end{smallmatrix}$ 6 $\begin{smallmatrix}7\\\sharp\end{smallmatrix}$ $\begin{smallmatrix}4\!\!\!/\\2\end{smallmatrix}$ 6 6 $\begin{smallmatrix}6\\4\end{smallmatrix}$ - $\begin{smallmatrix}5\\\sharp\end{smallmatrix}$ $\begin{smallmatrix}7\\\sharp\end{smallmatrix}$

R.N.:

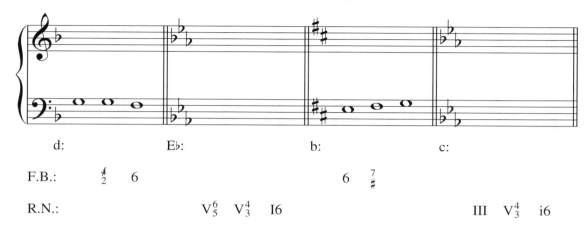

6 6 $\begin{smallmatrix}6\\5\end{smallmatrix}$ ♯ 6̸ $\begin{smallmatrix}7\\\sharp\end{smallmatrix}$ ♯

R.N.:

CHAPTER 9 OTHER SEVENTH CHORDS

The two most important seventh chords in tonal music next to the V7 chord are the **supertonic** and **leading tone seventh chords**. These will be examined in turn, followed by the remaining seventh chords, all of which are far less often found. The principles learned in dealing with the V7 are much the same: the seventh may be approached freely, resolves down by step, and the chords may be used in any inversion. The supertonic seventh chord in major keys is a minor seventh chord, while in minor keys it is a half diminished seventh chord:

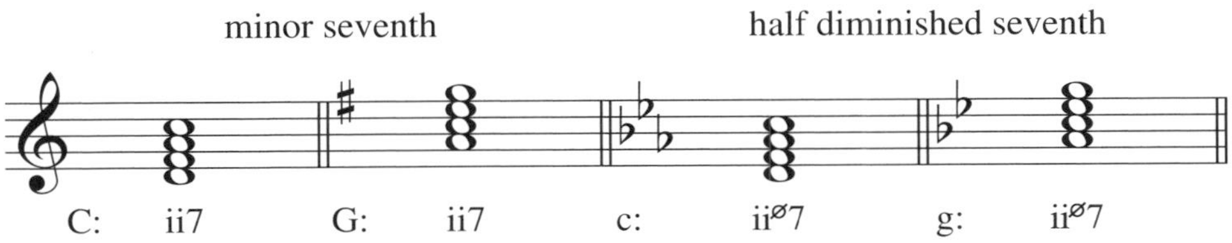

THE SUPERTONIC SEVENTH CHORD

Notice the symbol used to denote the half diminished seventh chord: a small circle with a line diagonally through it. Many students find it difficult to remember to add this to the chord when they come across it in analysis. The ii7 and ii⌀7 chords, in root position or any inversion, have a strong tendency to move to the dominant chord, either as a triad or as a seventh chord:

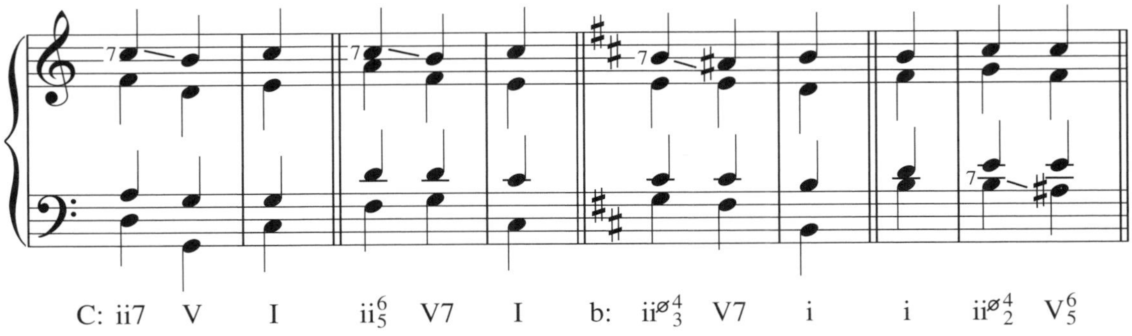

Tonic, submediant, or subdominant are the usual approaches to the **supertonic seventh chord**. All are effective:

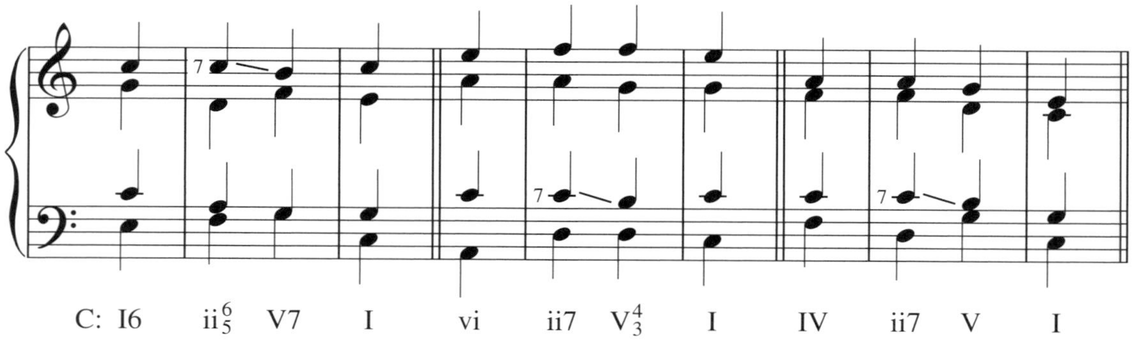

When ii7 (iiø7) precedes the cadential six-four chord, the resolution of the seventh may be delayed (Example A). In fact, however, composers have treated the seventh quite freely in this situation, and the six-four chord is free to move without any obligation to resolve the seventh (Example B). Furthermore, the seventh need not be held over in the same voice (Example C):

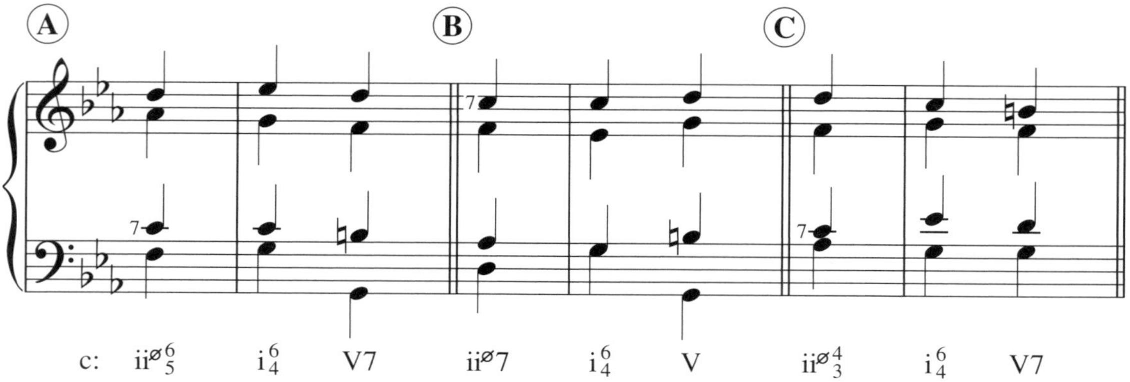

THE LEADING TONE SEVENTH CHORD

In major keys, the **LT seventh chord** is a half diminished seventh, while in minor keys, it forms a fully diminished seventh chord. This chord contains two strong tendency tones—the LT and a seventh; accordingly, attention must be given to both in the resolution, using the same principles discussed earlier.

Example A below shows the half diminished seventh chord on the LT. Example B shows the Roman numeral notation for the fully diminished seventh chord. This chord, here confined to the LT in minor, will take on great importancein *Hal Leonard Harmony & Theory, Part 2*, which deals with chromatic harmony. The only instance of it in diatonic harmony is as vii°7 in minor keys. The resolution is strongly to the tonic chord, and inversions are all used (Example C).

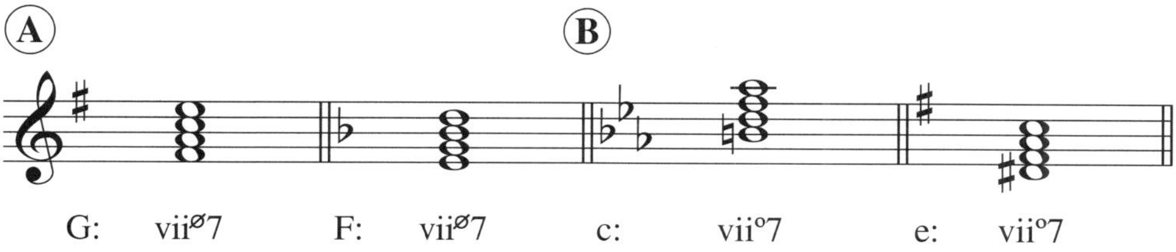

Example C3 shows the more usual resolution of the LT seventh in first inversion to I6. In Example C6, we see the less common resolution to root position i. The unequal fifths between bass and alto are acceptable. In Example C7, the resolution of vii$^{\circ 4}_{2}$ must go to i$^6_4$; in this instance, be sure that the i$^6_4$ is one of the four forms of this chord!

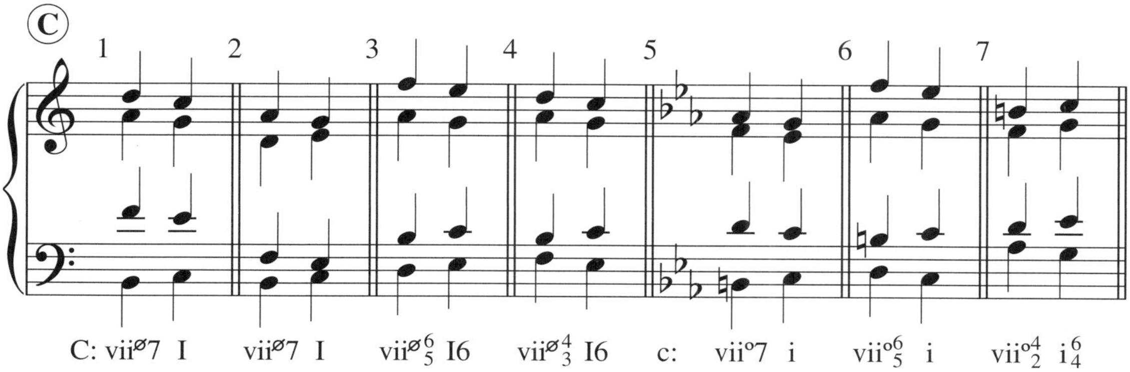

Example D shows the potential problem of parallel fifths in the resolution of $vii^{ø}7$ to I. In this case, double the third of I to avoid the parallels. There is one form of "unequal" fifths that should always be avoided; this is seen in Example E. The diminished fifth moving to a perfect fifth in this one circumstance is not satisfactory. The conditions are: 1) the interval involves the bass and an upper part; 2) the LT is in the bass in the first chord; 3) the bass moves to the tonic note on the second chord. The reverse direction is acceptable, however.

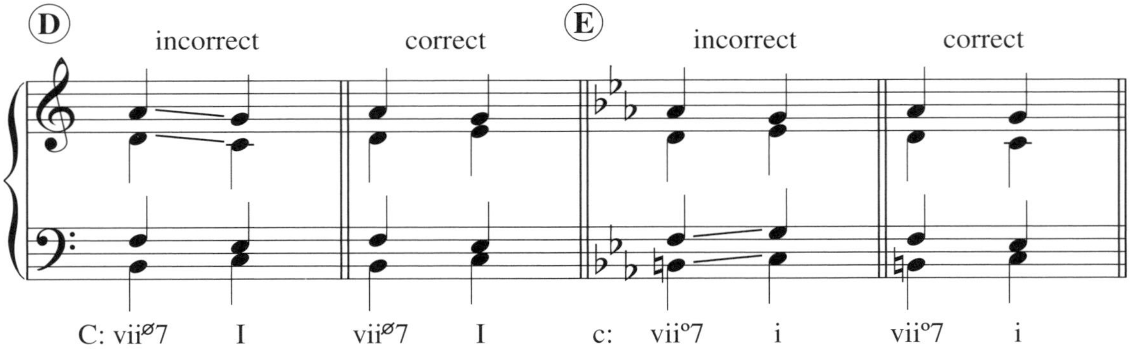

All of the following are good:

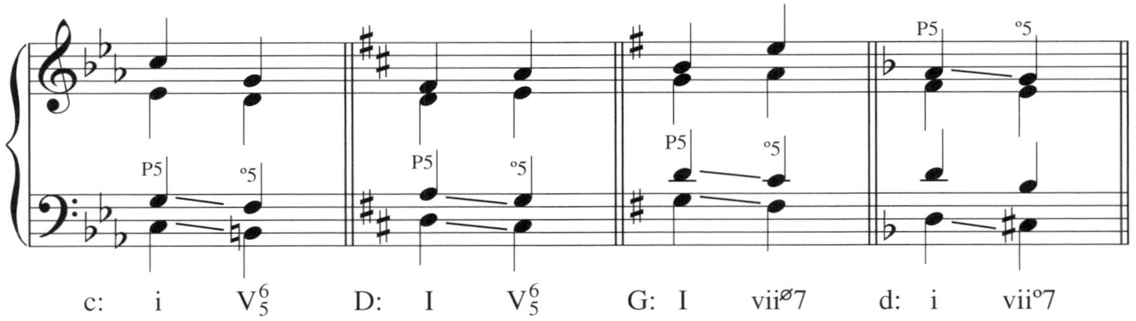

A FEW MORE SEVENTH CHORDS

In classical tonality, the **tonic**, **subdominant**, **submediant**, and **mediant seventh chords** occur much less frequently than the dominant, supertonic, and leading tone seventh chords. The approach to the seventh is as before: free. The resolution is the same: down by step. The key here is not to overuse these chords. They may be used in any inversion. The following examples demonstrate:

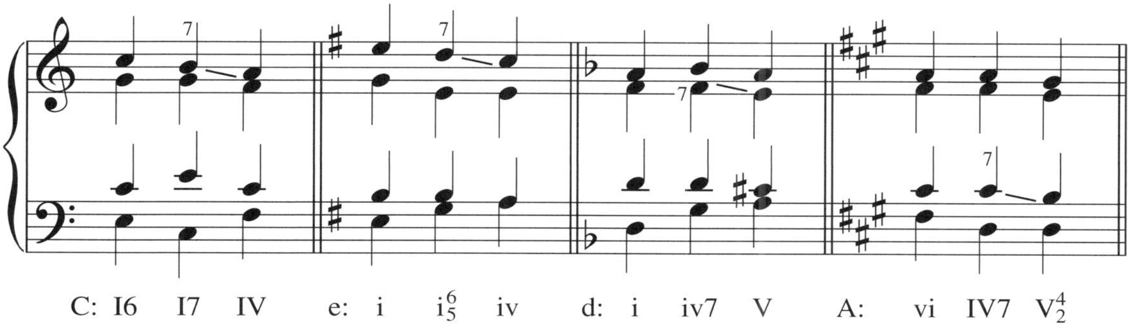

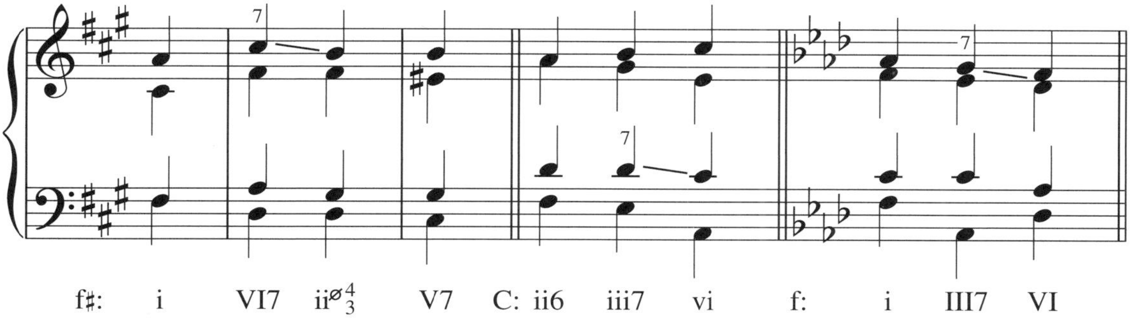

Seventh chords may be used in continuous succession, following Circle of Fifths root movement (roots moving down a fifth or up a fourth). In each chord, the seventh resolves as expected:

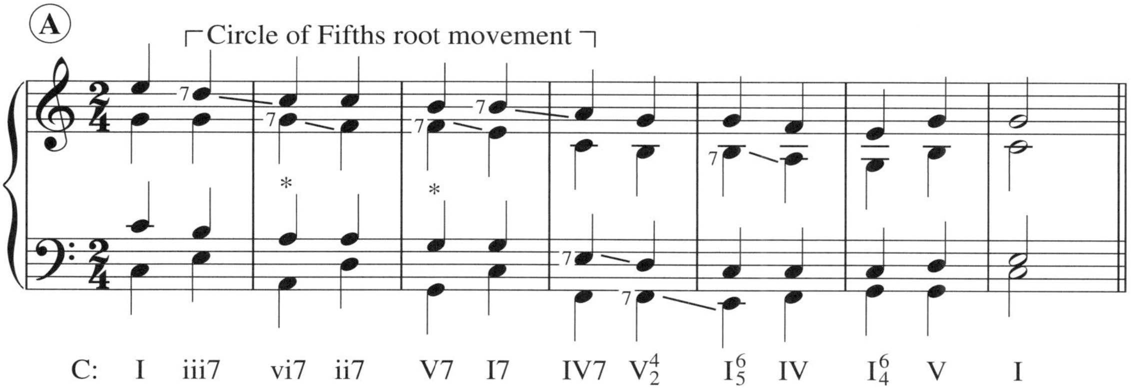

(B)

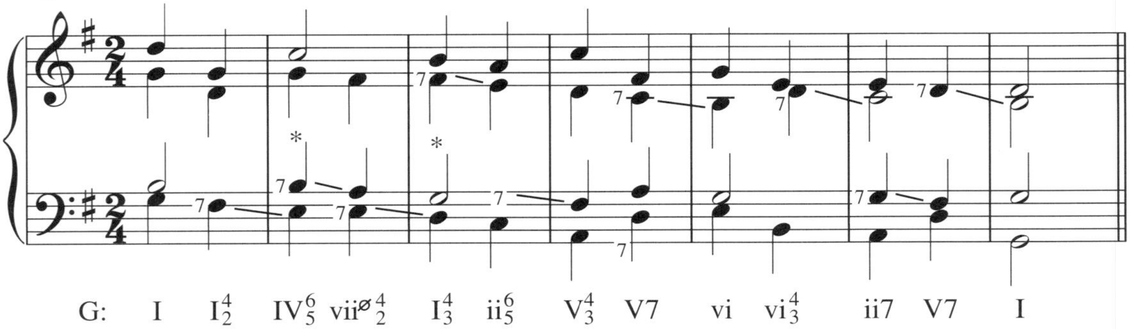

In Example A above, the asterisks denote "incomplete" seventh chords, which are frequently needed to avoid parallels. In Example B, various inversions are illustrated. Such concentrations of seventh chords of all kinds are more representative of procedures used in popular music than in the traditional masterworks; the intention here is merely to show how these chords are approached and resolved.

We have learned that the seventh must rise in the progression V7–I6 (i6). The same principle applies to transpositions of this progression, such as ii7–V6, I7–IV6, iii7–vi6, and vi7–ii6. (All these are Circle of Fifths progressions.) Several examples of the rising seventh are shown below:

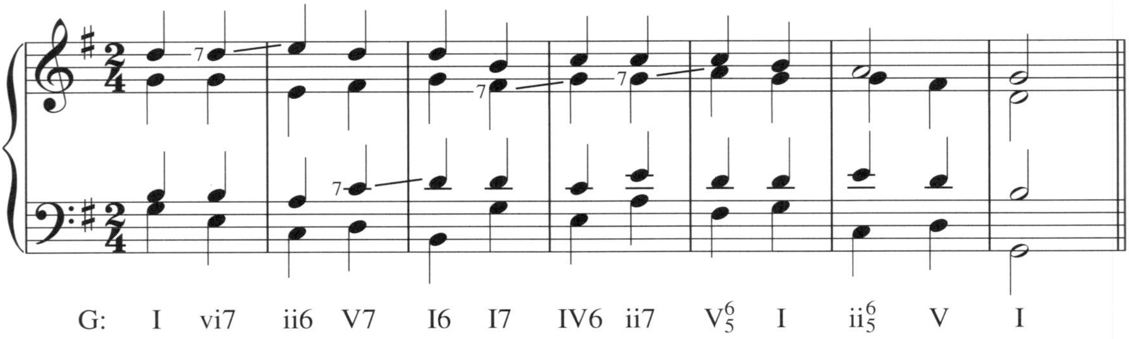

In summary, seventh chords form an important part of the harmonic vocabulary. All five types (see page 11) play a role in adding richness to harmony. The V7 chord is by far the most common seventh chord in tonal music, followed by the supertonic and leading tone seventh chords. The remaining degrees (I7, iii7, IV7, and vi7) are used sparingly. The seventh may be approached freely but must resolve down by step. Exceptions to this have been discussed and should be committed to memory.

FIGURED BASS AND THE LEADING TONE SEVENTH CHORD

There is a direct correspondence between **figured bass symbols** and Roman numeral symbols for any unaltered chords—that is, chords that have no accidentals outside the key signature. This is true for seventh chords as well as triads: the Arabic numerals denoting inversions are identical. The following example, showing a figured bass line and its corresponding Roman numeral analysis, demonstrates:

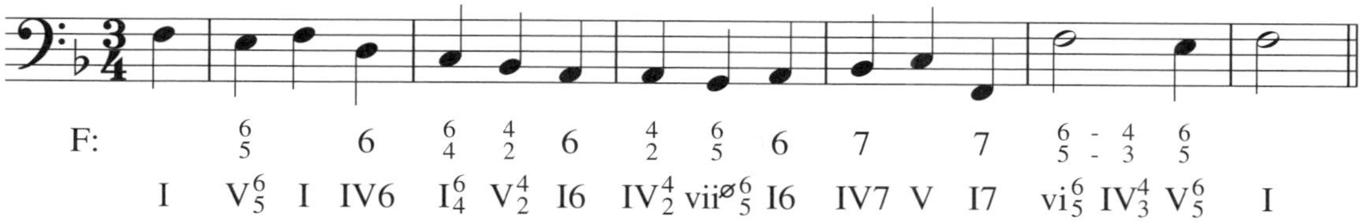

But in minor keys, the LT must be accounted for, as we know, in forms of V and vii°. The leading tone seventh chord, vii°7, presents additional obligations when committed to figured bass. In vii°7, the LT is in the bass, so no added symbols are needed. In vii°6/5 the LT is a sixth above the bass and must be accounted for. In vii°4/3 the LT is a fourth above the bass and must be accounted for, and in vii°4/2 it is a second above the bass and must be accounted for:

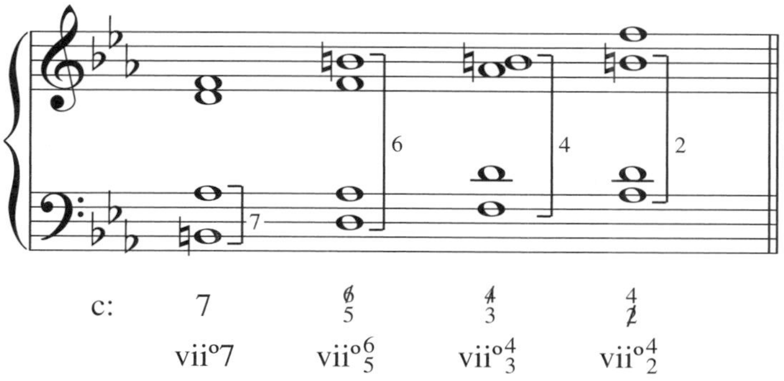

With this survey of seventh chords, we come to the end of the diatonic materials of tonal harmony and are ready to proceed to *Hal Leonard Harmony & Theory, Part 2*. Before moving on to that book, read the Appendix that follows, and do the exercises for Chapter Nine. A thorough review of all material presented thus far should be done before moving into the very exciting regions of chromatic harmony.

EXERCISES

1. Analyze these progressions:

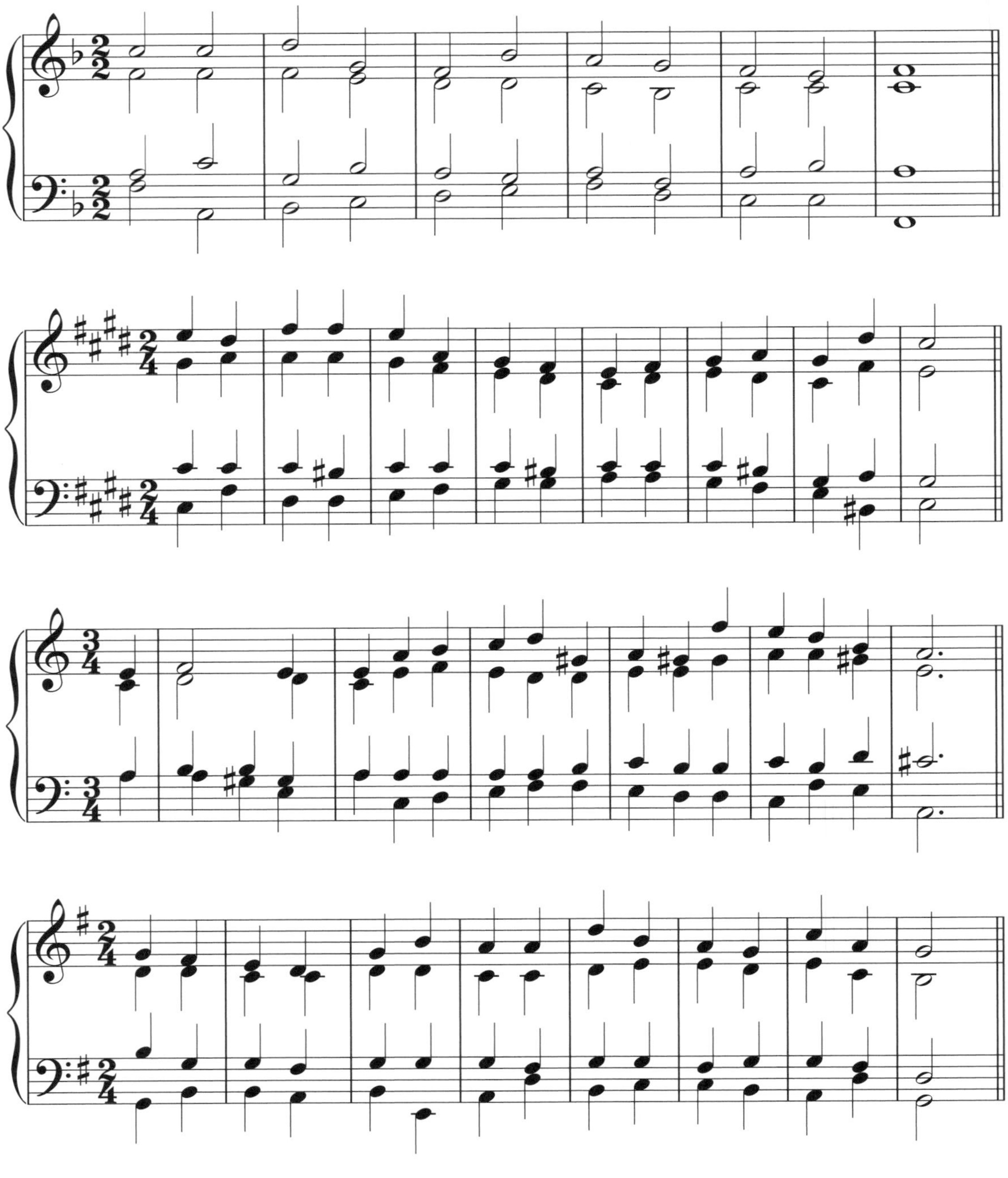

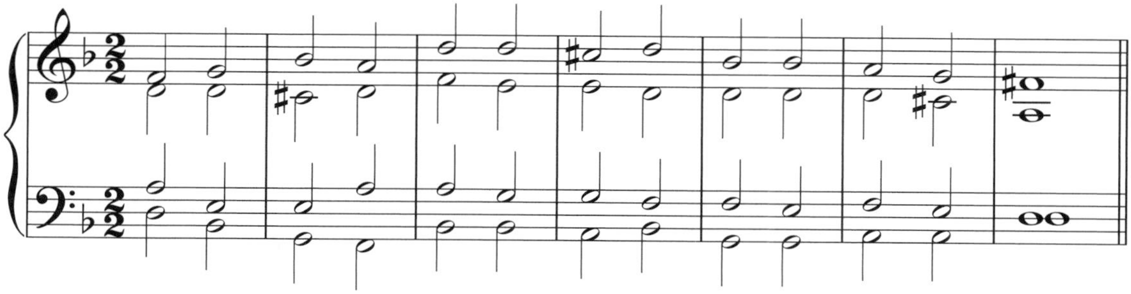

2. Fill out in four-part harmony:

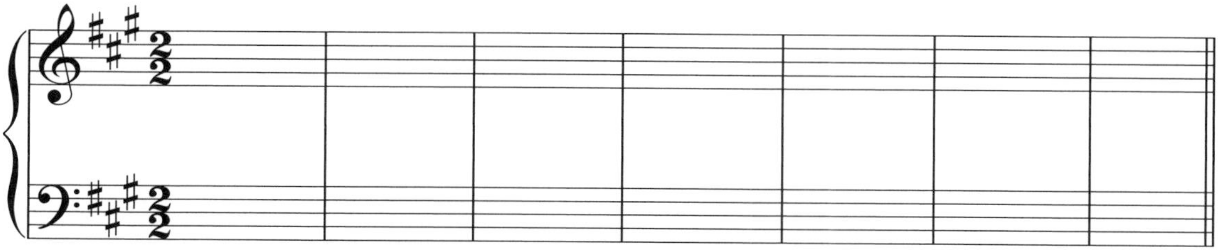

A: I $vii^{\varnothing}{}^{6}_{5}$ I6 ii^{6}_{5} I^{6}_{4} V^{4}_{2} I^{6}_{5} IV7 $vii^{\varnothing}{}^{4}_{3}$ I6 ii^{4}_{3} V7 I

3. Analyze the harmony and add upper voices:

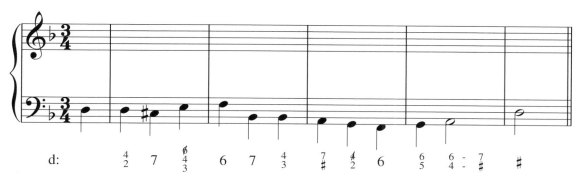

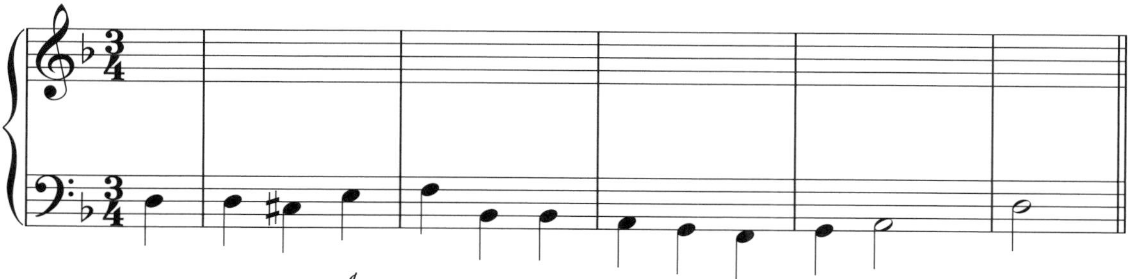

d: $^{4}_{2}$ 7 $^{6\!\!/}_{\,4\,3}$ 6 7 $^{4}_{3}$ $^{7}_{\sharp}$ $^{4\!\!/}_{2}$ 6 $^{6}_{5}$ $^{6\,-\,7}_{4\,-\,\sharp}$ ♯

R.N.:

4. Work out a solid harmony for this melody. Add alto, tenor and bass. Analyze. Use ii7 and vii$^{\varnothing}$7 chords in suitable forms.

D:

5. As above. Use ii$^{\varnothing}$7 and vii° chords in suitable forms. Analyze the harmony.

c:

6. For the following three Examples:
Analyze the harmony and provide a figured bass, then copy out on a separate piece of manuscript paper and enrich with NHTs and additional chord tones. Use some strong-beat NHTs.

a:

F.B.:

R.N.:

e:

F.B.:

R.N.:

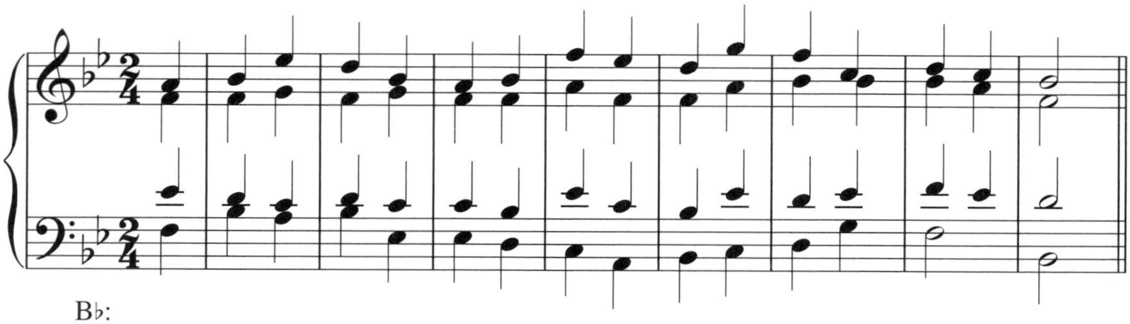

B♭:

F.B.:

R.N.:

7. The following two Examples have the same harmony. Analyze the harmony and NHTs.

d:

d:

8. Analyze the harmony:

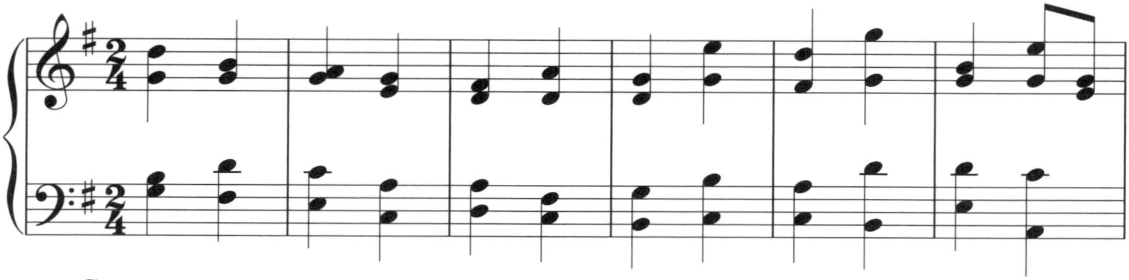

G:

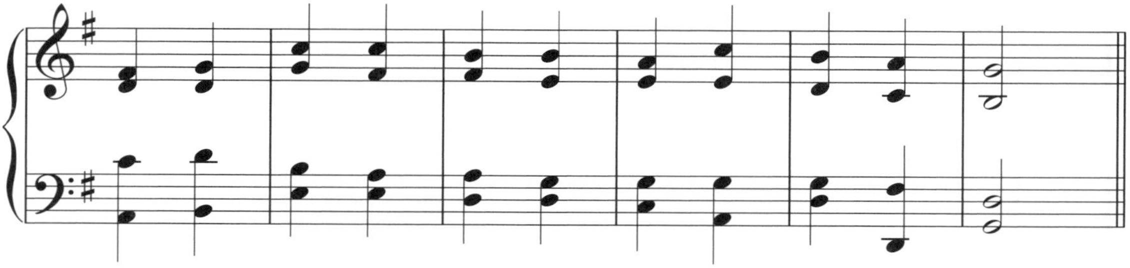

9. Fill out in four-part harmony. Add a few suspensions, but no other NHTs and no intervening chord tone skips. Try to develop a good melodic line. Be sure to resolve all sevenths correctly (down by step).

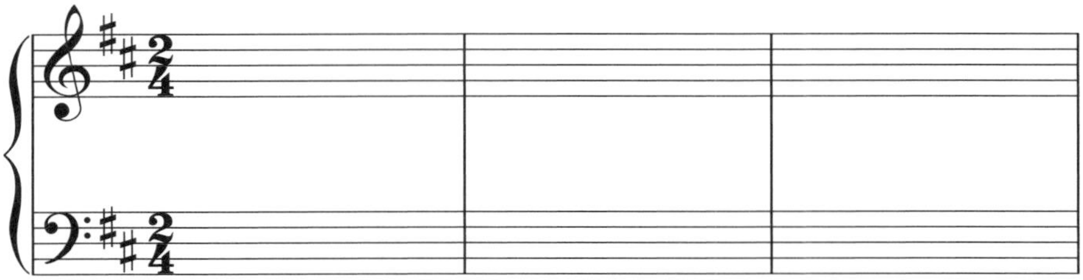

D: I I^{6}_{5} IV^{4}_{2} ii7 I^{6}_{4} V7

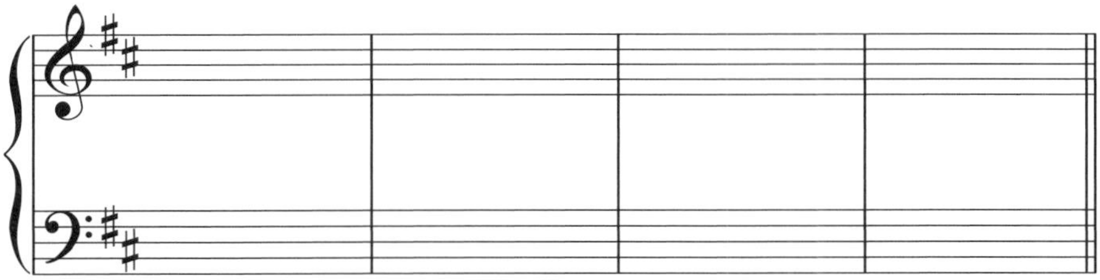

vi vi^{4}_{2} IV7 $vii^{ø4}_{3}$ I6 V^{4}_{3} I

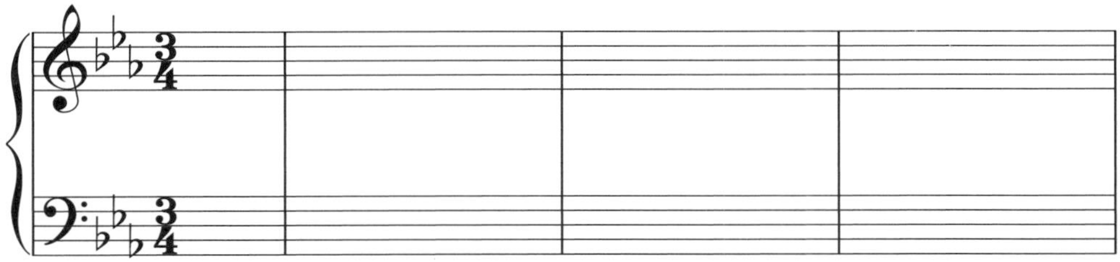

c: V i $ii^{ø4}_{2}$ V^{6}_{5} i ______ i^{4}_{2} $ii^{ø4}_{3}$ iv7 V

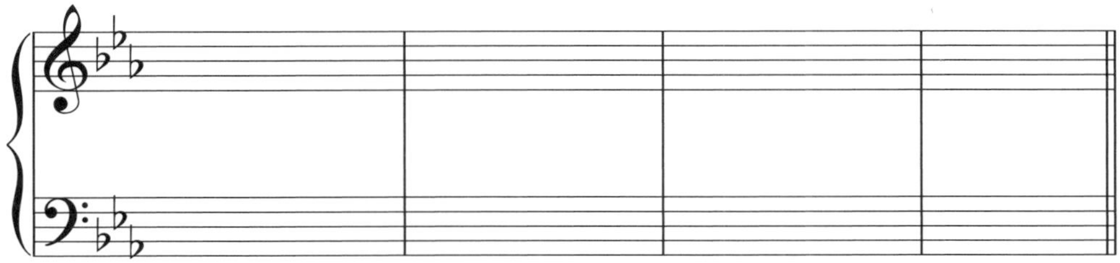

VI VI^{6}_{5} vii°7 V^{4}_{3} i6 $ii^{ø6}_{5}$ i^{6}_{4} ______ V7 I

APPENDIX

EXPOSED FIFTHS AND EXPOSED OCTAVES

More often called **direct**, **covered**, or **hidden** fifths or octaves, the term **exposed** most clearly defines this particular aspect of voice leading. It involves the approach to a fifth or octave between the bass and the soprano. If both voices move in similar motion to a P5 or P8, and the soprano skips a third or more, the "exposed" interval occurs. Indeed the motion of the voices does "expose" the interval and this is the reason for the questionable nature of the effect. Some examples:

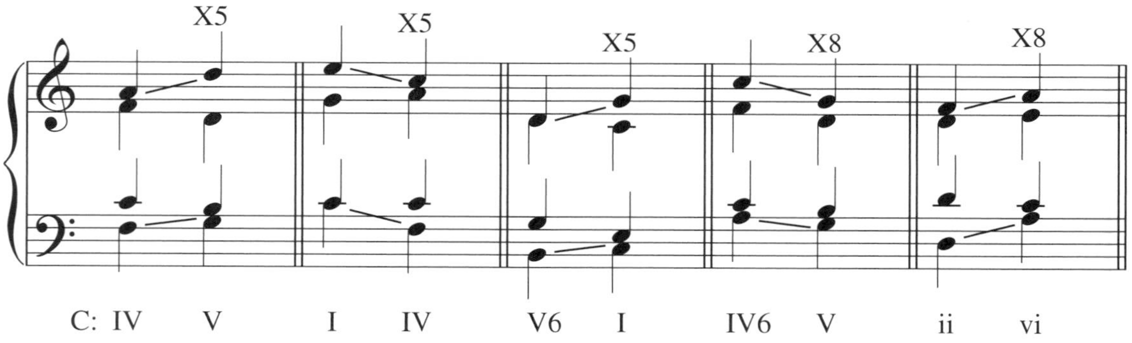

If the soprano moves by step, there is no problem (Example A). If there is no change of harmony, no problem exists (Example B). In Example C, the effect is so slight as to be acceptable. The progression in Example D was very common in the 16th century; as such, there seems no good reason to frown upon it.

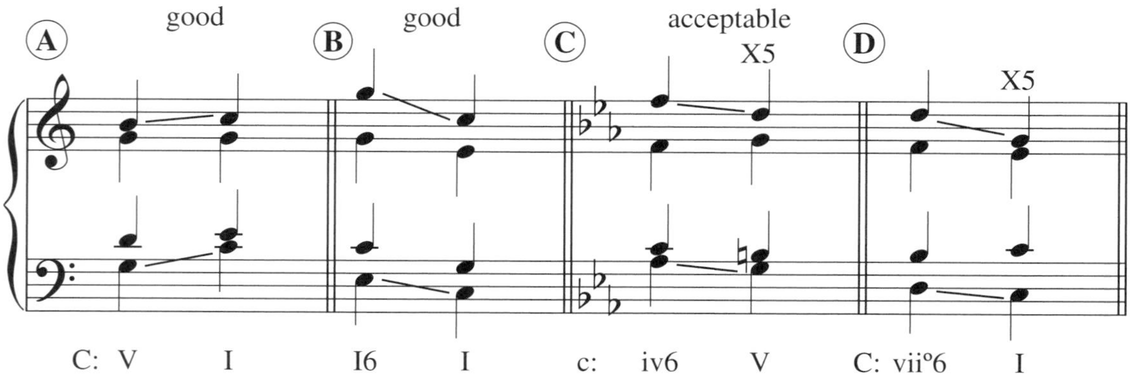

LESS COMMON CHORDS IN MINOR

The Subtonic Triad

Instead of the vii°6, VII, built upon the natural seventh degree of the scale, is occasionally used in minor keys. It is usually approached from the tonic triad and resolves to III (Example A). It sometimes resolves to VI or iv6 on its way to V (Example B):

(A)

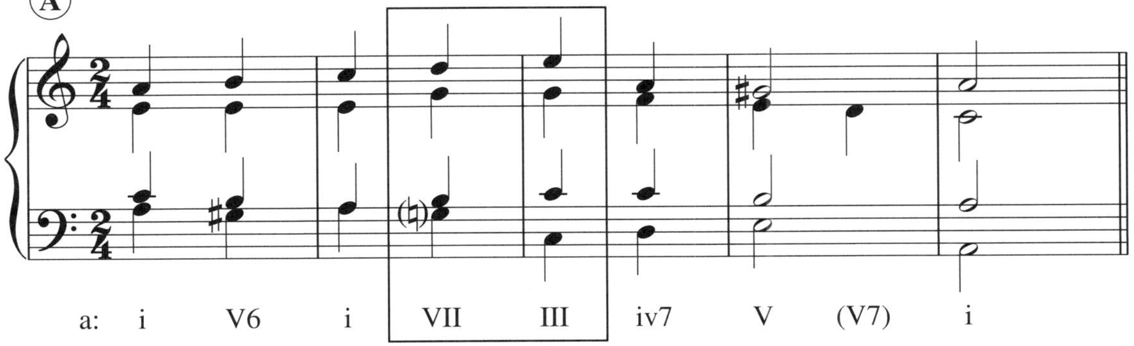

(B)

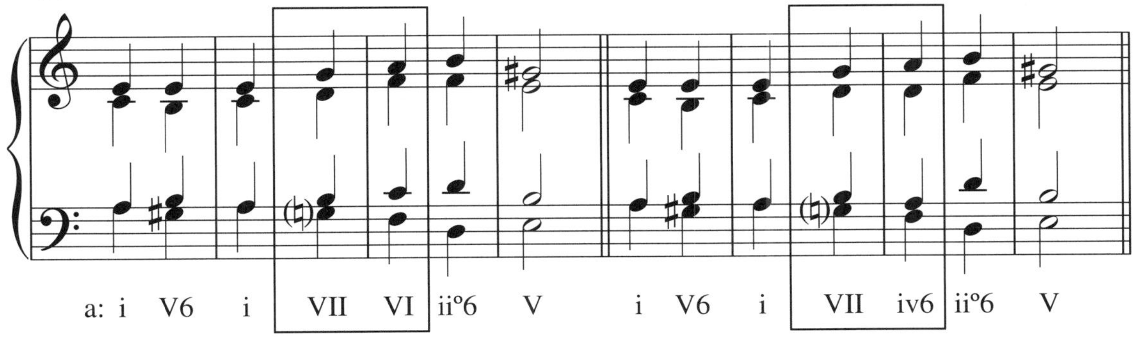

The Mediant Augmented Triad

Labeled III+, this chord uses the LT instead of the natural seventh degree. The approach is usually from i or from a chord already containing the LT. Resolution is to VI or iv6. Resolution to i6 gives the LT the impression of being a NHT:

CHROMATIC INFLECTION

It is possible in minor keys to move from III to either dominant or leading tone chords. The unraised seventh degree in the III chord changes **chromatically** upward to become the LT in the next chord. This can be a very effective progression:

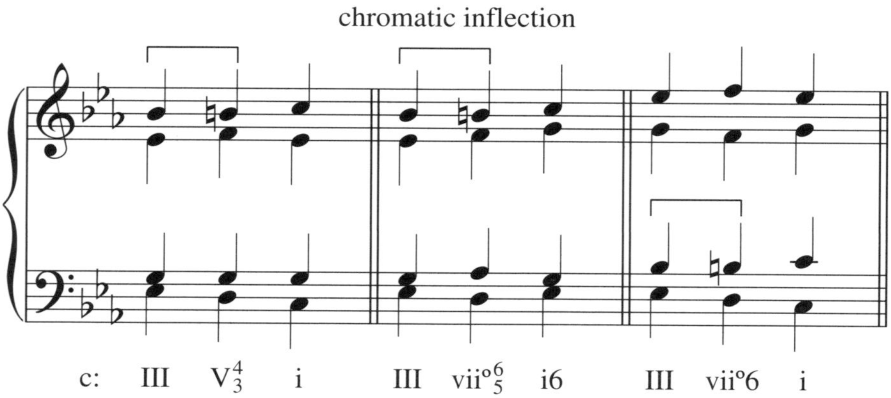

CROSS RELATION

Cross relation occurs when a chromatic change takes place at the distance of an octave (or compound octave), forming a diminished or augmented octave. In this case, one perceives the harsh effect of this interval. When a cross relation occurs between two triads, they should generally be avoided (Example A). If the second chord has the richness of a seventh chord, the cross relation is often quite acceptable. The ear must act as judge here (Example B):

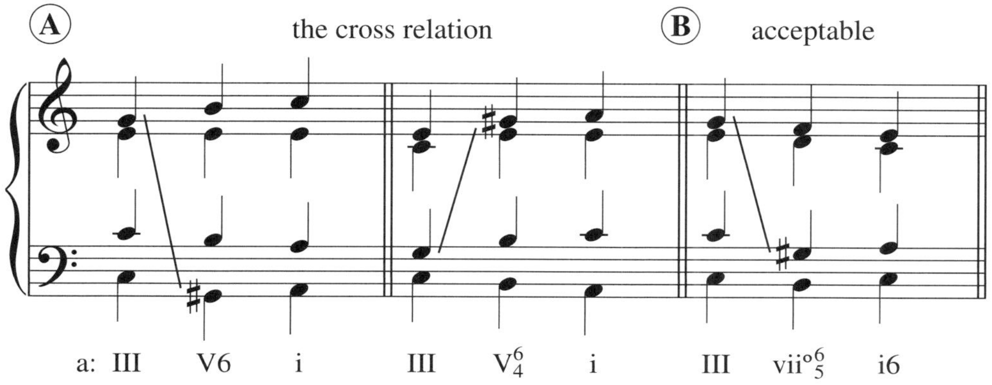

ROOT MOVEMENT IN HARMONIC PROGRESSIONS

Strong Progressions

1. Up a perfect fourth (down a perfect fifth):
   I–IV, ii–V, iii–vi, V–I, vi–ii. vii°–iii is rare.
   Up an augmented fourth is okay in sequences. IV–vii°6 is good.

2. Up a second: I–ii, ii–iii, iii–IV, IV–V, V–vi, vii°6–I.
   vi–vii°6 is rare but usable. Watch voice leading!

3. Down a third: I–vi, ii–vii°6, iii–I, IV–ii, V–iii, vi-–V, vii°6–V7

4. Down a second: I–vii°6, ii–I, iii–ii, IV–iii, V–IV6, vi–V, vii°6–vi

"Weak" Progressions

1. Up a third: I–iii, ii–IV, iii–V, IV–vi, V–vii°6, vi–I, vii°6–ii
   For best effect, follow a weak progression with a strong progression: I–iii–IV, I–iii–vi, etc.
   Very usable: vi–I6, I–iii6, etc.

2. Up a perfect fifth (down a perfect fourth):
   ii–vi, iii–vii°6, V–ii, vi–iii, vii°6–IV (up a diminished fifth)
   I–V and IV–I are very common. All the others are rare.

GENERAL OBSERVATIONS

1. Tonic triads can move to any chord, including any secondary dominant.
2. Use of inversions can make a poor progression good.
3. Chords that precede V:
    - a. IV
    - b. ii
    - c. vi
    - d. I
    - e. V (chord repetition)
4. Six-four chords are treated in only one of four ways:
    - a. passing
    - b. stationary
    - c. cadential
    - d. chord prolongation (arpeggiated)

THE SEQUENCE

The **sequence** is a common method of achieving unity in music. A sequence involves transposed repetition. A pattern (or "model") forms the basis of a sequence. The pattern may be very short or may extend over several beats or even measures. Once stated, the pattern is then transposed—up or down—to other scale degrees. The interval of transposition is usually one of three possibilities:

1) down a second
2) down a third
3) up a second

This is especially true if the pattern is repeated (by transposition) two or more times. Examples A, B, and C clarify:

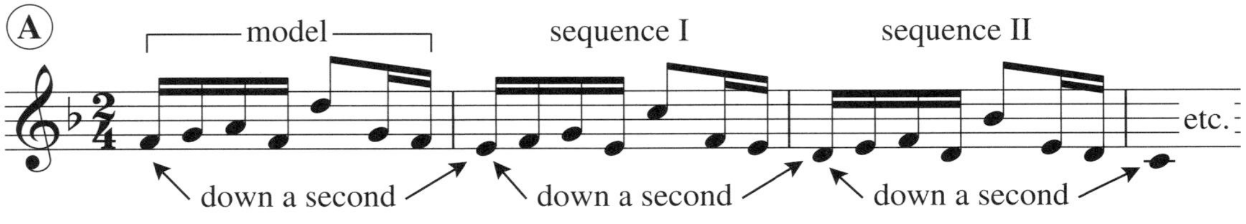

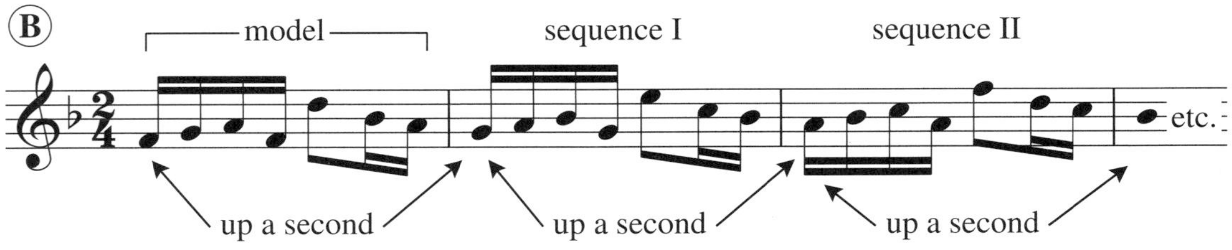

C

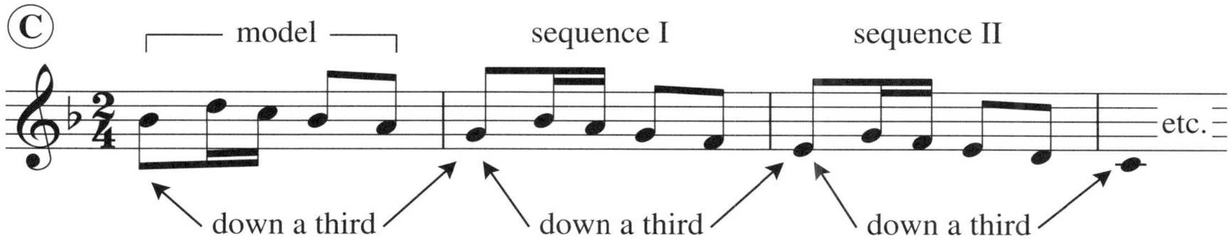

If there is but one transposition of the pattern, the interval of transposition could be, in addition to the above-mentioned, a fourth, fifth, or sixth. Examples D, E, and F demonstrate. If the pattern continues to be transposed at these intervals, the overall melodic line suffers. Such occurrences as are seen in Example G are very rare.

D

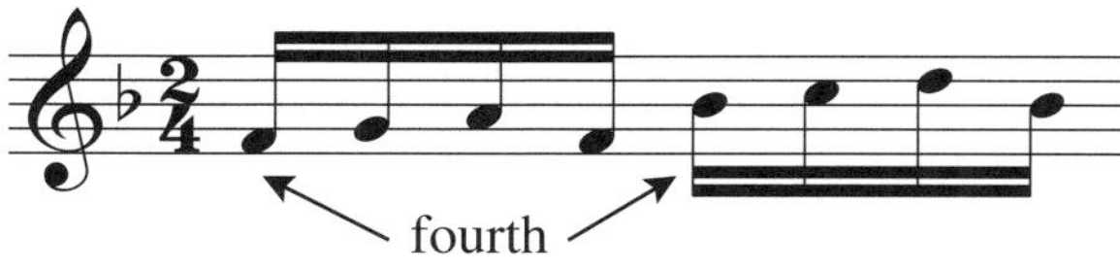

E

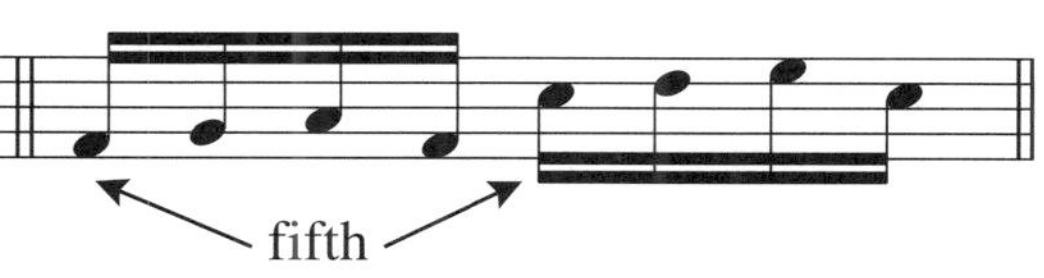

F

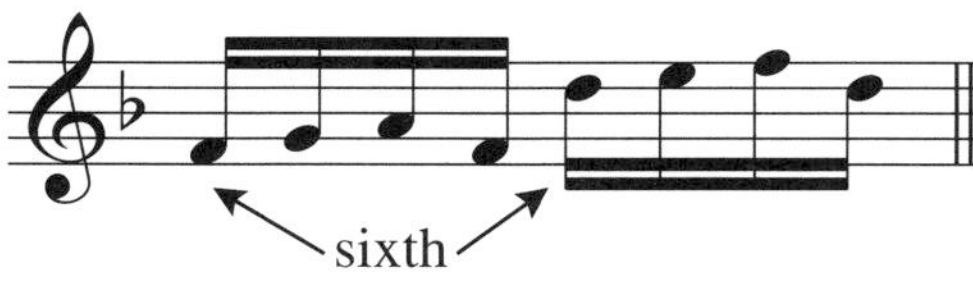

G

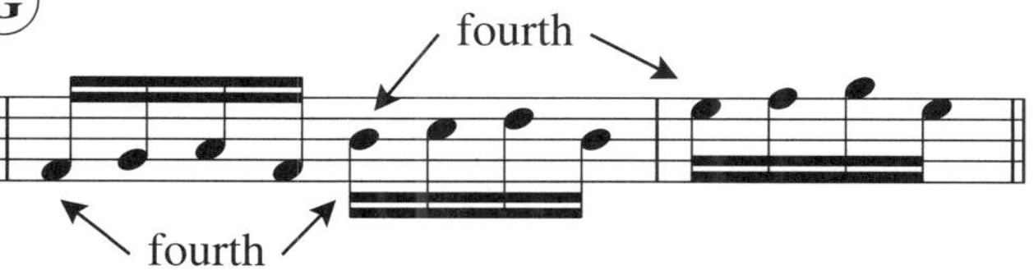

Sequences may be purely melodic, as in all the foregoing examples. They are also melodic and harmonic, in which all the voices participate in the sequence. In these instances, the patterns of the harmonic progression are usually also sequential. This may involve as little as one chord only, or, more commonly, two or more chords in the pattern:

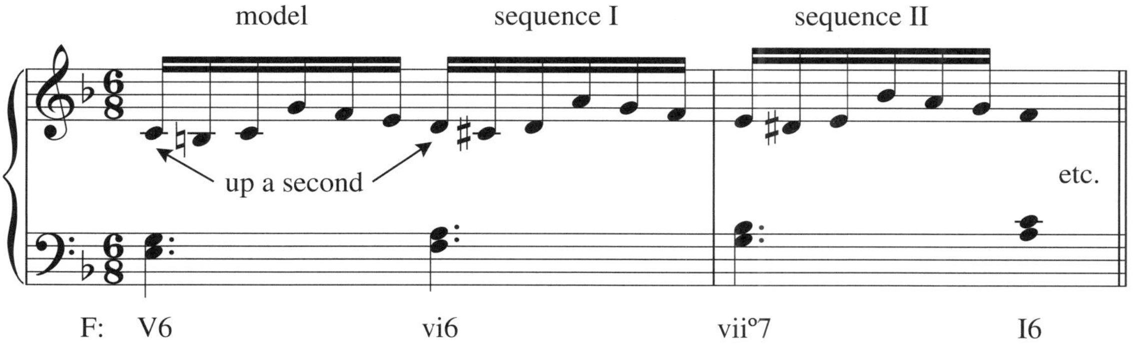

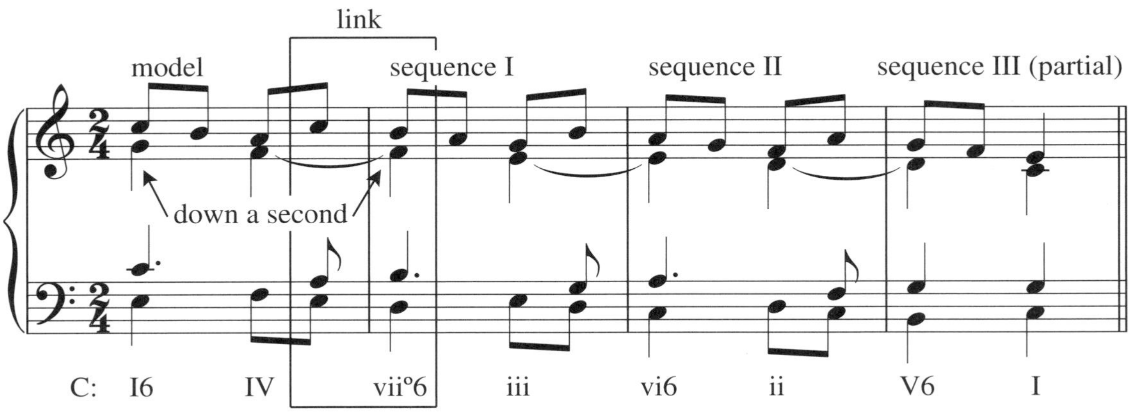

In order to be effective musically, there must be a smooth, error-free connection between the end of the model and the beginning of the sequence. In the previous example, this "link" is boxed in. The link must be convincing harmonically, with good voice leading, etc. You will notice that the vii°6 chord at the beginning of the second measure has a doubled LT. Irregular doubling is acceptable in sequence for the same reason that the awkward melodic intervals are acceptable: the unifying effect of the sequence justifies them. Once the link is achieved with musical results, the sequence may then be carried out as desired. In general, sequences limit themselves to three transpositions of the model, but the literature is full of sequences with four and more transpositions as well.

The sequence plays a very important role in chromatic harmony, so we will be returning to it in the pages of *Hal Leonard Harmony & Theory, Part 2.*

A final example shows a sequence with four chords in the model:

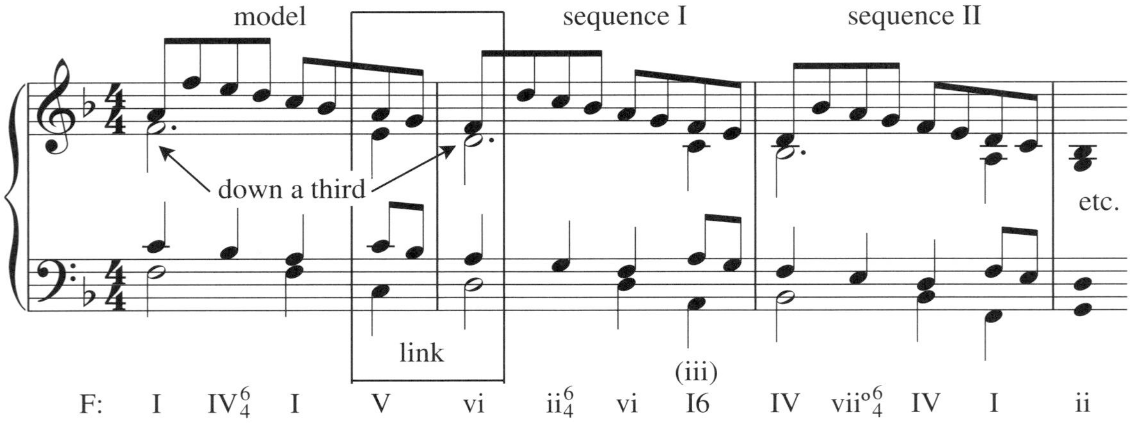

INDEX

ABOUT THE AUTHOR

George Heussenstamm (b. 1926) received all his musical training in the Southern California area. Winner of numerous national and international composition competitions, he is a member of ASCAP, an honorary member of the international music fraternity, Sigma Alpha Iota, a former member of the American Society of University Composers (now called SCI), and the International Society for Contemporary Music. He was a member of NACUSA (National Association of Composers, USA), in which he served as vice president for many years. In 1976 and 1981 he was the recipient of Fellowship Grants from the National Endowment for the Arts. From 1971 to 1984 he was Manager of the Coleman Chamber Music Association, the oldest continuing chamber music series in the country. Eight of his compositions were recorded on LP and four of these have been committed to CD.

Since 1976 Heussenstamm taught music theory and composition at Cal State Dominguez Hills, Cal State Los Angeles, Ambassador College, and steadily for 17 years at California State University, Northridge, prior to his retirement in June 2000.

Composer of more than 85 published works, he is the author of *The Norton Manual of Music Notation*, released by W.W. Norton and Co. in 1987 and still a mainstay in the literature about the notation of music, making Heussenstamm one of the leading authorities in this field.

Though perhaps best known for his large-scale works for saxophone and brass ensembles, Heussenstamm has composed in a wide spectrum of media. His compositions have been performed with regularity both in the United States and abroad.